Best Places to Go

A Family Destination Guide

by Nan Jeffrey

9 780935 701753

51495

Foghorn Press
BOOKS BUILDING COMMUNITY

Avalon House

Foghorn Press, Inc./Avalon House Publishing

Copyright © 1993 by Nan Jeffrey

Foghorn Press
555 DeHaro Street #220
The Boiler Room
San Francisco, CA 94107
(415) 241-9550

Credits
Managing Editor—**Ann-Marie Brown**
Illustrations—**Jeff Camish**
Maps—**Chuck Steacy**
Copy Editing—**Howard Rabinowitz**

Library of Congress Cataloging-in-Publication Data

Jeffrey, Nan, 1949-
Best Places to go: a family destination guide/
Nan Jeffrey. p. cm.
Includes bibliographical references and index.
ISBN 0-935701-75-3 (v. 1): $14.95
1. Voyages and travels—1981—Guidebooks.
2. Family recreation—Guidebooks. I. Title.
G153.4.J43 1993
910'.2'02—dc20

Best Places to Go

A Family Destination Guide

by Nan Jeffrey

BOOKS BUILDING COMMUNITY

Avalon House

Acknowledgments

I wish to thank everyone who shared their travel experiences or insight with me during the course of this project, including members of the various tourist boards who contributed their time and materials. In particular, I would like to thank the tourist boards of Finland, Norway, Ireland, Newfoundland and Prince Edward Island.

A special thank-you goes out to the following people for their help and enthusiasm:

Andrea Wang of the Globe Corner Bookstore, Cambridge, Massachusetts; Chuck Steacy and the staff at Map-Link, Santa Barbara, California; Jeff Camish; Kim Grant, a free-lance travel writer and photographer; John Seigel Boettner, author of *Hey Mom, Can I Ride My Bike Across America*; Don Knight, founder and director of Scholé, an alternative school on Cape Breton; Barbara Maryniak, author of *Hiking in Newfoundland's National Parks*; Karl Luunta, author of Moon Publication's *Jamaica Handbook*; Les Belzer; and my sister, Lindy Coggeshall.

CONTENTS

Central America & The Yucatan Peninsula

The West Indies

Great Britain & Ireland

Scandinavia

Continental Europe

Northern Africa & The Island of Madeira

Appendix—p. 321
Author's Recommendations

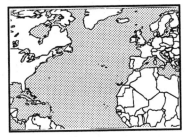

Introduction

Everywhere in the world has the potential for adventure travel. Some places offer an ethnic experience far removed from life at home. Others feature unspoiled wilderness and an expansive network of parks. One country might be best suited to newcomers, another more appropriate for experienced adventurers. Each area offers something of cultural interest to the traveler: its language, social norms, traditions, unique food, and historical background. Each also possesses certain environmental attributes, areas of natural beauty, be they protected, cultivated, or simply left untouched, that are waiting to be explored.

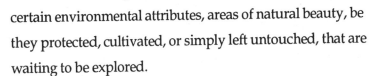

Some places might be seen in a more positive light than others, because of your level of experience, the ages of your children, your budget, or the season you plan to travel in. Political climates vary, determining the wisdom of one location over another. Certain places just seem to have a universal appeal, luring visitors to them year after year. The concept of adventure travel is a growing one, and places that were once regarded as inappropriate have met with new popularity. As communication and awareness between nations have increased, so has the availability of good, safe travel destinations. Fears are being set aside and prejudices abandoned as people recognize that despite nationality and race, language and cultural practice, we all share a common bond. Viewed this way, the whole world becomes a great destination.

In writing this book, we hope to meet the growing interest in world adventure travel, particularly for families with children. Wanting to adventure is one thing, but knowing how to start, where to go, how to travel, and what to expect is another. In choosing these destinations, we have selected a cross-section of what's available. Places that make travel simple and ones that demand much of you. Those for novices and those for veterans. The tried-and-true and the comparatively unknown. Countries that are expensive and those that can be traveled on a shoe-string. The orientation is an outdoor one, for this is a book about adventure travel, travel that strips away the normal barriers of tourism and subjects you to a country: physically, culturally, and socially. Once having tried it, you will discover this to be the most exciting travel of all; the kind best suited for families.

USE OF THE BOOK

Best Places To Go is principally a book about areas around the world and how they can best be traveled by a family adventuring together. The first two chapters deal with the mechanics of adventure travel: how it is defined, what its benefits are, how it applies to families and how it can be done. Because this is ultimately a book about destinations, we've covered these areas briefly. For more detailed information on how to adventure together as a family, refer to our handbook *Adventuring With Children*.

Following these introductory chapters, the book is divided into geographical areas around the world. A variety of countries, islands and regions have been described in detail, each one representing a specific destination. Readers are bound to pose questions about some omissions. Why, you might wonder, did we include Norway, but not Sweden, Portugal without Spain, Morocco instead of Tunisia? Choices for this edition were made based on travelers' requests and space limitations. Viewed as a whole, the book touches on many popular adventure travel destinations. Many places omitted, of course, will be featured in volume II, including the western United States and Canada, Mexico, South America, the Pacific region, and Asia.

GENERAL DESTINATION FORMAT

Each destination has been covered by the following categories. Remember, the emphasis here is on family adventure travel, and the purpose of the book to help you choose where to go, the best way to travel, and what to expect when you get there.

General Description. This orients the reader, supplying basic information about the area's location, terrain, climate, culture, and lifestyle. Included are seasonal changes and how they affect travel. What season is best for hiking the Alps or cruising the Bahamas or bicycling Prince Edward Island? When should you visit a Caribbean island or Mayan ruin or the coast of Greece? Most families feel bound by the traditional school year. Summer, they assume, is the only time to travel, with the possible exception of a quick trip at Christmas or mid-winter break. This not only limits where you can reasonably go, but subjects you to peak season in most destinations.

If there's one thing we'd like families to appreciate, it's the ease with which they can travel during the school year. The benefits are numerous. Prices are down, crowds non-existent, and people more receptive to you as a visitor. Destinations that once seemed an impossibility can be seriously considered. For those who live in the north, the long, cold winter can be temporarily escaped as you pack up the family for a trip to the tropics, the Far East, or the Southern Hemisphere. Perhaps most important of all, travel provides a wonderful educational experience, one that will far outweigh any academics the children are missing at home. For more information on how to teach your children while traveling during the school year, refer to our handbook *Adventuring With Children*. This includes correspondence school programs, curriculum planning, resource materials, teaching tips, and social concerns.

Practical Concerns. This covers all the concerns relevant to travel to each of the destinations: political conditions and safety, travel documents, money, travel costs, language, health, food and shopping, clothing, laundry and bathing, baby needs, and any special concerns for that region. On an organized tour, these are all taken care of, leaving you with little more to do than bring the appropriate clothing and have the prerequisite inoculations (if any). On your own, however, the concerns can be numerous, especially if you are venturing into the previously unfamiliar territory of traveling with your offspring. We've tried to include enough to make you feel comfortable before setting off for each destination, armed with a good idea of what to take and what to expect when you get there.

• *A Note on Political Conditions and Safety.* World politics always seem to be in a state of flux. While veteran travelers soon discover that people are all basically the same (something children inherently accept), governments rarely function at this fundamental level. Some places are routinely safe for travel, others seem to make a habit of political discord. One way to receive an update is by calling the U.S. State Department at (202) 647-5226. Bear in mind, however, that the State Dept.'s recommendations tend to be cautious and conservative, if not downright alarming. News coverage, many people's primary view of the world, can make almost anywhere sound high risk.

Conversely, risks in your home country are accepted as the norm and rarely thought about. Americans live with the highest crime rate in the world, yet are easily scared off visiting somewhere that is experiencing minor military skirmishes. Theft is commonplace in the U.S. and road accidents all too frequent, yet no one lets this interfere with their weekend travel plans. "Aren't you afraid to go there?" is the reaction we often elicit when acquaintances hear of our latest travel plans. Yet when viewed from a similar foreign perspective, America can seem like a dangerous destination. Avoid countries at war, stay away from politically sensitive areas (such as unfriendly border zones), then rely on your common sense. People are universally friendly and welcoming, particularly to families traveling with children. Almost anywhere is safer than it sounds and tourists are rarely targeted in political incidents. Don't let your fears of the unknown keep you from exploring a part of the world that lures you. Just as you wouldn't take a nighttime stroll through a city park in the United States, or leave your wallet exposed on a subway, so too can you learn the basic procedures for safety abroad.

• *A Note on Longlife Milk.* Frequent reference has been made under Food to a product called longlife milk. Widely available outside the United States, this refers to a sterilized milk that requires no refrigeration and is generally sold in small, one-liter cartons. Along with powdered whole milk (the kind sold outside of the U.S.), it provides an excellent, safe, pasteurized source of milk throughout most of the world.

Transportation. Transportation, of course, is all important when traveling, with the following three catagories dealt with in the book: how to get to your destination, what type of transport to use once you get there, and what the roads are like. When it comes to transportation, countries can vary tremendously: those with well-developed public transportation and those with practically none; places where travel is easy and painless and places where covering even minor distances can be a major undertaking; those with sleek dual highways and those with roads that even a four-wheel drive would balk at.

Because this is a book about adventuring, with an emphasis on low-cost travel, we've stressed the use of public transportation where it's available, rather than renting a car. Although travel by car is undeniably convenient, it is also expensive (when renting), confining, and limiting in the exposure it allows you to the people and places you are visiting. In developing countries particularly, people react differently when you step out of a rental car rather than off a bus or train. Perhaps most important, riding public transportation is a vehicle to adventure, allowing you to taste local life, to share an equal status with the natives, to experience the same conditions, even if only briefly. In a place such as Europe, public transportation is efficient, comfortable, convenient, and far less expensive than travel by rental car.

Bicycling could also be regarded as a viable mode of regional transport for many destinations, even when traveling with children. For the purposes of the book, however, we've included all information on bicycle touring in the Outdoor Activities section.

The general condition of roads has been covered both to benefit motorists and bicyclers and to give you some idea of which areas are easier to travel in than others. Belize, for instance, has two regions that are accessed by good roads and another that involves far more rigorous travel, whether by car, bus, or bike.

Accommodations. This covers all types of accommodations relevant to budget-oriented travel that are appropriate for families. These include campgrounds, hostels, Bed & Breakfast places, pensions, bungalows, cottages, and farm vacations. Hotels are available throughout the world, but few families can afford this type of accommodation long-term, nor do they lend themselves well to adventure. Remember, when choosing a place, that staying somewhere where you can cook your own meals will greatly help reduce costs on any trip. Avoiding renting a car and dining out (on a regular basis) are the two biggest money savers when it comes to family travel. Camping, of course, remains the least expensive means of accommodation and has therefore been given ample coverage. For those who prefer something different, other low-cost alternatives have been included.

Points of Interest. Visiting natural, cultural, and historic points of interest is a low-cost source of entertainment while traveling, as well as an opportunity to learn a great deal about an area. Museums, historic sites, festivals, fairs, parks and preserves all help broaden your understanding of a place and its people. Depending on your children's inclination, try a variety of activities or follow a certain theme. Our children's cultural interests are widespread, a reflection of their age, sex, inherent taste, upbringing, and level of travel experience. With our boys, anything of a military nature has always been a perennial favorite, as have ruins, music festivals, historic villages, and unspoiled areas of natural beauty.

Some children, unused to this type of attraction might show an initial lack of interest, particularly when it comes to visiting museums or ruins. After all, this is very different from the type of entertainment most children are exposed to. Whenever we mention to people that we are doing research on family adventure travel, they invariably point us in the direction of some amusement center, as though children were incapable of amusing themselves.

Unfortunately, this is all too true today when external devices have taken the place of internal capabilities, leaving children bereft of those very imaginative skills that must be called into play when visiting historic sites, exploring the outdoors, or just plain adventuring. To introduce your children to the more subtle entertainment of museums and ruins, historic sites and monuments, pick small places to start with, ones that won't quickly tire or bore them. Provide some entertaining background information beforehand about what you will be visiting. If your children like trains, visit railroad museums. If they're interested in old-fashioned things, try historic villages or houses. If they like music or play an instrument, attend a local festival. If soldiers and knights excite them, find a castle or fort. If dolls are their favorite thing, locate an antique doll and dollhouse exhibit. Any child can develop an interest in this sort of thing given proper encouragement.

Outdoor Activities. With adventure travel, the focus is not only environmental awareness and cultural sensitivity, but physical challenge. No matter how you travel or where you go, a certain amount of outdoor exposure can be expected. For some, it can mean tramping the streets and hiking the trails, bicycling backroads and braving the elements. In some countries, just renting a place and living simply can involve a series of outdoor activities as you shop in open-air markets, ride public buses, fetch water, do laundry, explore the countryside, and rely on your two feet, that most basic mode of transportation. Adventure is easy to come by when you travel this way, whether moving from place to place or just experiencing one small corner of a country or island or region. Exploring a place from an outdoor vantage makes it an adventure. Not only are you physically challenged, but the level of your travel experience and insight into a place are far more intimate and revealing. With children, the chances for a successful family trip are greatly increased, for children love the outdoors, finding it a natural environment for their innate enthusiasm, high energy level, and fertile imaginations.

The world abounds with opportunities for outdoor activities, from bicycling the backroads of Portugal to trekking in the Andes. As it was impossible to include all the outdoor activities, we chose hiking, bicycling, canoeing, sailing, swimming, and nature studies, ones popular with many families and capable of incorporating children of all ages.

• *Note on Sailing.* Many of the destinations included in this book have good opportunities for chartering boats. SAIL Magazine's August issue is an excellent resource for those seeking reliable boat charter operations worldwide.

Sidebars. Appearing at the end of each section is a sidebar, something that gives particular insight into that region or country. By including them we hope to provide readers with an extra guideline or tip about each area, something that will inspire them to travel to each corner of the world and create their own types of adventures.

Resource Section. Here you'll find supplemental information for the traveler, incorporated into the following categories:

• *Tourist Bureaus.* Listed with each destination is the national tourist bureau, in many cases an excellent resource and gold mine of information. Be sure to specify areas of interest, as many only send the standard tourist brochures unless they know what you're interested in. Places like Newfoundland, the Maritimes, Florida, England and Norway, for instance, have abundant useful material on outdoor activies and nature parks. Tourist bureaus will send information on anything from public transportation and camping to architecture and historic sites, greatly helping in your trip planning.

• *Consulates & Embassies.* The name, address, and phone number of national consulates or embassies are given here. You may use them to find out more specific information on traveling to that destination.

• *National Airlines.* Included in this section are the major carriers, including the national airlines, serving that destination. Flying with a national airline is always a fun experience, an early introduction to the country you are about to visit.

• *Suggested Reading.* Our suggested reading list includes the best guide books, along with books that provide insight or inspiration about the destination. Where applicable we have included books for children about a particular location.

• *Suggested Maps.* Accompanying each regional description is a small reference map of the destination, followed by a list of suggested maps for purchase. Carrying a good map is integral to any successful adventure, particularly when planning outdoor exploration like hiking, bicycling, or boating. As maps vary (both in detail and cost), we've suggested ones we feel are most appropriate for this type of travel.

Best Places To Go

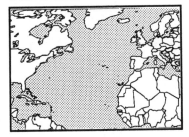

Why Adventure Travel?

Whҽn our twin sons, Tristan and Colin, were six, we took them on a five month backpacking trip through Greece and Turkey. As a family, we were used to traveling together, having taken our first camping trip when the boys were six months old. Since then, the children had lived much of their lives on a sailboat, cruising the waters of the eastern United States and the Bahamas. Now that they were old enough to shoulder a pack, we decided to explore further afield, taking only what we could fit into four packs. In addition to the normal challenges of a trip like this, both children were now in first grade. As the trip coincided with the second half of the school year, they required some form of schooling as we traveled.

While family and friends looked on in doubt, we made lists, allocated jobs, booked tickets, selected items, and finally squeezed everything from camping gear to an arsenal of school books into the four packs. The one thing we never considered was staying home. Since then we have continued to travel, planning some adventure each year that takes us far from home and the routines that bind us there. As the children have grown, so have the challenges, from a simple camping trip with babies in Florida to a 1,500 mile bicycle trip through Morocco, Spain and Portugal. Family adventuring, we've discovered, is one of life's greatest experiences. In a world grown seemingly complex and security-ridden, adventuring allows you a simplicity and freedom of old.

Ask a roomful of people to describe an adventure they've had and you'll hear a different answer every time. You might even begin, after a while, to wonder how they all qualify adventure. While some eagerly recount stories of trekking in Nepal or three month bicycle escapades, others make their adventures sound more like advertisements for *Travel & Leisure*. Ask a roomful of parents about adventure and you're bound to hear about the inevitable weekend camping trip or how they survived a visit to Disney World. In truth, adventure travel is a nebulous affair, ranging anywhere from cross-continental hitchhiking sagas to simple backpacking with babies. Adventure can be experienced on the homefront or the other side of the world, alone or with a group, spontaneously or by design. It's both fun and fearful, entertaining and grueling, physically demanding and wonderfully relaxing. In essence, it is an extension of life itself, life experienced in a heightened way.

Adventure travel opportunities have never been more plentiful, more accessible, or more appreciated than today. Gone are the days when adventuring was a man's prerogative, the destiny of just a few intrepid opportunists. Some people mistakenly feel the world has become too tame, the opportunities for true adventure too few. They scoff at the notion of "canned adventure"; how truly adventurous is driving around the African bush with a group of fellow tourists, or a guided tour of the Galapogas? How can adventure travel be something prepaid and prearranged?

The wonderful thing about adventure travel is that it has so many guises. For some, it's a trip with an adventure travel outfitter to an exotic land, experienced in an outdoor way: trekking ancient paths, bicycling backroads, or rafting wild rivers. For others, it's pursuing independent travel, braving new destinations, new countries, and new cultures on their own. For families with children, it's often the very notion of traveling together. The challenges loom as large for them as for any inveterate, globe-trotting backpacker. For us, adventure travel has taken many forms. We've adventured on land and by water, on foot and by bicycle, while camping and while renting, in hot climates and cold, with dependent babies and capable children, in familiar cultures and alien ones. Whatever the experience, all shared certain characteristics and attributes, things that bound them together as adventure travel. Ultimately, the experience was about stepping outside the normal structure of our day-to-day life, about meeting a challenge and overcoming it.

So you might well ask, "why adventure travel? Why pursue adventure instead of an easier, more conventional type of travel? Why make your vacation more rigorous than your normal lifestyle? Why not join the throng of vacationers that are doing their best to Winnebago the world?" Because in an era that seems sadly bereft of meaningful challenges, there is still one out there within reach of any willing family. Adventure travel offers so much. It's travel on a shoestring budget. It's seeing the world on its own terms. It's stripping away the cocoon of security most of us live in and allowing yourself to develop strengths you didn't know you had. It's families bound together in ways that generate understanding and respect and a new depth of feeling as they strive towards a common goal. It's learning to appreciate the value of small things. It's seeing the environment as something in its own right rather than just as a commodity solely for the use of man. It's the modern age of pioneering. Above all, for children and parents alike, it's fun.

Responsible adventure travel serves another purpose, one that benefits the areas you visit as well as yourselves. For the most part, tourism is a mixed blessing. While it often provides a welcome boost to the local economy and sometimes the only means of economic survival, it also threatens the integrity of the places it promotes. Because responsible adventure travel has such a low impact, by traveling this way you contribute much towards preserving the quality of the places you visit.

For us, family adventuring has come to mean both experiencing a place in an outdoor-oriented way and learning about its culture and environment. Understanding a place, accepting its cultural differences, and discovering its natural world are an integral part of any adventure. Museums and historic sites, festivals and fairs, parks and preserves, all teach about the culture and ecology of an area. Just visiting a few will broaden your children's understanding of a place, and in a larger sense, the world beyond it.

Academically, adventure travel is the world's best textbook, enriching your child in ways no stationary program possibly can. Crusaders' castles and Minoan ruins, Roman towns and Viking settlements have all been explored by our children, the remnants sparking their imaginations. Languages have been studied and cultural habits copied, foods sampled and lifestyles learned from. Each trip you embark on becomes a wealth of learning opportunities, not only in what you see and where you visit, but in how you live. Families are thrown together with time to talk and share ideas. Many of Colin and Tristan's most valuable lessons have taken place while hiking a trail or bicycling a backroad.

Many couples give up travel when they have children. Bound by their ingrained views of what a trip would be like as a family, they stay home or leave the children and go on their own. If they go as a family, the emphasis is on entertainment and amusement parks, as though children were incapable of entertaining themselves. Adventure travel forces parents to deviate from this conventional train of thought. On a trip, children become independent and responsible, imaginative and creative. Taking them away from a neighborhood playgroup or VCR no longer seems threatening. Divorced from the prevalence of their peers, children expand their social criteria to encompass everything from siblings to parents, toddlers to teenagers. Tristan and Colin have never had trouble finding playmates on a trip. No matter what country we visit, they always make friends. For a child, the language barrier means little. The language of play is universal.

Adventuring is travel at a child's pace. The emphasis is less on the amount of area covered than the depth of experience. While camping in Portugal on a bicycle trip, Tristan and Colin met two children from South Africa. Quick to make friends, as all traveling children are, they were soon swapping stories and sharing thoughts. Traveling all over Europe by camper with their parents, the South African children said they were miserable and bored, eager to get home. Later we asked our children about this. What made our trip different from theirs? The boys didn't experience a moment's hesitation in answering. "It's boring," they said, "just riding around in a car all day and stopping somewhere new every night. We'd hate it." They were right, of course. Parents often ask us, how do you get your children to hike up a mountain or bicycle 60 kilometers in a day? It's easy, we say. What they won't do is spend hours locked in a car, immobilized and isolated from the places they are passing through. Yet for most parents, that is the accepted mode of family travel.

Children respond well to a trip that places more emphasis on delving into an area than viewing it from the confines of a car. Cars, while undeniably convenient and sometimes necessary, can be a big inhibitor to adventure travel. If you take one, leave it behind whenever possible: for a hike, an overnight boat trip, a mini-bicycle tour, a trek through the backwoods.

Because adventuring is done modestly, contact with the people is made easy. Unlike conventional travel, which tends to isolate you from the local inhabitants other than on a commercial basis, adventure travel exposes you to them. Traveling simply, riding public transportation, bicycling or hiking, shopping in local markets, all help minimize the disparity between your lifestyle and theirs. As a family traveling together, you will also receive the warmest welcome, for children are the world's best ambassadors. While free-camping in an olive grove beside a Moroccan mountain village, we were quickly befriended by a group of Berber children. Happy to play with Tristan and Colin, they brought us food, showed us the sights, and escorted us to the local "souk," or market. Later, after watching them demand money from tourists for performing similar services, we asked them why they didn't charge us. Their answer was simple. "You are our friends."

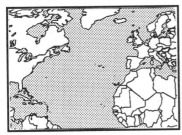

Reviewing The Basics

We will never forget the first time we took our children adventuring. Armed with a blue VW bug, two Mexican baby baskets, a diaper pail, sixty cloth diapers, and a handful of light-weight clothing, we loaded up both babies and headed south. Although well-versed in the rudiments of adventure travel, Kevin and I soon discovered

that doing it with children presented a whole new set of guide-lines. Instead of just a place to sleep, our tent became a play-room, with toys littering the sleeping bags and mobiles hung suspended from the roof. Running water and laundry facilities took on an aura of glamour, and neighboring campers flocked over with enthusiasm to see the babies. Adventuring with children, we learned, was quite different from adventuring alone.

Our next trip was on a sailboat, more challenging than camping and possessed of another new set of criteria. In subsequent years, we tried backpacking and canoeing, traveling by public transportation and bicycling, camping abroad and renting. Each experience built on the foundation of what had come before while also offering new challenges, new basics that had to be discovered, learned, and applied. What emerged was as broad a spectrum of procedures as there are different types of adventures. No matter where or how we traveled, however, the basic core of our adventure travels remained the same; certain characteristics, techniques, and attributes applied to all of them.

The following deals briefly with the basics of how to adventure travel, whether independently or with a group, living in one place or moving around, in a poor country or a modern one, with toddlers or teenagers. Having already written an entire book on the topic, we realize that one chapter can hardly suffice as a comprehensive resource. The purpose is rather to whet the appetite of other families who want to go adventuring by showing the basic mechanics of travel around the world.

INDEPENDENT TRAVEL

Although independent travel is potentially the most challenging, it can also be the most rewarding. For many families, this is the only way to travel. The pace is of your own choosing, the itinerary flexible, the needs of your children catered to, your spontaneity indulged. Everything you experience is uniquely your own, the result of your own abilities and labors. If you discover a wonderful hiking trail or special beach or deserted island, if a family befriends you or foreign children present you with a gift of food, you know the experience is special to you rather than the result of someone's well-planned itinerary. The same thing didn't happen to another group of families the week before and the week before that.

The more you travel independently, the more confident and capable you become. Suddenly the world seems a less intimidating place and nearly everywhere a potential destination. As a family, you develop strengths and skills you didn't know you had. Instead of being relegated to the backseat of a car or channeled into a series of child-oriented activities, adventuring children become capable participants in their own right. The adventuring child is a happy one because he's allowed a freedom that's very different from today's permissiveness. Working within the family unit, the child sees himself as an integral part of any adventure.

Adventure travel is similar to an Outward Bound experience. Unlike modern life, where the family is splintered and diversified, each member oriented in a different direction, the adventuring family traveling independently must work together in ways that are exciting, active and fulfilling to children and parents alike. Freedom becomes a matter of contribution and responsibility rather than indulgence and neglect. Children don't have a chance to be fussy, bored, or rebellious. Life becomes too stimulating and challenging.

Below are some tips for independent travelers:

Start Slowly. The best advice we can give beginning families is to start slowly. Plan your itinerary modestly and you will find it every bit as relaxing as any well-planned group tour.

Stay Flexible. Don't feel bound to a certain travel format. If you find somewhere you and your children enjoy, feel free to spend your entire trip there. That's one of the joys of independent travel. Remember that distance covered has very little to do with depth of experience. Children have a natural resistance to fast-paced, frequent travel. Take advantage of this proclivity to discover the advantages of slow, in-depth exposure to an area. You may not see nearly as much as the average tour-package tourist, but your experience will be far more enjoyable, revealing, and meaningful for you as a family.

Involve the Children. Children respond well to involvement in family affairs, particularly when it's something as exciting as adventuring. Cater to this natural interest and you will find even bored teenagers or rebellious toddlers becoming enthusiastic participants. This includes involving them with trip planning, packing, camping, and all outdoor activities. Allow them the freedom to bicycle and hike, sail and canoe, experiment and explore. Active children are happy ones, particularly when given the freedom to accept responsibility for themselves.

Travel Light. Take as little as possible. It's amazing what you find you can happily live without while traveling. This includes clothes, toys, household items, and entertainment devices. Traveling simply is synonymous with adventure travel. You learn to appreciate small things and soon find yourself wondering why you ever thought you needed so much at home. One exception is books. Take plenty of those for children when traveling to a foreign-speaking country. Adventuring children become voracious readers.

Relax. Remember, adventuring should be relaxing. Just because you're dealing with the unknown and meeting new challenges doesn't mean things have to be tense or fearful. The world is predominantly a safe place and the people in it inherently friendly. Although cultural differences and language barriers can pose momentary confusions, ultimately, people are welcoming the world over, especially to families with children.

Keep a Sense of Humor. Travel to foreign countries always involves some truly memorable experiences, moments that are horrendous to live through, but seem hilarious in retrospect. Keep a sense of humor when disaster strikes and you'll find yourself breezing through that appalling bus ride or a night spent in the world's worst dive.

We've laughed our way through some truly amazing escapades: the night both children wet their sleeping bags while camping in a thunderstorm in Spain; the Moroccan bus ride where we became mired in a goat path; the airplane flight that landed in the wrong place in the middle of the night; not being able to exchange money on a Greek island during the five-day Easter holiday; plus the usual epic bathroom experiences that defy imagination. As your travel exposure grows, so will your ability to cope with the unavoidable. In the meantime, seeing the humorous side of things will go a long way towards minimizing their effect on you.

ADVENTURE TRAVEL OUTFITTERS

Although we have always stressed the positive aspects of independent travel (low-cost, challenging, the freedom to plan your own itinerary and follow your own whim), adventure travel outfitters serve an equally valid purpose. For short-term adventures with a flexible budget, a trip with one can mean the difference between frustration and success: frustration because it took you most of your one or two week trip to find a place you liked or organize the activities you wanted to do. For beginners, traveling with someone else in charge can supply the necessary catalyst to get you going in the first place. A trip with an outfitter can help you gain the confidence to try one on your own next time.

Adventure travel outfitters supply many people's need for a ready-made itinerary while offering a welcome departure from the "package tour to a patch of sand" mentality. With the ever-increasing interest in adventuring, more and more options are being offered each year. Many include children above a certain age or run special family-oriented trips. Some have a strong environmental focus, others feature specific outdoor activities or unusual cultural contact. Research well before committing yourself to a certain trip. Not everything is the way it seems in the brochures. Despite what may seem like highly unusual itineraries, in many cases independent travel can supply the same experience at considerably less cost.

One notable exception is an African safari. Most game parks are closed to independent travel, so going with an outfitter is a must. This doesn't mean your entire trip has to be with a group. Many outfits operate locally and can be joined for a portion of your visit. Other locally-run operations include river rafting, sea kayaking, trail riding, mountain biking, and nature hikes. These are generally outdoor oriented activities that have little to do with cross-cultural contact. A hike or bicycle ride on your own will show you just as much of the physical beauty of an area for free. On the other hand, if you do join a group, meeting other travelers of like minds should make it a guaranteed success.

THE OUTDOOR ACTIVITIES

Children love the outdoors, making this an easy area to generate enthusiasm. Probably the single biggest mistake parents make is underestimating their children's capabilities when it comes to riding a bicycle or hiking a trail, shouldering a pack or paddling a canoe. Hiking guides continually suggest four or five kilometer hikes as ideal for families, as though children were incapable of covering longer distances. Bicycling is a universally favorite pastime for children, yet the idea of family touring borders on the revolutionary.

Coupled with their safety concerns, this low expectation among parents results in children who have almost no experience with long-term exposure to outdoor activities, particularly at a young age (the best time to get them hooked). The truth of the matter is that children, even very young ones, are almost as capable as adults when it comes to physical output. Keep them interested and they will go forever. Tristan and Colin always look far more exhausted after a day in the car than following a long hike or bike ride. The difference? They are happier, more stimulated, and allowed more responsibility for themselves when outdoors and active than cooped up in a vehicle.

The following are some brief recommendations concerning each of the outdoor activities included in the book. For more detailed information on how to get your children camping, hiking, bicycling, sailing, and canoeing refer to our handbook *Adventuring With Children*. Also included with each destination is information on swimming and nature studies. Although neither qualifies either as a means of travel or as a way to extensively explore the outdoors, both are integral to family adventure travel.

Hiking. Hiking can be done almost anywhere in the world. For some people it is a way of life, for others a means of exercise and escape from mankind's clutter: into a park, up a mountain, or along a deserted beach. Some trails are made specifically for hikers, others form ancient byways, used since time immemorial.

Like all outdoor activities, hiking brings you closer to a place, exposing you to things never experienced by most visitors. Children can make wonderful hikers, provided it's fun. Choose hikes with plenty of visual stimuli: grazing animals, cultivated fields, mountain villages, rushing brooks. All spark their interest and imagination and keep them endlessly entertained.

Bicycling. This is a great way for a family to travel. Some areas can be seen exclusively by bike, others best explored in a series of short trips or day outings. Even if you plan to base yourself in one place or travel by car or public transportation, bringing bicycles along is wonderfully liberating. Jaunts around the countryside, trips to the local market, or simply a need to exercise the children are all made easier with bicycles.

Once having discovered the joys of bicycle travel, we've rarely left ours behind. Any good ten-speed should be fine unless you plan extensive backcountry explorations on dirt roads. Children are capable of riding a fully loaded ten-speed by age nine. On a bicycle tour, expect them to cover an average of 50 km a day, a pace that leaves plenty of time for breaks, sightseeing, and play after reaching your destination. Be prepared for frequent stops, as children have a way of continually needing something: something to eat, something to drink, a bathroom break, clothes to put on, clothes to take off off.

Leave room in their handlebar pack for easy storage of whatever is in continual demand. A water bottle or two mounted on the bike with velcro is one way to cut down on repeated delays. Other helpful items to store in a handlebar pack for quick access are a reading book and a handful of small toys like matchbox cars, dolls, or a ball.

Sailing & Canoeing. Travel by water is always adventurous. Needs are reduced and ties to land severed, even if only temporarily. A sense of self-sufficiency and independence are keenly felt. Places take on a new aura, that of peace and elegance, isolation and beauty. The pace of travel is slowed and the forces of nature respected. Water travel is the antithesis to modern, face-paced, transient social trends. Children love water, deriving endless fascination and entertainment from it. Mud puddles and ponds, lakes and streams, rivers and oceans all lure them like magnets.

Getting your children out on the water is one of the easiest ways to interest them in adventuring. Whether it's for a day or a month, a weekend canoe trip or a two year cruise, don't hesitate to pack up the family and take to the water. Adventure and excitement, independence and self-sufficiency will be yours as you discover a unique view of the world hidden from most people.

With a sailboat, your home goes with you, making this one of the best ways to travel with infants or toddlers. Things that would normally have to be left home can be crammed aboard, giving young children a sense of security and familiarity as they travel. During our sons' first six years of life spent aboard a sailboat, I don't think they ever truly realized that we were going anywhere.

Children of any age can enjoy an outing in a canoe. Young ones can be carried as passengers. Older ones of about ten years and up can paddle well, given sufficient rest periods. As with all forms of outdoor activity, children like variety rather monotonous repetition. Negotiating a passage between rocks, landing at a beach, exploring close to shore, watching for signs of animal life, all help liven up a canoe trip for a child. Canoe travel, after all, is a lot more entertaining than car travel and children are expected to do that all the time.

Swimming. Although swimming hardly falls into the same category as the other outdoor activities, it's something most children love, even if they're doing little more than just playing along the water's edge. Children of all ages share an inherent love of water, delighting in its presence and deriving endless sources of entertainment from it. No matter where the destination, we've discovered, bringing along beachwear is always a good idea when traveling with children. Included with each destination is information on types of swimming areas (lakes, ocean, rivers, etc.), locations of good beaches, degree of safety, and water conditions. A number of tropical destinations also include information on snorkeling, the ideal way for children to discover the fascinating underwater world of the sea. Any child old enough to swim proficiently can learn to snorkel safely. Even timid ones seem to gain tremendous confidence when fitted out with a mask and fins. Introduce these first, than add the mouthpiece when the child feels comfortable. If traveling to an area like the Caribbean or Bahamas where snorkeling opportunities are plentiful, bringing your own gear is always best, particularly for children.

Nature Studies. Don't overlook this excellent teaching resource in many of the destinations. The possibility for nature studies exists worldwide, greatly increasing you and your children's understanding of a given area and the natural world it incorporates. As always, children enjoy learning about something they can see or experience firsthand, making travel the ideal time to help them develop a love and appreciation for the outdoors. Some areas offer numerous opportunities for nature studies, with group activities, interpretive nature walks, exhibits and parks. Others must be studied on your own, using whatever information you can glean from the surroundings. Parks and preserves remain the most valuable resources and are always well worth a visit. General details on environmental learning opportunities have been provided with each destination, offering insight into what is available in a given area.

EQUIPMENT RECOMMENDATIONS

Perhaps the single biggest question that looms in most parents' minds when contemplating a trip is what to take. It's a question I am continually asked. How did I know what clothes to take, what medicines to include, what sources of entertainment to choose? Did we take one tent or two, a kerosene stove or propane, hiking boots or sneakers? Confronted with the sheer magnitude of what they own and use daily, first-time adventurers wallow in confusion. Nor does a trip to the local outdoor retailer necessarily clarify the situation. If anything, the overabundance of specialty equipment (much of it costly) only intensifies the problem. Before long, the whole trip begins to look more like an expensive nightmare than your budget dream.

Choosing the right equipment needn't be the dilemma it initially seems. The cost can be kept as low as you want and much of the equipment limited to what you already own. Newcomers will have to spend the most, but console yourself with the fact that adventure equipment lasts a long time and will serve you well in future travels. All adventure travel equipment can be divided into three categories: basic family needs, general camping gear (not necessarily intended just for camping), and specialized outdoor gear for individual activities. Having tried a number of different activities as a basis for our travels, we've run the gamut of equipment acquisitions. Each time, however, the bulk of what we needed was similar, whether bicycling in North Africa or renting in Central America, hiking in Europe or cruising in the Caribbean. For more detailed information on equipment planning, refer to our book, *The Complete Buyer's Guide to the Best Travel & Outdoor Gear.*

Basic Family Needs. This covers all those indispensable items at home that you'll need to bring along: clothing, footwear, toiletries, first aid, reading material, photography equipment, toys, and food. Think small when packing. No one is going to care if your child wears the same two T-shirts the entire trip. If you're planning to do your own cooking, take along any indispensable seasonings your family likes when traveling to out-of-the-way places. Because the availability of basics varies from place to place, what you include will be somewhat dependent on where you go and how long you stay. Information concerning the availability of many everyday needs is included with each destination chapter.

General Camping Gear. Whether you plan to camp or not, we recommend taking all camping gear except a tent on any trip. Because independent adventure travel goes hand-in-hand with budget travel, guaranteeing yourself a clean place to sleep, plus the ability to cook, is a wonderful security. We can recall island-hopping on ferries through the Mediterranean when the whole family bedded down on deck with sleeping bags and pads. Early, predawn arrivals at a destination were always more enjoyable when hot drinks and breakfast could be served up right from our backpacks. With camping gear, the whole outdoors can serve as a place to spend the night, whether traveling by car, bike, or public bus. Include sleeping bags and pads, cooking gear, a reliable stove (a multi-fuel one is best for overseas travel), water carrier, water filter, and one or two tents (optional).

Specialized Gear. What specialized equipment to take will depend on what activities you plan. We always seem to find ourselves trying to juggle everything: bicycles and framepacks, boat equipment and tents. Some people do manage to travel that way, with canoe, bicycles, camping gear, and children popping out from all corners of their vehicle. Going foreign eliminates this possibility for the most part, forcing us to think smaller and more modestly. Here again, some overlap in equipment is possible, particularly with hiking and bicycling.

• *Hiking Gear.* Unless you plan some wilderness backpacking, decent shoes, day packs, and water carriers are all you will need. If traveling with a baby, choose your child carrier carefully for optimum comfort. Most hiking throughout the world can be done without full-frame packs.

• *Bicycling Gear.* Choose bicycles with at least 10 speeds and durable tires. 18 speeds are best. A good set of panniers, handlebar pack, spare parts, and tools should last you many trips. Carrying at least one large set of panniers is helpful even on day outings for transporting paraphernalia like food and extra clothing. Consider taking bicycles even if you plan to stay in one place. They're a great way to explore, shop, and exercise.

• *Canoeing Gear.* If you plan to travel by vehicle, taking your own canoe is a great idea. Without one, canoe travel is limited to those few areas that rent them. Fortunately, canoe rentals are available in many of the prime areas of exploration, particularly in North America where this sport is most popular. Beyond a reliable canoe, good paddles, and possibly a seat or two for passengers, little is needed specifically for canoe travel.

• *Sailing Gear.* This is the one exception to the "go modest" theory. There's nothing small about what you'll need if you plan to travel by sailboat. The rewards, however, will far outweigh the inconveniences of buying, outfitting, and traveling by sailboat. A variety of options are available: ocean-going yachts and coastal cruisers, monohulls and multihulls, day-sailors and trailerable craft. All have their advantages and suit certain needs. Choose a boat carefully, but don't feel compelled to buy all that endless arsenal of equipment that's available today. Sailing has been around a long time, long before the age of electronics, modern mechanized devices, and fuel-driven engines. As long as you are safe and comfortable, that's all that really counts.

LIVING ABROAD

Living abroad is probably the easiest way to adventure independently as a family. Depending on your chosen destination, the experience can range from relaxing to rigorous, from the modern and familiar to the primitive and unknown. Living abroad is always an adventure, no matter where the destination. Instead of moving from place to place, the destiny of most tourists, the emphasis is on delving into an area, a culture, a way of life. Lifestyle differences that are normally just seen while passing though become realities as you adapt yourselves to the ways of a community. It is the ultimate cross-cultural experience, an amalgamation of those habits that you already possess and those of the people around you. Children invariably thrive on this type of experience, seeing it as an extension of their homelife.

Like sailboat travel, a home is created, a familiarity and routine established. For first-time adventuring families, or when traveling to a vastly different culture, living in one place can alleviate many of the basic challenges, making the whole experience a more relaxing one. If you plan to travel during the school year, it's always easier to cope with academics from a base. As most of our travel is off-season while the children are doing school and both Kevin and I working on our writing, we usually live in one place for at least some of each trip, preferably the first part. That way we gently ease ourselves into a culture before taking on the added challenge of exploring the country more extensively, usually in an outdoor-oriented way like bicycling, sailing or backpacking.

Renting. Living abroad in one place usually means renting. Rentals are easier to find and more affordable than you might expect. Off-season travel to an area should get you the best price. To find a place, ask anyone: at the local tourist bureau, realtors, people off the streets, whoever. Check out the amenities before paying, then still expect the unexpected. This is all part of the foreign rental experience, discovering what works and what doesn't (how the stove works, how the hot water heater doesn't....).

If traveling to a place and seeking out a rental seems more than you can cope with, try contacting one of the following organizations, specializing in arranging worldwide house rentals. Keep in mind that these rentals will probably be more commodious and expensive than what you can find on your own.

• *Rent A Home International*, 7200-34th Ave. NW, Seattle, WA 98117.

• *At Home Abroad*, Sutton Town House, 405 East 56th Street, 6H, NY, NY 10022.

• *Interhome Inc.*, 124 Little Falls Road, Fairfield, NJ 07006.

• *Interhome Holidays*, 156 Randall Street, Oakville, Ontario, L6J 1P4, Canada.

House Exchange. If you own a home in a desirable area, one excellent way to try a stint abroad is to do an exchange. House conditions are bound to be good, if not downright luxurious, compared to most inexpensive rentals. To make the experience more of an adventure, choose a location that is different from where you live at home. There's not much point in traveling halfway around the world just to find yourself living in the same circumstances. Many people have seasonal cottages in excellent areas for a living abroad experience. House exchanges are a terrific introduction to adventuring for first-time travelers. Just coping with a foreign culture and language might seem challenging enough, without the added factor of finding a place to live. To arrange a home exchange, contact any of the following:

- *INTERVAC USA*, PO Box 590504, San Francisco, CA 94119.

- *West World Holiday Exchange*, 1707 Platt Crescent, North Vancouver, BC V7J 1X9, Canada.

- *Vacation Exchange Club*, PO Box 820, Haleiwa, HI 96712.

- *Better Homes & Travel*, PO Box Box 268, New York, NY 10-270.

- *INTERVAC Canada*, 606 Alexander Cr. NW, Calgary, Alberta, T2M 4T3, Canada.

Campgrounds. Another way to have all the advantages of basing yourself in one place at little cost is to stay at a campground. While amenities will be more basic, the sense of a home and routine can still be easily established. Many foreign campgrounds rent small bungalows for a nominal fee, a definite step up from tenting. In a warm, sunny climate, small accommodations won't seem much of an inconvenience when the children are spending most of the time outdoors.

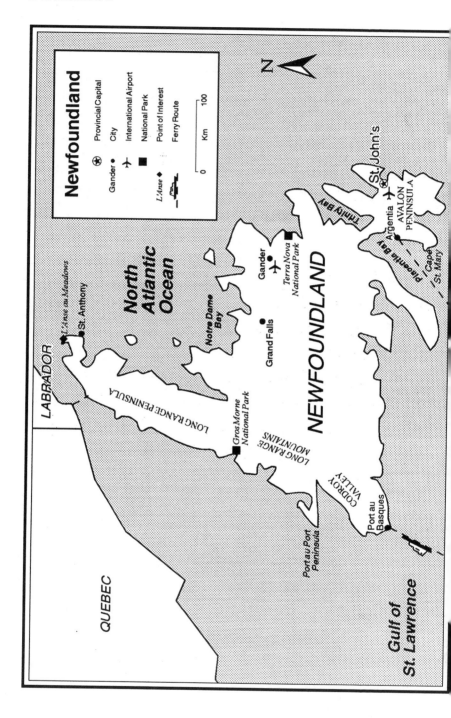

Newfoundland

Wild and indomitable, friendly and welcoming, Newfoundland is perhaps North America's best kept secret. The sea is a constant presence, shaping much of the character of this isolated Canadian province. It brought the first white settlers when the Vikings landed at L'Anse aux Meadows. Throughout history it has provided a livelihood that continues today. Its fog shrouds the southern shores and its waves have carved a series of rock-strewn coasts. Icebergs drift south from the Arctic in summer and pack ice forms an endless white prairie in winter. A place where man exists in the shadow of nature, Newfoundland offers endless opportunities for family adventure travel.

GENERAL DESCRIPTION

Location. Together with Labrador, Newfoundland forms Canada's most eastern, and perhaps most remote, province. An island, separated from its Maritime neighbors by the Gulf of St. Lawrence and Cabot Straits, Newfoundland seems adrift, a rugged, untamed piece of land cast out into the North Atlantic. The waters that surround it can be beset by storms and currents, fog, and icebergs. Crossing by ferry from Cape Breton, Nova Scotia is like stepping into another world.

Terrain. Terrain is varied, from the Long Range Mountains in the west to the barrens of the Avalon Peninsula in the east. There are mountains and fjords, lakes and rivers, forests and fertile valleys. The coast stretches endlessly, sometimes rocky and barren, sometimes wrapped in fog or edged with trees. To the north, islands lie scattered offshore like intrepid children straying from their parent. The interior remains dense and wooded, more the domain of moose and caribou than man.

Climate. Like most of Canada, Newfoundland is subject to extreme seasonal changes, from ice and snowbound winters to warm, comfortable summers. Due to its near proximity to the Gulf Stream, the weather is surprisingly mild for such a high latitude. Temperatures are noticeably cooler at the northern tip of the Long Range Peninsula than to the south and east. Summer is the best time to visit, with most parks and campgrounds only officially open during this time. Temperatures average in the mid to high 70's. Even at the height of the summer season, crowds are still virtually non-existent in this lovely, uncrowded province.

Culture & Lifestyle. Newfoundland's culture is uniquely its own, set apart and distinctive from the other provinces. It is a difference you sense immediately upon arrival, the product of years of isolation and hardship, of self-sufficiency and community spirit, the result of a heritage forged living with the forces of nature. After four hundred years of settlement, most Newfoundlanders still live along the shore, many making their living from the sea.

Regional accents are strong, the lifestyle unique, a delightful blend of modern amenities and ingrained traditions. It is a lifestyle reminiscent of pioneer days, but without most of the hardships. Clothes hang from clotheslines and housewives bake their own bread. People walk to village stores and children rule the roads on bicycles. Yet there are schools and health clinics, daily mail service and well-stocked shops. Homes are comfortable and modern, filled with every convenience. Newfoundlanders are deeply committed to their province, and have every reason to be. It is a wild, friendly, exuberant place.

Go to Newfoundland prepared to socialize. The people are open and welcoming. Casual meetings lead to invitations into homes, advice on places to see, gifts of food, quick friendships. Most country people the world over are open and welcoming to families traveling modestly on their own, but only a few have the advantage of being able to communicate with you beyond a basic level. Unless you are very fluent in a foreign language, this offers a rare opportunity when traveling. Don't be afraid to cross the line between tourist and inhabitant, for it is there that so many true adventures lie.

PRACTICAL CONCERNS

Political Conditions & Safety. Once the domain of early Maritime Indians and Dorset Eskimos, Newfoundland was first sparsely settled by fishermen from Europe around 400 years ago. The island maintained independence until 1949, becoming the last province to join Canada. Today it is a safe place to travel to. Parents have little to fear by letting their children roam a campground, village, or the countryside alone. About the biggest risk you run adventuring here is being bitten by blackflies.

Travel Documents. Proof of citizenship is the only requirement for American citizens. All other nationals except those from Greenland must have a valid passport and, in some cases, a visa (most EC countries and all Commonwealth ones are exempt). Visas are issued up to six months.

Money. Currency is the Canadian Dollar, comprised of 100 cents. Banks are widespread and located in all sizeable towns. Travelers checks are accepted everywhere and the safest way to carry your money. Credit cards can also be used to make withdrawals from a local bank. Travelers checks have a lower service charge than withdrawals in most instances.

Costs. Prices are no steeper in Newfoundland than elsewhere in Atlantic Canada. Coming from the States, expect food and fuel costs to be about 50% higher than at home. Locally produced foods cost less. Because government subsidies help support remote communities, food prices are equivalent throughout the province. Accommodation costs are inexpensive at camp-grounds, reasonable at Hospitality Homes and small hotels. Much of what you do in Newfoundland involves no money at all, including visits to a number of parks and historic sites. With its opportunities to explore the outdoors and easily interact with the local population, Newfoundland is an excellent destination for inexpensive family adventuring.

Language. With the exception of a small area on the Port au Port Peninsula, English is the principal language. As throughout Canada, all information is written in both French and English. The biggest communication challenge will be trying to understand the local dialects, some of which offer all the confusion of a foreign language.

Health. Newfoundland has no specific health concerns. No immunizations are necessary and both food and water safe. Health care facilities are widespread and excellent, although expensive for non-residents. Drug stores can be found in larger towns. Small general stores in rural communities also carry a good cross-section of basics if they're the only store in the area. Carry a good basic first aid kit to avoid being caught short at the wrong time, but don't worry about finding more. Consider bringing a water filter or purifying tablets. Necessary for backcountry camping, they will also come in handy at campgrounds where the water must be treated before using.

Food. Towns are excellently supplied for their size, perhaps because the people are so accustomed to isolation. With no large town down the road, each community has learned to take responsibility for its own supply. With few exceptions you'll find at least one well-stocked store in even the smallest village. The more isolated the place, the more dependable the store. If you want something like fresh bread or produce that isn't in the store, the chances are someone in the village can accommodate you. In one remote village we even managed a birthday cake for Tristan and Colin, baked by a local woman.

All the basic foods are available, including a surprising variety of fresh produce. Some areas, like the Codroy and Humber Valleys sell locally-grown products. Another excellent source of fresh food, one your children will enjoy, is wild fruit. Mid-summer in Newfoundland is filled with delicious strawberries, growing in meadows and along paths. Long-life milk is available, sold in one-liter cartons under the label Grand Pré (that's what the Newfoundlanders call it). Bought off the shelf, it will keep for months unrefrigerated. In isolated villages this is often all that's available.

Clothes. Newfoundland is one of those places where you need to go prepared for anything: hot sun and cold, wind and rain. The chances are you'll experience all of them during the course of even a short visit. Summer temperatures generally vary from hot to cool depending on the weather and proximity to the ocean, so plan your clothes accordingly. If you do leave something critical behind, finding clothing is easy in any large town or good general store.

Laundry & Bathing. This can pose a bit of a challenge in Newfoundland. Private campgrounds, those meccas of washing machines, are next to nonexistent. Only a couple of provincial and national park campgrounds have laundry facilities. Nor are towns necessarily better supplied. Take enough clothes so you can go at least a week between washings. Then do some searching. Fellow campers seem to have a laundry grapevine that can help you out. Bathing is only minimally easier if camping. Check the Tourist guide to discover which campgrounds offer hot showers. Other types of accommodations all supply hot water bathing facilites, including private campgrounds. If you're free camping in a remote village, don't be surprised if someone offers the use of their shower, just another example of Newfoundlanderss' inate hospitality. For the most part, the same places can provide both laundry and bathing facilities. During the course of our trip we found ourselves doing both in a variety of places: a provincial park, an historic village, a marina, a fishing town, in the sink. Adventuring is never dull in Newfoundland.

Baby Needs. All types of baby food and paraphernalia are available. Bring some kind of child carrier for hiking. The Tough Traveler child carriers are excellent choices with their optional Rain/Sun Hoods. This affords both protection from rain and a place to drape some netting when hiking in buggy areas. If camping, you will definitely want a dining fly for areas with black flies. Although active children might hardly notice them, an infant or sitting toddler is going to make a perfect target. Carrying a dining fly guarantees a bug-free play place for your baby while camped. Bring one with you, as they're hard to find in Newfoundland.

Blackflies. During warm summer months, blackflies can be a problem in some areas. Be sure to pack some effective bug repellant, but you can also avoid buggy areas by choosing open, exposed sites, preferably on the coast. Wind is the best deterrent.

TRANSPORTATION

Getting There. As an island, Newfoundland is only accessible by air or ferry. Ferries operate daily year-round from North Sydney, Nova Scotia to Port aux Basques and seasonally from North Sydney to Argentia in summer and early fall. St. John's has an international airport with connections to North America and Europe. If possible, go by ferry. The crossing is a pure delight, from the lively entertainment provided at the docks to the thrilling arrival on a coast often shrouded in dense fog.

Regional Transport. Regional travel is best done by car. Although public buses service much of the province, principally along the Trans Canada Highway, the most exciting areas of the island would be missed this way.

Roads. Roads come in a variety of guises. The Trans Canada Highway, linking together the far-flung communities between St. John's and Port aux Basques, is smooth, fast and modern, with two lanes and little traffic. Even in peak summer season the road is not overly crowded. Beyond the Trans Canada, communities are accessed either by paved or dirt roads. The Long Range Peninsula now has an excellent road all the way to its northern tip at L'Anse aux Meadows. Dirt roads range from smooth rides to back-jarring washboards. Some are long and arduous, but all are worth traveling for what you find at the end; some of the friendliest, most charming villages in the world.

ACCOMMODATIONS

Campgrounds. Camping is definitely the ideal way to explore this exquisite province filled with natural beauty. Facilities are available all over the province, including excellent choices at national and provincial parks. Facilities at provincial parks are usually minimal, with emphasis placed on natural surroundings. Picnic tables, cold running water, free fire wood, and gorgeous settings are the norm. All close after Labour Day, but can still be used provided you supply your own water. National park campgrounds vary from basic facilities to hot running water and hook-ups. During peak season, campgrounds at Terra Nova are more crowded than Gros Morne, due to proximity to St. John's. Camping goods are available at major towns like Corner Brook and St. John's. Bring whatever equipment and spare parts you need with you.

Hospitality Homes. These offer both inexpensive accommodations and an ideal way to meet local people. Located in small coastal communities, a stay in one allows you to experience this unique lifestyle. For a list of homes, see the *Newfoundland Travel Guide*.

POINTS OF INTEREST

Natural. Few places in the world can match the impact of experiencing Newfoundland firsthand; areas of natural beauty and animal habitats co-exist on an equal standing with man. Opportunities to see wildlife in its natural surroundings abound. Whales swim in to bays. Moose and caribou roam the interior. Seabirds nest along the coast. Parks and preserves are plentiful, among them the following:

• *Gros Morne National Park.* Perhaps Newfoundland's most spectacular area. Includes the province's highest mountains, an inland fjord, and unusual geological formations.

• *Terra Nova National Park.* A coastal park along the northeastern shore with beaches, forest, rivers, and wooded hills.

• *Avalon Wilderness Reserve.* Interior barrens and lakes of southern Avalon Peninsula. Home to thousands of caribou. Designated canoe route and hiking trails.

• *Witless Bay Ecological Reserve.* Three islands that make up one of the world's largest seabird breeding areas. Accessible only by boat.

• *Cape St. Mary's Ecological Area.* Coastal seabird nesting area accessible by land.

Cultural. Newfoundland's culture is thriving today, more reminiscent of what one sees in an ethnic culture than a modern, homogenous one. The signs are everywhere, the result of an inherent self-sufficiency and

resourcefulness than permeates presentday life. Poles rise stacked to dry teepee-style, destined for winter wood. Tiny potato plots line deserted roads, taking advantage of any patch of arable soil. Many cultural aspects reflect the province's link to the sea: rows of fish drying on flakes by the waterfronts; modest homes colored in bright pastels, a homing beacon for returning fishermen; boats everywhere, from small dories pulled up on the shore to large off-shore craft, their paintwork often indicative of the village they originate from.

• *Festivals.* Summertime is filled with festivals. Many are traditional music festivals, reflecting the strong Celtic heritage of the province. Others celebrate everything from the strawberry harvest to the fishing industry. Not only will you enjoy some wonderful entertainment, but chances are you'll meet local families as well.

Historic. Newfoundland has an abundance of museums and historic sites. All teach you something about this remote province and its intrepid people. The following are a few of the better known ones and only a smattering of what's available.

• *Port au Choix National Historic Park..* Burial ground of Maritime Archaic Indians, inhabitants from over 8,000 years ago.

• *L'Anse aux Meadows.* Original site of a Viking village, the earliest known European settlement in North America. Includes a reconstructed village, museum and exhibits. Impressively located at the northern tip of Newfoundland.

• *Mary March Regional Museum.* Many exhibits relevant to the province: natural history, geology, native peoples, European settlement.

• *Castle Hill National Historic Park.* Center of conflict between French and English for control of Newfoundland's fishing industry. Remains of both English and French fortifications.

• *Grenfell House.* Original headquarters of famous Grenfell Mission. Exhibits show history of mission's hospital work and provide great insight into life in remote coastal outports of Newfoundland and Labrador.

OUTDOOR ACTIVITIES

Backcountry Camping. As the least populated province in Canada, Newfoundland has endless scope for backcountry camping. Designated sites are available at Gros Morne National Park, Terra Nova National Park, and Barrachois Provincial Park. The one at Green Gardens in Gros Morne shouldn't be missed. Water is one thing you won't have trouble finding off the beaten track. Fresh water ponds and brooks are prolific. Carry a water filter to guard against Giardia and bacteria.

Hiking. Hiking in Newfoundland is as exciting as everything else about the province. A number of designated hiking areas have been developed, among them the following:

• *Gros Morne.* Hiking here should not be missed. With some of the province's most spectacular scenery, the park offers a variety of trails in contrasting surroundings. Most are appropriate for children of all ages.

• *Terra Nova.* A wide variety of trails are offered in this scenic, coastal setting.

• *St. George to Mainland Trail.* Of cultural significance, this footpath traverses rugged coastline on the Port au Port Peninsula, linking two Acadian communities.

Much of the province's hiking potential is of an informal nature. Short, easy walks are possible all over the province: out to a lighthouse, along the coast, to waterfalls, or around a village. Villages have a very community-oriented attitude towards private land that makes exploring on foot easy. Most common are paths radiating out along the coast, paths that once linked remote homes. While not designated hikes, they provide some of the best hiking in the province: scenic, adventurous, and imbued with insight into the lives and culture of the people of Newfoundland.

Bicycling. Despite its immense size and sparse settlement, Newfoundland has some excellent places for bicycling. Peninsulas, small coastal communities, islands, and near-deserted roads can all be explored by bike. We don't recommend bicycle touring as your sole means of transport. Too much of your trip would be spent covering long, dull distances on the Trans Canada. Although wide, smooth, and surprisingly free of traffic, this road acts as a transportation link between east and west, bypassing most areas of interest. It is out on the coast, down the many country roads that radiate away from the Trans Canada, that the thrill and essence of Newfoundland really lies. Places like the Codroy Valley, Bonavista Peninsula, the Notre Dame Bay area, and Port au Port Peninsula all offer exciting, short bicycle routes. Even the Northern Peninsula could comfortably be covered exclusively by bicycle, with easy riding on a level road skirting the shore of the Gulf of St. Lawrence.

The one exception to the "bicycle only" rule might be the Avalon Peninsula. Flying into St.John or taking the ferry to Argentia, you could do a comfortable two-week circum-navigation of the Avalon solely by bicycle. To avoid summer bugs and frequent fog, this route would be best in early fall.

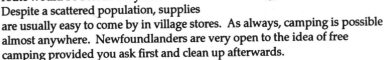

Despite a scattered population, supplies are usually easy to come by in village stores. As always, camping is possible almost anywhere. Newfoundlanders are very open to the idea of free camping provided you ask first and clean up afterwards.

Canoeing. Canoeing here generally requires bringing your own canoe. Of the many lakes, rivers, and ponds in the province, all are unspoiled and undeveloped, waiting for you to discover them on your own. As always in inland Newfoundland, blackflies can be a factor during the summer months. Day outings in the interior or in any bog areas won't be a problem, although you might find yourselves picnicking out on the water rather than on shore. Just launch your canoe where ever you see an appropriate spot. Leaving a loaded, parked car is generally not a problem. There may be an abundant number of blackflies, but there aren't many thieves.

The Tourist Bureau publishes a list of 11 possible rivers for canoe travel, some of which are appropriate for families. A few places are easily accessible for day trips or overnights. The Codroy Valley and St. Paul's Inlet are two good areas for canoeing on the west coast. Terra Nova National Park is the easiest place to canoe, with rentals and outlined routes that are ideal for families with children. Experienced families might want to consider an outing in the Avalon Wilderness Preserve along a designated canoe route. We strongly suggest doing this in fall after blackfly season, as much of this route is through interior bogs.

Sailing. Sailing in Newfoundland can be one of life's ultimate adventures. Although the province has a well-earned reputation for fog, this is only true for the south and east coasts. Other areas like the north coast stay virtually fog-free all summer.

• *Notre Dame Bay & Hamilton Sound.* This is one of the province's prime cruising grounds. With its many islands and lovely, clear weather, the area offers endless opportunities for exploration. Chartering is possible at Morton's Harbor Marina, a friendly family-run operation in the tiny village of Morton's Harbour.

• *Long Range Peninsula.* Sailing the east coast of the peninsula offers some never-to-be-forgotten cruising. Provisions are available at coastal villages scattered along the shore and tying up at government wharfs for the night will introduce you to local inhabitants.

• *Bonavista & Trinity Bays.* With their many small bays, islands, reaches, and sounds, these offer good sailing in relatively protected waters. Cruising is also possible in Terra Nova where docking facilities have been provided for sailors.

Swimming. Although swimming is hardly something you'll find yourselves doing a great deal of in Newfoundland, bringing along bathing suits is always a good idea. Numerous freshwater lakes and rivers offer the warmest swimming, while ocean beaches provide an endless source of entertainment for children, plus the opportunity for occasional quick dips. Despite visiting during an exceptionally cold summer, we managed a number of swims, from rivers and bog lakes to the Gulf of St. Lawrence. Good beaches are located along the southwest coast, at Gros Morne National Park, and on the east coast.

Nature Studies. Opportunities for nature studies seem to be everywhere in this province where the wildlife far outnumbers the inhabitants. As always, parks, preserves, and museums are the best resources.

• *Birdwatching.* Visit Cape St. Mary's Ecological Reserve and the Witless Bay Provincial Seabird Sanctuary, two of the largest seabird breeding areas in the world.

• *Whalewatching.* Humpback whales arrive in Trinity Bay each summmer, making this a prime area for whalewatching. Frequent boat tours are offered seasonally.

• *Mary March Museum.* Don't miss the fascinating display here depicting the unusual geological formation of Newfoundland.

• *Gros Morne National Park.* Park exhibits include information on the unique Tablelands, now a World Heritage Site.

Small Voyages of Discovery

Newfoundland's provincial ferry service is an adventure in itself. Nothing gets you into the mood of this isolated, awe-inspiring island faster than the initial approach by ferry from Nova Scotia. Fogs are frequent, and your first sight of the province is often nothing more than a shadowy glimpse of rocks before the ferry nudges the dock. Like a true-life Brigadoon, Newfoundland seems hidden in the mists, appearing only for those who venture this far.

Off the boat, the feeling persists that you have traveled much further, into another time and place. Sparsely populated along its rugged shore, Newfoundland has long relied on the sea to provide its livelihood and means of transportation. Although roads now penetrate to communities once all but cut off, ferries still service a number of isolated areas. A trip on one will provide you with the kind of experience that is the essence of adventure travel, personal challenge coupled with intimate cultural interaction.

Beginning with the ferry itself, the experience is unlike anything most tourists experience, traveling their more conventional route by car and road. Because the provincial ferry service is government operated, fares are kept extremly low to benefit the survival of these out- lying communities. Conse- quently, you can en- joy a one or two hour coastal trip for a fraction of what it would cost on a scenic tour boat. Boats come in a variety of guises, from small passenger affairs to large car ferries. Once on the water, Newfoundland's scenery takes on an added aura of grandeur, one that reinforces the presence and power of nature in this remote province. Coastal beauty only guessed at is now experienced firsthand as the ferry threads its way among wooded islands, along mountainous shores, or through the mysterious shrouded world of fog and rock. On some rides, icebergs loom across the water like giant cliffs and castles, floating in a blue calm that masks their size and strength. For people who have never seen icebergs, encountering them up close on a ferry is unforgetable.

Children love ferries, making this an easy way to excite them about your travels. Even the most apathetic, disinterested child is going to sit up and take notice on a trip that starts with something as exciting as a ferry ride. Because most of Newfoundland's ferries are simple passenger boats, your car can be left behind, a further indication to jaded car-traveling youth that this new experience is going to be something out of the ordinary. Most children will love everything about a ferry outing, from the anticipation of its arrival to the thrill of watching it load and get underway.

There's something about the mechanics of a ferry that keeps children of all ages riveted with interest. Older children will invariably disappear on an exploration of the premises, peering over rails and into corners while devising a host of nautical games. Like all boat transport, ferries are a wonderful vehicle for a child's imaginative play. Don't be surprised if they soon appear on excellent terms with the captain and crew, all of whom seem to welcome curious and enthusiastic children.

Any ferry ride is a miniature adventure, exposing you to a place and people in a way most tourists never experience. Despite a similarity of language and culture, habit and dress, a coastal community at the end of a ferry trip is as alien as any wildly ethnic corner of the world. In many ways it is even more rewarding, for the common language and ability to communicate, the cultural similarities and mutual lifestyle allow you to immerse yourself in the community, becoming a temporary part of it rather than just a social attraction.

Taking bicycles is one excellent way to explore the islands and villages at your destination, riding along quiet dirt roads with hardly a vehicle in sight. Camping is also always a possibility: beside a school, in someone's field, in a meadow where an isolated house once stood, nestled in a cove. Everywhere you will find the same generosity and willingness to extend a welcome.

Each ferry trip offers its own unique exerience, its own taste of Newfoundland culture. On one you might ride in lonely splendor, another amidst a crowd of local inhabitants. A third might regale you with traditional music as a crewman, temporarily freed from dock work, plays tunes on his concertina. Where you go or what ferry you choose makes little difference. All of them lead to adventure, to a special corner of the world, to a people you will never forget.

RESOURCE SECTION

TOURIST BUREAUS
Central Office: Canadian Government Office of Tourism: Federal Dept. of Regional Industrial Expansion, 235 Queen St., Ottawa K1A OH5, Canada Tel: (613) 995-9001.
Provincial Office: Department of Development and Tourism, PO Box 2016, St. Johns, Newfoundland A1C 5R8. Tel: (709) 576-2830. Use this address for requesting provincial travel information.

CONSULATES
Canadian Consulate General: 16th Floor, Exxon Bldg., 1251 Ave. of the Americas, New York, NY 10020. Tel: (212) 768-2400.
Other Canadian consulates located in most major North American cities.

NATIONAL AIRLINES
Air Canada: Place Air Canada, 500 Rene Levesque Blvd. West, Montreal PQ H2Z 1X5, Canada Tel: (800) 422-6232, (514) 393-3333.
Canadian Airlines International. Ste. 2800, 700-2nd St. S.W., Calgary, AB T2P 2W2, Canada   Tel: (800) 426-7000, (403) 294-2000. *Air Atlantic* is an affiliate airline serving Atlantic Canada.

SUGGESTED READING
"Them Days" Series: Magazine format; anthology of stories about early life in northern Newfoundland and Labrador. Contact: Newfoundland Emporium, 7 Broadway, Corner Brook, NFLD A2H 4C2, Canada.
Real Guide: Canada by Lee, Jepson & Smith. New York: Prentice Hall Travel.
Canada: A Travel Survival Kit by T. Smallman. Berkeley: Lonely Planet Publications.

SUGGESTED MAPS
Atlantic Provinces by Map Art. Scale: 1,500,000:1, Approx. price: $3.
Good Travel maps for Newfoundland & Labrador are also available from the provincial tourist office.

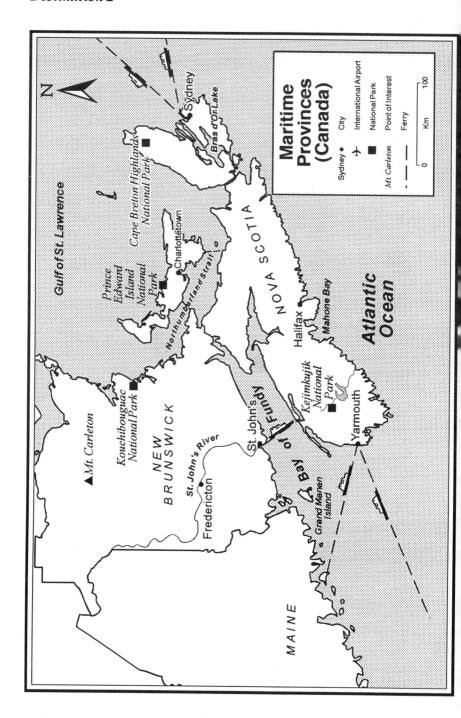

The Canadian Maritimes

The Canadian Maritime Provinces abound with opportunities for rewarding adventure travel. Some are well-suited to novice adventures, others offer all the challenge of a trek in the Himalayas. For those who seek to gain confidence and hone their adventuring skills, the Maritimes offer a wonderful learning experience. The challenges are nature-oriented and exhilarating: adventure in an outdoor environment. Children will take to it like ducks to water, always a key to any successful family outing.

GENERAL DESCRIPTION

Location. Made up of the three provinces along Canada's east coast, the Maritimes are comprised of Nova Scotia, Prince Edward Island and New Brunswick. Nova Scotia forms a 350-mile long peninsula, including Cape Breton Island in the north. Prince Edward Island lies in the Gulf of St. Lawrence, north of Nova Scotia and New Brunswick across the narrow Northumberland Strait. New Brunswick, the largest of the three provinces, is located on the mainland and bordered by Maine, Quebec, the Bay of Fundy and the Gulf of St. Lawrence.

Terrain. The area is diverse, ranging from the white sand beaches of P.E.I. to the interior mountains of New Brunswick. Nova Scotia and New Brunswick are both regions of contrasts: dense forests and cultivated valleys, huge tides and tranquil lakes, rocky headlands and gentle backwaters. One moment the area seems tamed and settled, the next on the brink of wilderness. Prince Edward Island is an island of pastoral farms that spread across the undulating land like a giant patchwork quilt, edged by red cliffs and beaches, within reach of the sea.

Climate. The Maritimes are warmer in the fall and cooler in the spring and summer than inland Canada. Comfortable outdoor travel is limited to spring through fall. Summer temperatures vary from hot to cool depending on the weather and proximity to the cooling effects of the ocean. September is probably the best time of all to travel to the Maritimes; the tourist season is over and the weather still at its zenith, with warm days and cool nights. Although summer is not overly crowded, travel is always more pleasant off-season when people are more relaxed and facilities almost empty.

Culture & Lifestyle. The Maritimes' culture is very much that of the New World, an amalgamation of emigrant cultures coupled with its original native population. Micmac Indian settlements still dot the provinces. French Acadians form a highly visible minority, contrasting with the predominant Anglo culture, with New Brunswick representing the one truly bilingual province in Canada. One reason the Acadians stand so distinctly apart is their use of French as a primary language. Other minority cultures retain a strong link to their heritage, something visitors can enjoy at the abundant local festivals celebrated each summer. The provinces are proud of their cultural diversity and do much to preserve and celebrate it. Their desire to maintain a cultural identity is authentic and can be fascinating for visitors. What makes an area like this unique is that right around the corner from a Scottish Highland community might be a completely French-speaking one of Acadians.

Visiting the Maritime Provinces has been described by some as stepping back fifty years. The comparison is a complimentary one. Coming from the fast-paced, often frenetic pace that has come to typify modern life, the Maritimes seem delightfully old-fashioned. The pace is still slow, the sense of community strong. Rural communities predominate and country friendliness prevails. People take the time to greet each other, to linger and talk, to extend a welcome to strangers. As with any rural area, the countryside is filled with things to see, places to explore and friendly people to meet. Children will love it.

PRACTICAL CONCERNS

Political Update & Safety. Canada is a safe place to travel. There are no political hazards, nor is the lifestyle a threatening one. The Maritimes are predominantly rural, the ideal environment for children to safely explore, both with parents and alone. Canadians are friendly people—don't let any misplaced paranoia keep you from responding openly to that friendliness. You'll encounter it everywhere, even in heavily touristed areas where you might expect more reticence towards visitors. This is a refreshing attitude in a world grown jaded with overtourism.

Travel Documents. Proof of citizenship is the only requirement for American citizens traveling to the Maritimes. All other nationals except those from Greenland must have a valid passport and, in some cases, a visa (most EC countries and all Commonwealth ones are exempt). Visas are issued up to six months. Border crossings from the States are quick, although American officials can be sticklers under what they consider suspicious-looking circumstances. We once had our car thoroughly searched when I took a wrong turn and mistakenly drove us back to the border in the middle of the night after crossing over from Canada.

Money. Currency is the Canadian dollar, consisting of 100 cents. Banks are widespread and located in all sizeable towns. Travelers checks are accepted everywhere and the safest way to carry your money. Credit cards can also be used to make withdrawals from a local bank. Visa seems to be the most widely accepted in the Maritime area. Travelers checks have a lower service charge than cash withdrawals in most instances.

Costs. To calculate the cost of a trip to the Maritimes is fairly simple. If you're coming from the States, fuel and some food (including milk) and specialty items will be about twice the price; most food and goods will be 30 to 50% higher. Visitors from Europe will find less of a discrepancy. Public transportation (including ferries), campgrounds, park fees and museums are all inexpensive. Compared to a trip to Disney World, a family adventure to the Maritimes should seem like a real bargain.

Language. With two official languages, all information is written in both English and French. For English-speaking families who have never traveled abroad, a visit to the Maritimes offers a gentle introduction to coping with a language other than their own. Although most Acadians are fluent in English, French is always the preferred choice.

Health. There are no specific health concerns. No immunizations are necessary and both food and water safe. Health care facilities are widespread and excellent, although expensive for non-residents. Drug stores can be found in all large towns. Small general stores in rural communities also carry a good cross-section of basics if they're the only store in the area.

Food. All basic western foods can be found throughout the provinces. Shopping varies from big supermarkets to tiny shops in rural towns. Obviously, the smaller the store, the more limited the choice of foods. The variety may suffer, but rarely the quality. The experience is always more pleasant on a small scale, with none of the depersonalization that plagues modern shopping centers. What you may have trouble finding at most stores is good natural foods, if that's something you like. The natural food movement doesn't seem to have ignited in the Maritimes yet, other than at a smattering of specialty stores, so if unsweetened peanut butter or trail mix is something your family craves, bring a supply with you if possible.

In rural areas, it's sometimes anyone's guess which towns have stores and which don't. Usually one town in an area will have all the amenities: general store, school, post office. One way to track down stores is with the help of the tourist guide book. The recommended "auto routes" mention any facilities along the way. We finally learned to buy food when we found it, especially when traveling by bicycle.

Clothes. Clothing for a trip to the Maritimes should include everything from swimming suits to warm jackets. During the fall, nights and early mornings can be cold, so bring hats and mittens if camping. Days are usually very warm spring through fall. We've found ourselves swimming at midday and huddled around a fire by evening. Basic clothing is easy to find in any large town. General stores are also a great place to buy clothes. You can still find them in the Maritimes, the kind that carry a bit of everything, from food to underwear. On Cape Breton we executed one epic shopping spree, buying shoes, socks, bug repellant, a rain jacket, snack food and matchbox cars, all under one roof.

Laundry & Bathing. Unless you plan some backcountry adventuring, laundromats are readily available. Private campgrounds often have washing machines and dryers. Check the individual campground listings in the Tourist Guides available at all tourist bureaus in the provinces. Campground facilities are the easiest to use because you can do your laundry while camped for the night. National park campgrounds also sometimes have laundromats. In the absence of a campground (or if not camping), find a large town. Hanging your clothes on a clothesline at your campsite can get you out of the laundromat a lot earlier and save on drying costs. Carry a piece of clothesline and a handful of pins. Bathing is almost always available at all types of accommodations except provincial parks in Nova Scotia. Expect hot showers and all the modern amenities in B & Bs, farms, and private campgrounds. Provincial parks in New Brunswick and Prince Edward Island also usually include bathing facilities, as do most national park campgrounds in all three provinces. If camping off-season, finding a place to bathe can be a bit trickier.

Baby Needs. All types of baby food and paraphernalia are available. Bring some kind of backpack for hiking. Otherwise, there are no special considerations. Diapers are easy to deal with at the many laundromats and babies can easily be kept clean with washing facilities at campgrounds or other accommodations.

TRANSPORTATION

Getting There. The Maritimes can be reached by car, airplane, train or ferry depending on the province. Located on the mainland, New Brunswick is the most accessible. Nova Scotia can be reached by car on the Trans Canada Highway or by ferry from Portland and Bar Harbor, ME or Saint John, N.B.. Daily ferries service Prince Edward Island from Caribou, N.S. and Tormentine, N.B.. There are international airports at Fredericton, N.B. and Halifax, N.S..

Regional Travel. All three provinces have public buses. New Brunswick also has a train service linking Fredericton, Saint John and Moncton. Because most local inhabitants rely on their own cars, bus service is not frequent or widespread. Travel this way is possible, but not ideal for families. Figure on bringing your own car, renting one while there, or better yet, traveling by bicycle.

Roads. Most roads are scenic, rural and easy to drive or bicycle. If you're tired of highway travel, these will seem like pure joy. These roads will force you to slow your pace and get into the relaxed mode of adventure travel. Dirt roads, where they exist, are usually well groomed and easy to travel, even on bicycles. P.E.I. in particular is a land of rural, scenic roads. Everywhere you turn there's another picturesque lane leading off across the countryside. Scenic routes have been designated around each of the three counties: Kings, Queens and Prince. Queens is by far the most heavily visited during peak season. To benefit tourists, Nova Scotia has been broken up into a series of "Trails" highlighting areas of particular interest. Most follow rural routes that are fun and adventurous to travel in a car or by bicycle. Because distances are greater between points of interest in New Brunswick, it's best to choose an area, like the St. John River Valley or Fundy Shore, and explore it in depth. This will keep you from making the mistake of driving like mad from place to place on the highways, then returning home afterwards feeling like your adventure turned into just another car trip.

ACCOMMODATIONS

Campgrounds. The Maritimes are loaded with campgrounds. Provincial park ones are widespread, with the emphasis on outdoor enjoyment rather than all the conveniences of home. All try to work closely within the context of their natural surroundings, particularly in Nova Scotia where facilities are basic. Sites are blended in whenever possible and fairly private. Provincial park campgrounds in New Brunswick and P.E.I. tend to be less rustic than those in Nova Scotia. Hot water and showers, for instance, are the norm. Campgrounds are also abundant in five national parks. During peak summer season, Prince Edward Island, Kejimkujik, and Kouchibouguac National Parks tend to be more crowded than the others. Off-season they're all a perfect delight. Private campgrounds are plentiful, although best used off-season when near-empty (unless you don't mind tenting in a sea of RVs). Most have a small store with fresh milk and basic foods. Firewood is available at most campgrounds, a welcome treat during cool autumn camping.

Bed & Breakfast. B&Bs are located all over the Maritimes. With accommodations right in private homes (usually two or three bedrooms with a shared bath), they provide an opportunity to meet some of the locals while offering a reasonably inexpensive alternative to camping. Unlike their American counterparts, where the emphasis is on gourmet dining, elegant accommodations, no children, and a hefty price, these B&Bs are well suited to budget-minded families. A combination of camping and B&Bs can provide a nice balance to a trip between outdoor living and a hint of luxury. People who run B&Bs tend to be friendly, outgoing and interested in strangers. A night in one can teach you much about a place.

Farm Vacation. These provide an unusual and enjoyable type of accommodation for families who really want an intimate insight into the rural life of the Maritimes. With this type of experience, you are treated like one of the family, living in their home, eating together and participating with farm chores if you wish. It's a rare child that doesn't enjoy this type of adventure, particularly if you don't live in a rural area yourselves. Contact the individual tourist bureaus for a list of participating homes.

POINTS OF INTEREST

Natural. The natural beauty of this area predominates, making it an ideal environmental learning experience for children. Despite their active tourist industry, the provinces remain committed to preserving the predominantly rural quality of their land. All three feature long stretches of unspoiled shorefront, while both New Brunswick and Nova Scotia have large tracts of wilderness in their interiors. Opportunities to see wildlife are plentiful. Whales arrive each year to their summer feeding grounds. Seals play in the waters and bask on rocks along the shore. On a hike through the woods, you might cross paths with a moose or bear. Over 300 species of birds visit Grand Manan Island, N.B. alone. There are five national parks and numerous provincial ones throughout the provinces, offering endless opportunities for outdoor activities and enjoying the Maritimes' wildlife and beauty. The following are just a few of the many wonderful natural points of interest.

• *Prince Edward Island National Park.* Located along the north coast, this is the area made famous by L.M. Mongomery and the setting for her book, *Anne of Green Gables.* Includes over 40 km of beach, camping, bicycle trails, walks, and hiking trails. Best visited off-season to avoid crowds.

• *Fundy National Park (New Brunswick).* Isolated, beautifully located, unspoiled and uncrowded (especially off-season). On the dramatic Bay of Fundy. Offers camping, hiking and nature studies, including a major network of trails with challenging, diverse hikes.

• *Cape Breton Highlands National Park (Nova Scotia).* Encompasses most of Cape Breton's impressive highlands. Stark headlands, forests, rocky coastline, beaches, and an isolated interior. Camping and extensive hiking, among the best in the Maritime provinces.

• *Kejimkujik National Park (Nova Scotia).* Located in the heart of Nova Scotia's interior lake district. An isolated park with fresh water lakes and forests. Camping, hiking, canoeing and abundant wildlife. Opportunities for overnight canoe trips or hikes to backcountry campsites.

• *Provincial Parks.* All three provinces have many of these, with 31 on Prince Edward Island alone. All are attractivly located and a wonderful way to explore the abundant natural areas of the Maritimes. In Nova Scotia, the emphasis is always on unspoiled natural surroundings and basic facilities, while those on Prince Edward Island often feature beach areas. Visiting provincial parks is an excellent way to avoid peak season crowds in national parks.

Cultural. Intensely aware of their diverse cultural background, the people of the Maritimes have done much to preserve it through a variety of ways. Festivals and museums, regional dialects and habits, the preservation of languages and celebration of music all offer numerous opportunities for savoring the rich culture of this fascinating region.

• *Festivals.* Summertime is festival time in the Maritimes, with celebrations all over the provinces honoring their heritage. With a strong Celtic background, many feature traditional Scottish and Irish music activities like fiddling, stepdancing, highland dancing and piping. Others pay tribute to the Acadian culture. Some celebrate the area's harvests, from fishing to farming. Attending at least one will help you and your children gain a greater understanding of the area you are visiting, both its past and present. Cultural events are always listed for each calendar year in the tourist guide books for each province.

• *Ceilidhs (pronounced "kay-lee's").* Gaelic in origin, ceilidhs evolved as social get-togethers in small communitities. Traditional activities include fiddling, dancing, singing and storytelling. Unlike more formal events, performers at ceilidhs are usually local talent of all ages. One summertime ceilidh worth attending is the weekly performance at Cape Breton Highlands National Park (Cheticamp headquarters). An evening there is pure magic for the whole family.

• *Cape Breton.* Settled by descendents of Scottish crofters and Acadians fleeing English persecution, Cape Breton's communities are among the most interesting in the Maritimes.

• *Acadian Communities.* These are most common along the southwest shore of Nova Scotia and northeast coast of New Brunswick. Visit the area to experience an intense change of culture.

Historic. As the oldest settlement region in Canada, the Maritimes have their share of historic sites and museums. Just about anywhere you go has at least one small museum: an historic house, a one-room school, an old mill, or a collection of artifacts. Others are well-known and frequented by many. The Nova Scotia Museum Complex maintains a variety of sites, from a pioneer farm to a fur traders' settlement. In addition to its museums and historic sites, Prince Edward Island has 30 historic lighthouses, all of them still in working order and three open to the public. Equally unusual are the plethora of covered bridges of New Brunswick, with 32 alone in the accessible Saint John's River Valley. The following are a handful of the many wonderful historic places in the region.

• *The Habitation, N.S.* A reconstruction of Canada's first permanent settlement, the second oldest in North America. Gives an insight into the French fur trading era.

• *Kings Landing Historical Settlement, New Brunswick.* Restoration of a Loyalist settlement from mid-18th to late 19th centuries. Includes many live demonstrations.

• *Fisheries Museum, N. S.* History and displays of Nova Scotia's schooner fishing industry.

• *Orwell Corner Historic Village, P.E.I.* Recreation of a village that once thrived in this agricultural district. Includes many original buildings, farm animals and gardens.

• *Fortress of Louisburg, N.S.* Canada's largest historical reconstruction project. An 18th century French fortified town. Includes 23 km of walking trails.

OUTDOOR ACTIVITIES

Backcountry Camping. Official backcountry camping is possible in both Nova Scotia and New Brunswick. Kejimkujik, Cape Breton Highlands, Kouchibouguac and Fundy National Parks all have designated sites. The ones in Keji can be reached on foot or by canoe. Cape Breton has a really lovely one at Fishing Cove on the west coast. Even little children can manage the hike. More intrepid families might want to try a venture into Mt. Carleton Provincial Park in the wilderness interior of New Brunswick.

Hiking. There's dozens of designated hiking trails all over the Maritime Provinces, none of which are too strenuous or technical for children of any age. The national parks have the widest choice, varying from easy day hikes to overnight or longer expeditions to wilderness campsites. For shorter walks, most provincial parks have at least one brief hike. The following offer some of the best hiking in the region.

• *Cape Breton Highlands National Park, N.S.* Trails are abundant, some offering spectacular views across the highlands and Northumberland Straits, others passing through woods or along rocky shores lined with wild blueberries. This is probably the prime hiking area in the entire Maritimes.

• *Fundy National Park, N.B.* These trails are wonderfully varied: along the rocky shore with its immense tides, across high bogs, through quiet woods, past unspoiled lakes.

• *Grand Manan Island, N.B.* Originally devised as access routes along the island shores for boat rescue operations. A complete guide to the 70 km of trails is available on the island.

• *Kejimkujik National Park, N.S.* A variety of lovely, easy-to-hike trails in the forested lake district.

Bicycling. The Maritimes must be one of the best places in the world for bicycling. Terrain is easy to cope with, backroads plentiful, the scenery lovely, and conditions safe for children. Some areas like Prince Edward

Island or
southern
Nova Scotia
seem made
for bicycling.
Others, like
New
Brunswick
and Cape Breton, are

better suited to a series of short trips. On bicycle tours, campgrounds and
inns are spaced for easy day rides and provisions readily available in most
parts. For an exciting two to three week bicycle tour, try a circumnavigation
of southern Nova Scotia, a combination of the Evangeline Trail and Lighthouse Route. Prince Edward Island is a bicycler's paradise, with gently
rolling hills, pastoral scenery, and an abundance of rural roads. Don't even
bother bringing a car. Any of the three counties can be circumnavigated in a
comfortable three to four days. To cover the whole island, allow about two
weeks. In New Brunswick, Grand Manan Island offers an exciting three
day tour of this isolated, awe-inspiring island with its misty fogs and 50-foot
tides. Day outings along the Fundy Shore or up the Saint John's River
Valley are also good choices. Remember that the key to fun bicycling is
getting off the main roads, something that's easy to do in the Maritimes.

Canoeing. Canoeing can be done in all three provinces. In each case, the
type of canoeing reflects the individual characteristics of each province.
Perhaps the best region in the entire Maritimes is Nova Scotia's interior lake
district in the south. Here, even families with very small children can
comfortably and safely explore the wilderness through a series of lakes and
rivers. Outings can vary from day trips to weeklong adventures. Canoes
can be rented in and around Kejimkujik National Park. New Brunswick's
canoeing ranges from wilderness river expeditions to gentle explorations. A
list of 26 outlined canoe trips, many of which are appropriate for families, is
available from the Dept. of Tourism. Canoe rentals are available in a
number of desirable locations. Canoeing on Prince Edward Island features
easy river explorations through rural farming country. Launching is
possible at any bridge crossing. Both Brudenell River and Mill River
Provincial Parks rent canoes and offer weekly group outings. Prince
Edward Island's gentle, scenic rivers offer ideal canoeing for families with
young children.

Sailing. The Maritimes have some of the most desirable cruising grounds
in North America. Nova Scotia offers the best sailing, principally along the
rocky East Coast with its numerous protected coves, wooded shoreline, and
small villages. The coastal region north of Halifax is particularly appealing,
with endless places to gunkhole. Sailing is popular with local Nova Scotians
and the Halifax/Mahone Bay area serves as the boating center of the

province. Up on Cape Breton, the Bras D'Or Lake offers the tranquillity of cruising on an inland sea. Because the sailing is protected, this is an excellent choice for families new to sailing or with young children. Boats can be chartered in the Baddeck area at Baddeck Catamaran, a pleasant, family-run operation. For more experienced sailors, a two or three day cruise to Grand Manan Island is an adventure. The combination of fierce currents, immense tides, and the likelihood of fog, coupled with that first glimpse of the island's 30-meter high cliffs, makes this an exciting landfall. A night spent tied up with huge fishing boats can't help but thrill children. Chartering is available in the area on New Brunswick's Fundy shore.

Swimming. Swimming is excellent in all three provinces, with the best on Prince Edward Island. Renowned for its endless sand beaches and warm water, this is the place for beach lovers, with plenty of private beaches to discover on your own. Swimming in Nova Scotia is best on inland lakes and along the Northumberland Coast where the best beaches and warmest water are found. New Brunswick offers lake swimming inland and excellent seashore at Kouchibouguac National Park.

Nature Studies. These can provide an important firsthand learning experience for children. All national parks have interpretive nature walks you can do on your own, evening nature programs, and guided outings. Other possibilities include whale-watching, bird-watching, beachcombing and seal watching trips with naturalists. A complete listing of activities is available in the tourist guides provided for each province.

Children's Hiking Challenge

Although numerous places in the Maritime Provinces are rich in opportunities for excellent family hiking, two areas in particular offer more than the usual variety: Fundy and Cape Breton Highlands National Parks. Not only are the trail selections and landscapes diverse, but both have a hiking incentive program for children that is ambitious, fun and rewarding.

Cape Breton Highlands National Park is made for exploring on foot, no matter what age you are. Babies and toddlers can ride in back packs, children age five and up can hike. Hikes here vary from high coastal paths with impressive scenic overlooks to woodland rambles, hikes of historic import, and paths along the water's rocky edge. Take your pick of what to see and you can probably find a trail with just that: a waterfall, stream, lake or beach; open meadow or closed forest; level ground or rigorous climb. Benjies Lake Trail is almost guaranteed to give you a glimpse of a moose - or more than a glimpse if one strolls out on the path the way it did to us. Hiking Aspy Trail in August can quickly deteriorate into an orgy of blueberry picking.

The Coastal Trail is driftwood heaven for children who like to construct things and play elaborate imaginary games (parents can console themselves while waiting with yet another blueberry bonanza). Both the Lone Shieling and Le Buttereau Trails are a trip into Cape Breton's past, one commemorating Scottish Highland settlers, the other traversing the site of an early Acadian coastal village. To help promote family hiking, the park has an incentive program for children, one that's ambitious, given the fact that most families only spend a couple of days in the park. Children up to age ten must hike 20 km, older children 50 km. A form at the back of each hiking guide (available at the park headquarters) should be filled out to record each child's performance.

Upon completion of the total required distance, the child receives a badge for his or her achievement. This is a fun way to introduce young children to hiking and a welcome change from the more prevalent attitude that two to three km represents the average child's hiking capacity. One little girl met along the way was enthusiastically striding her way through 20 km in 24 hours while her pained and resigned looking parents followed in her wake. Inherently attune to the reward system, children usually find the prospect of receiving a badge acts as a powerful incentive.

Fundy National Park in New Brunswick is equally beautiful, rich in hiking potential, and even more ambitious. Set off by itself along the notorious Fundy Shore, this park caters to true nature-oriented souls. Hiking here reflects the remote location and dominant feature of the world's highest tides. Again, there's invariably something of interest along each trail: the massive tidal change (up to 50 feet), the site of an old logging operation, inland lakes and bogs, a series of streams and waterfalls (15 on one hike alone), eerie rock formations dubbed the Devil's Half Acre, and nesting boxes to benefit the return of the peregrine falcon. For the most part the hiking is level and easy, well within the capabilities of any child. Experienced hiking children, or those already inaugurated by the Cape Breton Highlands program, will be equally stimulated by the Fundy Challenge. Intended for hikers of all ages, the goal here is an ambitious 100 km. Only 10 km, however, need be hiked in Fundy National Park. The rest can be hiked in any Canadian national park over the course of one year.

Children who have already done 50 km on Cape Breton will be well on their way towards earning the official looking certificate and pin that comes with completion of the Fundy Challenge. Each subsequent 100 km earns an additional attachment to the pin. Again, a record is kept and distances totaled before submitting for official approval. Let your children play a part in deciding what hikes to do. They respond well to a feeling of contribution and control, always performing better the more involved they are. Ours had very definite ideas of where they wanted to go each day, the result of long sessions spent pouring over the map and guide book: a coastal walk one day, inland to a lake the next, an old logging road that sparked imaginative games, a self-guided trail through a 1,000 year old bog. By providing some interesting background information, giving them responsibility, and offering a reward, programs like the Fundy Challenge and Cape Breton Highland's badge do far more than just motivate children. They turn them into lifelong hikers.

RESOURCE SECTION

TOURIST BUREAUS
Central Office: Canadian Government Office of Tourism: Federal Dept. of Regional Industrial Expansion, 235 Queen St., Ottawa K1A OH5, Canada Tel: (613) 995-9001. *Provincial Offices*. New Brunswick - Dept. of Tourism, Recreation, & Heritage, P.O. Box 12345, Fredricton, NB E3B 5C3, Tel: (800) 561-0123, (506)-453-2444. Nova Scotia - Dept. of Tourism, P.O. Box 456, Halifax, NS B3J 2R5, Tel: (800) 341-6096, (902) 425-5781. Prince Edward Island - Dept. of Tourism & Parks, P.O. Box 2000, Charlottetown, PEI C1A 7N8, Tel: (800) 565-9060, (902) 368-5500. Use these addresses when requesting provincial information.

CONSULATES
Canadian Consulate General: 16th Floor, Exxon Bldg., 1251 Ave. of the Americas, New York, NY 10020. Tel: (212) 768-2400. Other Canadian consulates located in most major North American cities.

NATIONAL AIRLINES
Air Canada: Place Air Canada, 500 Rene Levesque Blvd. West, Montreal PQ H2Z 1X5, Canada Tel: (800) 422-6232, (514) 393-3333. *Canadian Airlines International*. Ste. 2800, 700-2nd St. S.W., Calgary, AB T2P 2W2, Canada Tel: (800) 426-7000, (403) 294-2000. *Air Atlantic* is an affiliate airline serving Atlantic Canada.

SUGGESTED READING
Real Guide: Canada by Lee, Jepson & Smith. New York: Prentice Hall Travel. *Canada: A Travel Survival Kit* by T. Smallman. Berkeley: Lonely Planet Publications.

SUGGESTED MAPS
Atlantic Provinces by Map Art. Scale: 1,500,000:1, Approx. price: $3. Good travel maps for the Maritime Provinces are also available from the provincial tourist offices.

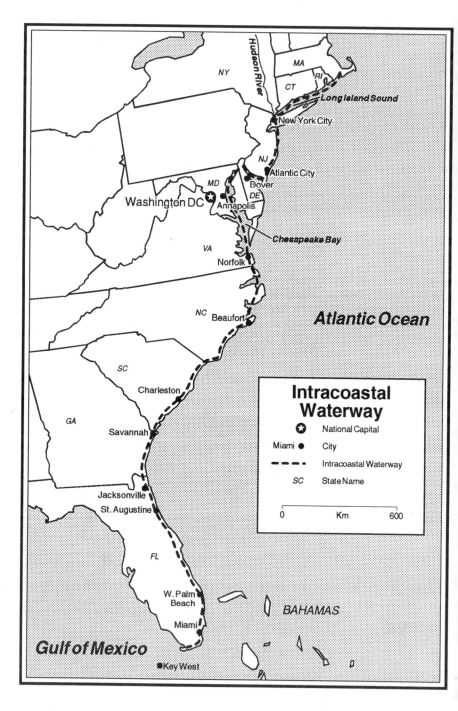

Intracoastal Waterway

⭐ National Capital

Miami ● City

- - - Intracoastal Waterway

SC State Name

0 ————— Km ————— 600

Intracoastal Waterway

Located on the east coast of the United States, the Intracoastal Waterway offers a unique opportunity for adventure. In an area typified by urban centers, multiple highways, overdevelopment, and dense population, the Waterway's charms are as pronounced as they are unexpected. Situated among the rivers, marshes, sounds, and bays that penetrate the east coast, it exposes you to a facet of the region that remains hidden to

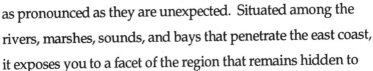

land-based travelers, one of beauty and tranquility. Both experienced and novice sailors will find a cruise on the Waterway an exciting, unusual way to explore this corner of the United States.

GENERAL DESCRIPTION

Location. Stretching along much of the East Coast of the United States, the Intracoastal Waterway passes through twelve states, from Cape Cod to the Florida Keys. The more well-known and most sheltered section extends 1095 miles from Norfolk, Virginia to Miami, Florida. Both a commercial transportation route for barges and a popular passage for sail boats migrating seasonally between northern and southern cruising grounds, the Waterway offers a protected passage along the Eastern Seaboard.

Terrain. The Intracoastal is as varied as the landscape it flows through. Depending on which section you choose to travel, you might find yourself sailing the open waters of the Chesapeake or navigating a man-made canal, running a sea-swept inlet or gliding along gentle creeks.

• *New Jersey.* Only shallow draft (4' or less) boats can navigate this section. Following the creeks and marshes that lie behind the outer barrier beach, it seems another world from Atlantic City and other popular coastal areas.

• *Chesapeake Bay.* One of the East Coast's prime cruising grounds, the Chesapeake is entered from the north via Delaware Bay. Despite its proximity to a number of major urban centers, the bay remains an unspoiled, natural place with an abundance of lovely anchorages, quiet towns, and rural countryside.

• *Virginia.* Beyond the Chesapeake, the Waterway becomes a combination of man-made canals linking natural bodies of water. Travel the Dismal Swamp Canal, a magical, mysterious route. A number of sizeable sounds and rivers help make up this section of the route, all easily navigated in a day.

• *North Carolina.* A combination of open water and canals, this is one of the lovliest sections of the Waterway. The land is sparsely populated, the anchorages cozy and quiet.

• *South Carolina.* Here the route narrows, depending more on man-made waterways than natural ones. As always, the surroundings are lovely, imbued with a southern charm far removed from the overdeveloped style of its outer beaches.

• *Georgia.* Georgia offers the most remote reaches of the Waterway route. Surrounded by a vast labyrinth of salt marshes and creeks, the landscape here seems untouched by human forces. Practically the only signs of habitation glimpsed are large shrimp boats heading to and from sea.

• *Florida.* The tempo in Florida varies widely from the quiet north to the frenetic south. Much of the northern route follows the Indian River, a lovely wide body of water with peaceful sailing and numerous anchorages. Approaching Palm Beach, the pace quickens. Moving south, the Waterway is principally man-made, passing through one of the most populated, affluent areas along the East Coast. Natural surroundings give way to views of elegant backyards and yachts tied to private docks. In this area where the number of boats rival the number of cars, even the Waterway can experience a nautical version of "rush hour".

Climate. Due to the Waterway's north and south orientation, it's best to travel south in the fall and north in spring and summer. This takes advantage of the prevailing seasonal winds, allowing the most sailing time. Despite the fact that most migratory boats do the route this way, crowded conditions are rarely a problem. Northern reaches are best cruised from May-November. Florida can be sailed all winter, with summer being the least desirable time due to heat, lack of wind, and crowded conditions. We traveled south from September to January and enjoyed pleasant fall weather the whole way. Winds were usually out of the north, allowing for plenty of sailing time. The reverse is true for springtime travel heading north, driven by prevailing southerly winds.

Culture & Lifestyle. Cruising the Intracoastal offers a backdoor view of communities along the East Coast. The exposure is the reverse of what most people see, viewed through the normal channels of road transportation. Backdoors and backyards literally face the Waterway. Docks lie scattered along the waterfront and people poke lazily about in boats. Communities can be pleasantly explored as you row ashore and explore on foot or by bicycle. More than just a vehicle for pleasure craft, the Waterway exhibits its commercial side as shrimp boats ply the inland waters and tugboats chug past pulling an impressive line of barges. Be aware while cruising that commercial craft always have the right-of-way.

PRACTICAL CONCERNS

Political Update and Safety. Travel here is very safe. Given the epidemic state of crime in the United States, a trip on the Intracoastal is a welcome respite from the concerns that plague most heavily populated areas. Normal precautions should be taken against theft if leaving the boat unattended, especially in Florida and near urban areas.

Travel Documents. Travel on the Waterway is the same for all travel in the United States. Foreign visitors must have a visa before entering the country. Those arriving by sailboat can obtain a cruising permit at customs. Separate permits are required for each state upon entry.

Travel Costs. Like most travel, a cruise on the Waterway can be as budget-oriented or extravagant as you choose. Traveling with your own sailboat and enjoying the numerous free anchorages will keep costs low.

Fuel is a consideration, as motoring a good portion of the time is unavoidable. Nightly dockage at marinas will increase costs, although the occasional overnight stop won't hurt. Consider paying for a few daytime hours of use to do laundry, provisioning, or shower the whole family. This provides the convenience of a marina at a fraction of the cost.

Health. As in all of the United States, health is not a concern. Medical supplies and services are always available along the route.

Food. Food is plentiful over most of the route, with a supermarket usually within easy walking distance of any town anchorage. For shorter trips, fill up with provisions prior to departure to avoid spending too much time having to stop and replenish supplies. One of the Intracoastal's greatest assets is the opportunity it offers to discover lovely, isolated anchorages, something you can't do if you're constantly stopping for a quick trip to the store. If your dream is to travel to more remote areas like the Bahamas or South Pacific, the Waterway offers a good opportunity to experiment with long-term provisioning.

Fuel. Gas, diesel, and propane are all readily available along most of the route at frequent marinas. Georgia is the one place you might need to carry extra engine fuel, as the remote marshlands offer few facilities.

Clothes. Depending on the season, you can need anything from bathing suits to parkas. We ran the gamut of clothing during our fall trip, beginning in T-shirts and sunshades and ending up in wool hats and mittens. Bear in mind that temperatures are cooler out on the water where the wind is blowing, so some warm clothing should always be included, even in summer.

Laundry & Bathing. With numerous town anchorages and marinas, laundry facilities are easy to find on a weekly basis. To keep time and costs spent in laundromats down, do like experienced live-aboard boaters do and convert your rigging into a clothesline. Sun and wind will dry your clothes in recordbreaking time. For baby diapers, rinse soiled ones in a bucket of seawater (try adding some Borax) until laundry day. Bathing is easy with the help of a solar shower (available at boat equipment stores and catalogs). Filled and left on the deck, it can provide the whole family with a quick shower by evening. Even if the sun's not out, just heat some water on the stove. One full shower will easily do one adult or two children, including a hair wash. Marinas along the Waterway will also often let you tie up for an hour or two at minimal cost so the whole family can utilize their shower facilities.

Baby Needs. Babies and boats really can mix, contrary to many people's belief. Include a dependable harness for toddlers or babies old enough to crawl. Netting along the lifelines provides a measure of security. Netting strung along a bunk will also keep little ones from falling out of bed when undersail. Don't worry about entertainment and toys. They'll have plenty to keep them occupied in the visually stimulating environment of Waterway travel.

Type of Boat. Because of the Waterway's protected waters, everything from large cruisers to small trailerable boats can safely sail there. Shallow draft boats will have the advantage of not having to worry so much about keeping to the central channel, or finding deep anchorages.

Length of Travel Time. Any amount of time can be spent on a cruise of the Waterway. The more relaxed your schedule, the more fun you'll have. Don't be influenced by migratory boats making their 60 to 70 miles a day (mostly under power). For the entire trip, plan on two months. This will allow you time to take advantage of the winds (without worrying how fast you're sailing) and to explore ashore while avoiding any feeling of pressure, the antithesis of enjoyable Waterway travel.

Boater Behavior. Maintaining a certain code of behavior can go a long way towards ensuring a continued welcome to boaters in communities along the route. Particularly in the south, where overcrowding can be a problem, some negative feeling has been generated. Ask first before landing a dinghy, disposing of trash, or walking across private property. Maintain your boat's appearance so it's aesthetically pleasing to homeowners who have to look at it at anchor. Go out of your way to find out what is acceptable and act accordingly.

TRANSPORTATION

Getting There. With a large cruising boat, the Waterway can be entered at a number of spots depending on where you're coming from. Coming from the north, enter at Long Island Sound or the Hudson River (if coming from the Great Lakes area). Chesapeake Bay is another easy entry place, as is almost anywhere in southern Florida if beginning in the south. Trailerable boats, of course, have infinite possibilities and can put in just about anywhere.

Regional Travel. Once cruising, no other means of transportation is necessary as everything is available for boaters on the Waterway itself. Inquire about things like restaurants that provide free transport for dining cruisers, and grocery stores that do dockside deliveries. Conveniences like this are common in many areas.

ACCOMMODATIONS

Anchoring. Anchoring is possible nearly everywhere on the Waterway. Most places are free, although during the summer major boating areas like Long Island Sound do charge a fee for town anchorages. Expect some crowding in areas like this during peak season. Cruising guides for the Intracoastal Waterway recommend popular spots along the route. A shallow draft boat will be able to poke into numerous others. Anchoring just about anywhere outside the marked channel is fine. Some anchorages are perennial favorites with cruisers doing the seasonal passage, offering a good opportunity for some socializing with fellow boaters. Long Island Sound and the Chesapeake have the most variety, being large, natural bodies of water. Expect some cozy anchoring in southern Florida where town anchorages can have a sizeable live-aboard community. Using two anchors (in a Bahamian moor) is the norm to avoid bumping hulls in the night.

Marinas. These are plentiful along much of the route, a convenient source of fuel, water, hot showers, laundry facilities, trash disposal, and nightly dockage. Although usually expensive (especially compared to a free anchorage), they can be worth the occasional splurge, especially after a long day or spell of bad weather. Prices vary widely, with some very reasonable if facilities are simple.

POINTS OF INTEREST

Natural. As a waterway, the Intracoastal is filled with areas of natural interest. More than almost anywhere on the East Coast, here nature has been left principally unspoiled by the effects of man's presence. With the exception of southern Florida, the Waterway provides a ribbon of nature weaving through one of the most populated regions of the world, something you will have a hard time believing as you cruise its peaceful waters. There are seabirds and dolphins, fish and manatees. Marshes spread away to distant horizons and rivers wind past forest lined shores. Particular areas of interest include Chesapeake Bay, the Elizabeth Islands, the Carolina Sounds, and the marshes of New Jersey and Georgia.

Cultural & Historic. The Intracoastal offers an unusual gateway into many areas of interest along the East Coast, a region steeped in culture and early American history.

• *Mystic Seaport.* Explore this complete replica of an early New England seaport while docked along its waterfront. A very exciting place for children, with live demonstrations and docked ships. Dockage fee includes entry to the seaport.

- *New York City.* Explore the city while docked at one of the marinas in downtown Manhatten, or just enjoy the thrill of sailing along the East or Hudson Rivers.

- *Baltimore.* Anchoring is available in the heart of the historic district from which the city can be explored.

- *Annapolis.* Anchor or dock at this pleasant town, the boating center of the Chesapeake.

- *Washington, D.C.* A side trip is possible up the Potomac for a visit to the capital city. Both dockage and anchoring are attractively located near the central parks.

- *Charleston & Savannah.* Both historic southern cities lie along the Intracoastal, waiting to be explored.

- *St. Augustine.* Visit the oldest settlement in North America, with its lovely historic district, museums and Spanish fort. Both anchoring and dockage are available.

OUTDOOR ACTIVITIES

Rowing. Children of all ages will enjoy poking around anchorages in a rowing dinghy. Despite the popularity of engines on dinghies, we suggest using oars with children. It's quieter, less obnoxious to fellow boaters (just wait until you're buzzed at seven a.m. by someone else's child gleefully at the controls of a dinghy outboard), and good exercise. It's also the only way to enjoy your natural surroundings while exploring.

Swimming. Swimming is possible just about anywhere along the Waterway except in the Chesapeake (due to the abundant stinging nettles) and urban areas. Although there won't be any beaches, swimming off the boat is an excellent way for children to hone their swimming skills. Little ones can always wear a lifejacket or swim with a kickboard. Be sure you have a good boarding ladder, suitable for children when getting out of the water.

Walking. Without a car, you'll soon find yourselves walking everywhere on shore: to shop, do laundry or just get some exercise. Take advantage of the situation by exploring the surrounding area on foot.

Bicycling. Many boaters enjoy bringing along bicycles for shore explorations. On a large boat, lash a few old bicycles to the life lines for children to use in port. They'll love the independence and you'll love the break from close family quarters. Special folding bicycles, available through marine chandleries and boating equipment catalogs, can be easily stored on board.

Playgrounds. Though hardly an outdoor activity for the whole family, young children will love the abundance of playgrounds along the Waterway in Florida. Many are located beside anchorages.

Waterway Magic

Sandwiched between Hampton Roads, Virginia and Albemarle Sound in North Carolina lies one of the Waterway's most peaceful, magical regions. Entering the Intracoastal at Norfolk from Chesapeake Bay, there's little hint of what lies just ahead as you pass through teeming Hampton Roads. Freighters from all over the world lie anchored at the entrance, while naval ships and submarines line the shore. For newcomers to Waterway travel, the huge lift bridges that span the river in rapid succession can be an awesome sight, particularly as they rise in unison to allow passage of your boat. Beyond the bridges, the noise and confusion, the excitement and activity are all left behind as you arrive at the first major junction along the Waterway. Here boaters have a choice between the Dismal Swamp Canal and what is commonly called the Virginia Cut, the first of many man-made land-cuts that help make up a continual protected waterway down the East Coast from Chesapeake Bay to Miami, Florida. By all means, choose the Dismal Swamp Canal route, a lovely area that, together with the connecting Pasquotank River, winds through an continuous stretch of unspoiled, wooded countryside. Don't be misled by its seemingly unprepossessing name, derived from the local colloquial word for swamp land. Surveyed by George Washington and hand-dug by slaves in the late eighteenth century, the canal has been used commercially since 1805. Despite the close proximity of a major road paralleling the first portion of the route, the feeling of isolation is complete as you travel down the narrow, tree-lined canal. With little traffic compared to the busy Virginia Cut, the Dismal Swamp Canal provides an early introduction to the peacefulness and gentle pace of Intracoastal Waterway travel.

Twenty-six and a half miles in length, the canal is best transited by starting in the morning, allowing plenty of time to arrive at one of the two anchorages along the Pasquotank River. There's a quiet anchorage less than a mile past the Virginia Cut junction where you can spend the night before beginning transit. With a total day's distance of thirty-five miles, including two locks, there's no need to hurry along the way. The entire route is one of the loveliest you'll find on the Intracoastal and should be savored accordingly; a serene ribbon of water winding through the Virginia and North Carolina countryside.

The first lock is reached almost immediately, a few miles past the anchorage. Locking procedure is simple and always exciting for children. Have fenders and bow and stern docklines in place before approaching the entrance. Southbound boats tie to starboard, northbound to port, similar to standard boating Rules of the Road. As water level rises or falls while locking through, you'll need one person on each dockline to make the necessary adjustments. Both locks frequently operate on a set schedule, so be prepared to wait once you are tied up. You might find yourselves enjoying breakfast in the company of fellow boaters at the first lock, then lunch at the second lock, a pleasant, congenial interlude. Tieing up and waiting for a while also offers a nice opportunity for active children to burn up some energy on shore.

Once locked through at the far end of the canal, you enter the narrow, twisting Pasquotank River. Here the feeling of remoteness intensifies as you glide along past densely-wooded shores. Traffic is almost nonexistent, consisting mainly of barges hauling wood from a nearby logging operation. Meeting a tug along the way, towing its massive chain of barges piled high with logs, is a definite thrill as you scramble to get well out of the way. Commercial traffic always has the right-of-way over pleasure craft. It's best to familiarize yourselves beforehand with correct boating Rules of the Road before undertaking any Waterway travel. This avoids confusion and panic if a huge tug or fishing boat suddenly starts bearing down on you, accompanied by a mysterious series of toots on its horn.

Two overnight anchorages lie just short of Elizabeth City, one to the right behind navigation marker #13, the other four miles beyond in a creek off to the left. Although Elizabeth City offers all the usual marina and downtown facilities, lingering overnight along the river provides the perfect ending to the peaceful interlude of travel along the Dismal Swamp Canal. If your children are lucky, they might even get to watch one last tug go past, pulling its immense load of barges. Enjoying sunset while anchored along the quiet, deserted shore epitomizes the freedom and beauty of life aboard a sailboat.

Before embarking on the Dismal Swamp Canal route, be sure to check that it's open. Low rainfall occasionally requires a temporary closing, as normal water levels in the canal only average of seven to nine feet. Either call the Corps of Engineers Department of Waterway Maintenance in Norfolk, or ask fellow boaters. Be sure to carry not only a chart of the area, but a good cruising guide as well. Highly recommended are *The Intracoastal Waterway: Norfolk to Miami* by Jan and Bill Moeller (covers Norfolk to Key Biscayne in an easy mile-by-mile format) and the four volume *Waterway Guide Series* put out by Communication Channels, Inc. of Atlanta, GA . The Mid- Atlantic edition covers the Dismal Swamp route. Other recommended guides are listed in the following Resource Section. We advise carrying several guides for Waterway travel, as they tend to be very useful in different ways. All locking and anchoring facilities along the route are free. Provisions, fuel and water are available at Hampton Roads and Elizabeth City.

RESOURCE SECTION

TOURIST BUREAUS

Virginia Division of Tourism, 1021 East Cary St., 14th Fl., Richmond, VA 23219   Tel: (804) 786-2051.
North Carolina Div. of Travel & Tourism, 430 N. Salisbury St., Raleigh, NC 27611   Tel: (800) VISIT NC.
South Carolina Dept. of Parks, Recreation, & Tourism, 1205 Pendleton St., Columbia, SC 29201   Tel: (803) 734-0122.
Georgia Dept. of Industry, Trade, & Tourism, P.O. Box 1776, Atlanta, GA 30301-1776   Tel: (800) 841-6586.
Florida Dept. of Commerce, Div. of Tourism, 126 Van Buren St., Tallahassee, FL 32399-2000   Tel: (904) 487-1462.

SUGGESTED READING

Cruising Guide to the Chesapeke: A Gunkholer's Guide by Shellenberger. Camden, ME: International Marine Publishing.
The Intracoastal Waterway: Norfolk to Miami by J. & B. Moeller. Camden, ME: International Marine Publishing.
The Waterway Guide Series. Atlanta, GA: Communication Channels, Inc.
Intracoastal Waterway Facilities Guide by R. D. Smith. Ludlow, MA: Paradox.

SUGGESTED MAPS

Nautical charts for each section of the Waterway are available separately at most marine chandleries or in convenient chart kit form.
Chart Kit for Cape Cod to NYC, Chart Kit for NJ to Cheasapeke Bay, Chart Kit for Norfolk to Miami. Better Boating Association, Needham, MA, 1-800-CHART KIT.
Intracoastal Waterway Chartbook by Kettlewell & Kettlewell. International Marine Publishing, Camden, ME.

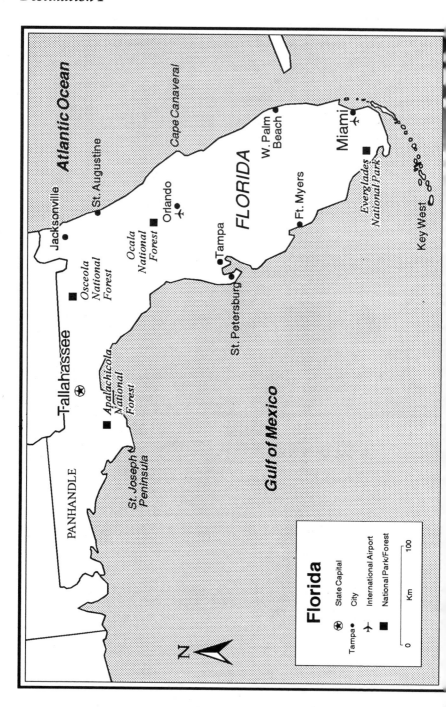

Atlantic Ocean

Cape Canaveral

St. Augustine

Jacksonville

FLORIDA

W. Palm
Beach

Miami

Orlando

Ocala
National
Forest

Ft. Myers

Everglades
National Park

Osceola
National
Forest

Tampa

Key West

Tallahassee

St. Petersburg

Apalachicola
National
Forest

Gulf of Mexico

St. Joseph
Peninsula

PANHANDLE

Florida

Tampa   State Capital
•   City
✈   International Airport
■   National Park/Forest

Km   100

0

N

Florida

Florida has much to offer the adventuring family in the way of outdoor activities, pockets of natural beauty, and quiet areas far removed from the resorts, crowded beaches, and condominiums that dominate its coastline. An adventure there can be the ideal antidote to mid-winter blues. Affordable, accessible and modern, it serves as an excellent proving ground for families new to adventuring, one we've thoroughly enjoyed a number of times, beginning when our children were six months old. For Americans and foreigners alike, Florida offers much more to families than just a vacation in the sun or a trip to Disney World.

GENERAL DESCRIPTION

Location. Florida lies at the extreme south of the eastern United States, extending out into the water like a corner of the country reaching towards the tropics. Bordered on land by Georgia and Alabama, the rest of the state faces the water, with the Atlantic to the east and the gentler waters of the Gulf of New Mexico to the west.

Terrain. After years of widespread settlement, Florida's terrain has undergone many changes, molded into cattle ranches and citrus orchards, clipped lawns and artfully-placed shrubs. Where left untouched by development, much of the landscape is lovely and tropical, a testament to its unique contribution to the eastern United States. Principally a flat state, the land flows south, past woods and wide open plains, a string of lakes and the dense marine environment of the everglades. There are pine forests and coral reefs, rivers and lagoons, white sand beaches and dense mangrove shores.

Climate. Climate varies from temperate to subtropical, with noticeably cooler temperatures in the northern portion of the state. December through May is the ideal time to visit the south, prior to the intense summer heat. Miami and the Keys enjoy summer temperatures almost year round. Swimming weather in the rest of the state begins about mid-March. Weather is warmer inland than along the coast with its cooling sea breezes.

Culture & Lifestyle. Like everything else about Florida, the culture and lifestyle is a study in contrasts: retired northerners and live-aboard boaters, Seminole Indians and immigrant Cubans, citrus growers and cattle ranchers. Each area has its pocket of culture, with no one thing completely defining the state. For the most part, the affluent lifestyle circles the state like a belt, following the line of the coast. Behind it lies another Florida, one that existed long before the influx of new residents seeking its sun and warmth. In many ways it is the interior that reveals Florida's more interesting side, a truer picture of its culture and lifestyle behind the scenes of migratory northerners. Here the lifestyle is more modest, the pace of life slower.

PRACTICAL CONCERNS

Political Update & Safety. Florida presents no major safety concerns other than what exists throughout the rest of the United States. This includes taking normal precautions against theft. Certain areas of Miami should be avoided and all cities treated with circumspection at night.

Travel Documents. These are the same as for travel anywhere in the United States. Foreign visitors (except Canadians) must have a visa prior to arrival. Visas are issued for three months. Canadians need only some form of identification.

Money. Money is best carried in travelers checks. Banks are located in most towns, while retail shops, restaurants and hotels also usually accept travelers checks. Credit cards are also widely accepted throughout the state.

Travel Costs. Travel costs here are similar to anywhere else in the U.S.. Food and fuel are relatively inexpensive. Campgrounds are reasonable, particularly in the many state parks. Stay away from Disney World and the myriad other amusement centers and your trip should be a bargain.

Language. English is the primary language. Miami is one place you might feel you've suddenly changed countries, with many residents speaking Spanish. Foreign-speaking visitors will need some English, as few Americans are proficient in a foreign language.

Health. The only health concern is sun protection. Florida's sun can be devastating, particularly for visitors escaping the winter cold. Use plenty of sunscreen, especially between 11 a.m. and 3 p.m. Sunhats and cotton T-shirts are another must if you plan any beach or boating time. Good sunscreens are available in drug stores all over the state. Use a #15 or higher.

Food. Florida has some of the biggest grocery stores imaginable, especially in coastal communities. Publix is the fanciest, the place where you'll see all the retirement people shopping. Finding food is never a problem, nor is finding that one item your child insists upon eating. Foreign visitors find the variety in an American supermarket overwhelming at first. Your biggest problem will be deciding which of the many brands of each item to buy. Whether traveling by boat, bicycle, or car, food shopping presents no difficulties.

Clothes. Bring lightweight clothing. This is heaven for parents with little children. They hardly need to wear a thing. Even in northern Florida in mid-winter, a heavy sweater is about the most you'll need. Include a rain jacket and bathing suit, no matter when or where you go. You'll need both. Clothes are easy to buy throughout the state at frequent shopping centers. Good buys include bathing suits, easy to find and surprisingly low cost compared to some other parts of the country.

Laundry & Bathing. Laundromats are located in most main towns as well as many private campgrounds. Getting your clothes washed won't be a problem. Nor will bathing. Nearly all campgrounds, including state parks, have hot showers. Keeping clean will generally be easy anyway due to the amount of time you'll spend in the water. Be sure to rinse children off at the end of day if they've been swimming in salt water. This keeps salt from getting into clothing and bedding.

Baby Needs. You'll love Florida for babies. Even diapers can practically be avoided as they bask naked in the sun and warmth. All baby foods are available. If camping, just bathe the baby in a dishpan or bucket. Diapers can be washed easily at a laundromat or campground. Include a piece of clothesline and handful of pins for drying. Bring something like a quilt for the baby to lie on, also a beach umbrella for naps at the beach. Sunhats are a must as well. For sunscreen, choose one like Johnson & Johnson that's specially designed for babies.

TRANSPORTATION

Getting There. Florida can be reached by car, bus, train or airplane. Driving is easy on any of the major highways that service the state from the north and west. Flights to Miami, Ft. Lauderdale, Tampa, Orlando and Jacksonville are frequent from all over the United States. Miami also has an international airport with flights from foreign countries. Amtrack has a daily train that runs between Boston and West Palm Beach, stopping at most major cities along the route. If arriving by public transportation, a rental car will be needed for the duration of your stay.

Regional Travel. With the possible exception of bicycle and sailboat travel, a car is a necessity. Car rentals are relatively inexpensive in Florida and fuel costs reasonable.

Roads. Like everywhere in the United States, Florida places great value on its roads. Highways reach all major corners of the state, allowing for quick travel from place to place. To avoid getting trapped into just another car trip, take to some backroads in the interior, finding places to get out and walk, do a short bicycle outing, or explore the inland waterways. Roads can be crowded along the coast, particularly during peak season (January-April). Inland backroads have little traffic.

ACCOMMODATIONS

Campgrounds. Although all the usual motel, hotel, and cottage accommodations are widely available, camping offers the best option for families. Campgrounds are widespread, with an extraordinary number located in attractive state parks. We definitely recommend these, infinitely preferable to the RV focus of almost all private campgrounds. During peak season, campgrounds in the extreme south or near beaches can be filled to capacity, so book a reservation if possible. State parks allow a set number of sites to be booked in advance. Otherwise, stay somewhere nearby for the night, then arrive mid-morning the following day just as people are leaving. Better yet, head to the parks in the northwest or inland where campgrounds are nearly empty. Facilities usually include private sites, water, hot showers, and picnic tables. Other attractive camping options include Everglades National Park and those in state forests, also nicely situated in natural settings.

POINTS OF INTEREST

Natural. Florida has many areas of natural beauty: everglades and pine forests; coral reefs and mangrove swamps, sand dunes and inland lakes.

Many are preserved in parks and national forests, waiting to be explored in a variety of ways.

• *Everglades National Park.* Ecologically unique, the everglades is a vast labyrinth of mangroves and natural waterways. Spreading over acres of coastal and inland area, the park is inhabited by a variety of wildlife, from manatees and aligators to panthers and abundant birds. Travel within the park is principally by boat, with only limited hiking. Explore by canoe, sailboat, or on one of the park's airboats, high-speed crafts that penetrate the interior without threatening its ecology.

• *State Parks.* These are truly impressive, an immense network of parks throughout the state. One of best run park systems we've ever experienced, it offers a gateway into the natural wonders of Florida. Among the best are those in the interior, along the southwest coast, and in the Panhandle. A far cry from the crowds of Florida's southern beach areas, these feature quiet and solitude, unspoiled beauty and few visitors. Some, like Falling Waters State Recreation Area and Florida Caverns State Park, feature unusual geological sights like a 67-foot waterfall or series of interconnected caves. The Florida State Park Guide includes a complete listing of parks and their natural features and wildlife. For more information, see the sidebar.

• *National Forests.* Both Ocala and Osceola National Forests feature camping, canoeing and extensive hiking. A visit to either is a nice contrast to coastal areas; expanses of pine forests and open spaces, inland lakes and gentle rivers.

• *Intracoastal Waterway (see Destination 3).* Extending the length of Florida's east coast and a portion of the northern Gulf shore, this offers scenic, protected sailing and a unique opportunity for coastal exploration. Rivers, canals, lakes and bays are all incorporated into this unusual cruising ground, one you can enjoy on anything from small, trailerable daysailers to large ocean-going craft.

Cultural. Florida's culture is an amalgamation of many eras: its conquest by the Spanish, the early years of intense forestry, the later development of cattle ranching, the rise of cotton plantations, its discovery by northern retirees, the arrival of vast numbers of Cubans, the survival of a proud Indian culture. Today it encompasses all those and more, cultural characteristics you can quickly discover by delving into the state. Various festivals and events also provide fascinating cultural background as well as entertainment. A schedule of events throughout the year is available from the state park service. The following are a few of the many interesting places to visit. A number of historic sites also reflect the rich culture of this diverse state.

- *Seminole Indian Reservation.* Located north of the Everglades, a visit here provides an insight into a native culture that has survived to the present. A number of locally made handicrafts are available.

- *Kennedy Space Center, Cape Canaveral.* The headquarters of the U.S. space shuttle program, this is a fascinating place for children and adults alike. A tour includes an informative movie and exhibits of earlier space crafts.

- *Stephen Foster State Folk Culture Center.* Dedicated to preserving the culture of Florida, both past and present, the center hosts a variety of exhibits and events throughout the year.

- *Forest Capital State Museum.* Depicts the history of forestry in Florida, beginning in the early 1800s, including a replica of an early forest homestead.

Historical. Florida's many historical points of interest reflect a heritage that extends back to prehistoric times. Any are worth a visit and fascinating for children. As many visitors mistakenly overlook the state's historic sites, the absence of crowds makes them more enjoyable and authentic to see.

- *Crystal River State Archaeological Site.* Florida's earliest evidence of human occupation. Once an important prehistoric ceremonial site, excavated mounds remain, built by pre-Columbian inhabitants.

- *St. Augustine.* As North America's oldest permanent settlement, this pleasant town offers much of historic interest. Located along the Intracoastal Waterway, it is accessible by boat or car. Children will love the horse-drawn carriages, historic buildings, period dress, and Spanish fort.

- *Fort Clinch State Park.* This features a fort built in the mid-1800s, occupied by both sides during the course of the Civil War. Attractively located on the northeast coast of Florida.

- *Olustee Battlefield State Historic Site.* The site of Florida's biggest Civil War battle. Includes an interpretive trail along the lines of the battlefield.

- *Marjorie Kinnan Rawlings State Historic Site.* Once the home of the famous children's author who wrote the classic novel *The Yearling*.

- *Kingsley Plantation State Historic Site.* Located on an original plantation, including the oldest plantation house in the state.

OUTDOOR ACTIVITIES

Backcountry Camping. Official backcountry camping sites are located in a number of state parks. For families with little experience, this is a wonderful opportunity to try an overnight or two at a primitive campsite without the rigors of a long or strenuous hike first. Children usually love this sort of thing, finding the whole experience exciting and adventurous. Parks with backcountry camping include St. George Island State Park, Torreya State Park, Waccasassa Bay State Preserve, Fort Cooper State Park, Lower Wekiva River State Reserve, and Rock Springs Run State Reserve.

Hiking. The level terrain makes this an easy place to introduce very young children to the pleasures of hiking. With little children, try to pick areas with something to look at other than just trees. Nature trails with interpretive signs, common in state parks, are always a hit. For more ambitious families, the most extensive hiking is along the Florida National Scenic Trail, destined upon completion to extend the length of the state from Big Cypress Swamp in southern Florida to Gulf Islands National Seashore in the northwest. Much of the trail passes through state parks and national forest, all clearly marked. Day hikes or overnights are possible in Osceola and Ocala National Forests, some of it along portions of the Florida Trail. The hiking is easy here through flat pine forests. Watch out for deer ticks, the kind that unfortunately can carry Lymes disease. Hiking opportunities are numerous throughout the state parks, with at least one good hike provided in nearly all of them. Others offer sizeable, all-day outings. The Florida State Park Guide includes a complete listing of parks that offer hiking. Informal coastal walking can also be done along beaches, always interesting for children (although you may have trouble keeping them moving, always a hazard at the beach).

Bicycling. Although many of Florida's roads are too busy to want to bicycle, particularly along the coast, inland backroads can be fun and safe to explore. Bringing bicycles is even worthwhile just so your children can ride around the campground roads, something they love to do. The Florida Recreational Trails System is presently converting a number of old railroad lines to bicycle paths, with one segment completed so far on the Tallahassee-to-St. Marks Historic Railroad State Trail. This 16-mile bicycle path offers scenic, easy biking, appropriate for children of all ages.

Canoeing. Florida has some lovely canoeing, most of it appropriate even for amateurs or families with very young children. Numerous state parks offer places to canoe, including 13 with rental services. For families with their own canoe, The Florida Canoe Trail Guide, available at state parks, now lists 36 designated canoe routes through state park waters. Canoeing is one of the best ways to explore portions of the Everglades National Park, with its labyrinth of mangrove-lined waterways and rich wildlife. One of the loveliest canoe routes in the state begins at Juniper Springs in Ocala National Forest. This is a magical three to four hour trip through dense tropical forest. Canoe rentals are available and the route suitable for even very young children.

Sailing. This is undoubtedly the best way to adventure in Florida. Like all water travel, the exposure is completely different, and, in this case, vastly improved over land-based travel along coastal areas. Gone are the crowded roads and noise, the development and highways, the retirement villages and RVs. Best areas to cruise include the Indian River (part of the Intracoastal Waterway), the Florida Keys, and the southwest coast. The sailing is protected, anchorages numerous, supplies readily available, and the waters inviting. Be sure to include snorkeling gear for children. They'll practically live in the water. Don't feel compelled to move fast. We often spend weeks exploring small areas of coastline on a boat.

Swimming. Swimming and Florida are synonymous. With miles of sand beach coastline, its not hard to find somewhere to swim, although the trick will be finding somewhere that a hundred people didn't already beat you to. The best technique is to walk, away from the parking lot, the fast food stands, the bodies sprawled on the beach. It's truely amazing how few people are willing to walk that extra few minutes that separate the crowds from lonely expanses of unspoiled beach. Bring backpacks or good shoulder bags for carrying things.

Swimming is best for little children on the west coast, free from surf. The east coast is excellent for body surfing, something older children love to do. Beaches along the Panhandle are the most deserted, with warm water and lovely sand dunes. There's also excellent freshwater swimming in the many inland lakes, a number of them located in state parks or national forests. Everglades National Park has no beaches. Swimming weather in Florida begins about mid-March.

Nature Studies. All state parks, forests, and Everglades National Park offer opportunities for nature studies. Many supply nature pamphlets and at least one self-guided walk. Have your children play "naturalist", carrying binoculars, magnifying glasses, notebooks and other official looking paraphernalia of their choosing. It's amazing how much they'll remember when the whole occasion is turned into a game.

State Park Gems

With over 100 state parks, Florida offers an almost unprecedented wealth of protected natural areas to explore in the southeastern United States. Although many are well-known and heavily visited by the crush of tourists that descend yearly on the state, others remain unspoiled and sparsely used. Happily, the state park system has taken the guesswork out of finding out which is which. The Florida State Park Guide, available from tourist bureaus or Florida Welcome Centers (located at the border) includes a complete descriptive list of parks, many of which are labeled state park gems. "State Park Gems", the guide writes, "indicate under-utilized parks and camping facilities that offer you greater adventure." It didn't take us long on a recent camping trip to Florida to decide to try some. Traveling during peak season in March, we'd already been turned away from a number of campgrounds, seen too many packed beaches, fought our way through too much congested traffic, and generally questioned the wisdom of our entire trip. Throwing all previous plans to the wind, we sought refuge at our first state park gem, lured by the promises of something unspoiled and nature-oriented.

Located a mere ten minutes from the coast, the park we choose was peacefully situated on the shores of a reservoir lake. Around it spread an expanse of low land and wild grasses, shade trees and thick brush, lulled by the soft sounds of nature. With a near empty campground, we had our pick of sites. Neighbors were quiet, content to just enjoy their surroundings. Even Easter Weekend failed to rouse the park from its tranquil state. Freshwater swimming was perfect for children, the beach edged by grass under cool shade trees. Rarely did we share the beach with anyone else. Directed by the resident park ranger, we discovered an unpublicized hike, skirting the lake's shore and winding through the dry grasses like a trip across the African veld. The children turned the expedition into an academic exercise, dashing about with

their "naturalist" paraphernalia, dutifully recording everything in attendant notebooks. Being eleven-year-old boys, their interest peaked upon discovering the unmistakable signs of wild boar.

Once discovered, state park gems became the dominant itinerary planner for our trip, culminating in a visit to St. Joseph Peninsula State Park. As with a number of parks located in the Panhandle, St. Joseph has all the appeal of a seaside park. With over 2,000 acres of protected barrier beach, the park is isolated and best enjoyed by those who don't require outside sources of entertainment.

Children will have their time filled just exploring the beach. Deer grazing beside your campsite at dawn, pleasant nature walks, high sand dunes, warm water, and endless stretches of empty beach are characteristics of this lovely park, and others like it along the Gulf coast. One word of warning - the midgies (or no-see-ums) can be rampant around the campsites, particularly in warm, damp weather. Arm yourself with Avon "Skin So Soft," or buy some at one of the nearby stores. This non-pesticide product works wonders and is safe for children and babies, its only drawback being that your whole family will smell like a toddler let loose in someone's prize perfumery.

If your vision of a family trip to Florida features snorkeling around the Keys and basking on southern beaches, don't be afraid of adjusting it to include some state park gems. Located in out-of-the-way places, or hidden among the vast stretches of lesser-known inland areas, they can offer a true picture of Florida's natural wonders, an enjoyable destination, and a memorable family adventure.

RESOURCE SECTION

TOURIST BUREAUS
Florida Dept. of Commerce, Div. of Tourism, 126 Van Buren St., Tallahassee, FL 32399-2000   Tel: (904) 487-1462.

NATIONAL AIRLINES
Of the national carriers that service Florida, Delta, American, & USAir provide the most regular service.

SUGGESTED READING
Hidden Florida, The Adventurer's Guide by R. Riegert. Berkeley: Ulysses Press.
Adventuring In Florida by A. de Hart. San Francisco: Sierra Club.
Real Guide To Florida by M. Sinclair. New York: Prentice Hall.

SUGGESTED MAPS
The Florida State tourist maps are sufficient to suit most travel needs. Other maps include:
U.S. Road Atlas by Rand McNally, scale varies.
Florida State Map by Gousha, scale N/A.

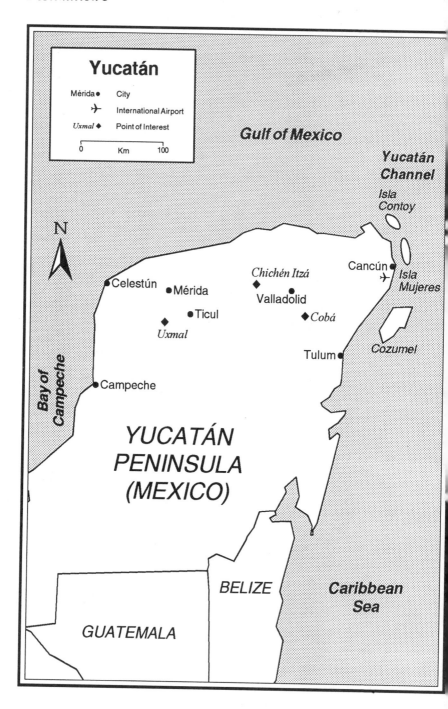

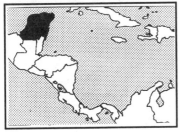

The Yucatán Peninsula

Mayan ruins, white sand beaches, warm weather, and peaceful, agricultural communities typify the Yucatán peninsula. Easily accessible from North America, the area has become a popular winter vacation spot for northerners escaping the winter blues. Although an enclave of resorts has sprung up in the vicinity of Cancún and Cozumel on the northeast coast, the bulk of the Yucatán remains untouched by excessive tourism. Adventuring is easy and safe in this quiet, friendly corner of Mexico.

GENERAL DESCRIPTION

Location. Thrusting out into the Caribbean Sea like the tail of a fish, the Yucatán Peninsula forms the southeastern portion of Mexico. To the north lies the Gulf of Mexico, to the south the country of Belize. Separated from the rest of Mexico by a ridge of mountains in the west, the Yucatán retains its own individuality, both physically and culturally.

Terrain. The Yucatán is predominantly flat, the vegetation lush and tropical. What appear on the landscape as hills are invariably Mayan ruins, still buried under thick tropical growth. Coastal areas are often lined with gorgeous sand beaches, a major reason for the recent development as a winter resort area. A small handful of islands lie off the northeast coast, with coral reefs and sandy beaches. Inland, areas given over to agriculture have citrus groves and henequen plantations, cattle ranches and small, varied farms. Border areas to the west have more hills, a hint of what exists throughout the rest of Mexico.

Climate. As in all subtropical areas, little seasonal change occurs, although passing winter northers can bring clouds and rain, similar to the Bahamas and Florida. Sea breezes keep coastal areas cooler than elsewhere, while inland regions can be unbelievably humid at times. The rainy season extends from late spring through summer. Fall is an excellent time to visit, after the rains, with less humidity, and before the tourist season.

Culture & Lifestyle. Culturally distinguished from rest of Mexico, the Yucatán was cut off and isolated until as recently as 30 years ago. Long inhabited by Mayans, the Peninsula was once the center of a thriving, advanced Indian civilization, with abundant cities, ceremonial sites, and a well-developed road system. Today, while scores of Mayan ruins lie hidden and crumbling in the jungle, testimony to this previous developed age, the present lifestyle is simple, primarily based on an agricultural economy. Inland, Indians till fields of corn and live in stone, thatched-roof houses. Villages are small and poor, the people hard-working, quiet and shy.

PRACTICAL CONCERNS

Political Update & Safety. In a country notoRíous for its bandits (mythical or otherwise), the Yucatán is a completely safe place to travel. The people are quiet and peaceful, welcoming to foreigners. As in any poor country, theft is always a concern and valuables should be kept with you at all times. The Mayans, however, do not have the same zestful enthusiasm for stealing that one finds throughout other parts of Mexico. Families will find the Peninsula a gentle introduction to travel in Central America, an area renowned for its tumultuous politics and frequent military activities, although these ills seem to be happily on the wane at the moment.

Travel Documents. Canadian and U.S. citizens need only some form of identification to enter the Yucatán. Most others, including EC countries, need a passport. Visas are also required in some instances. Contact the nearest consulate for details.

Money. Currency is the peso. Travelers checks are the best and safest way to carry money. Credit cards are usually acceptable in the larger hotels and restaurants of resort areas. Banks are found only in major towns or tourist areas, so be sure you have exchanged enough money before heading out into the countryside.

Travel Costs. Outside the Cancún area, travel is inexpensive. Bicycle or bus travel can keep transportation costs to a minimum. Staying in the tourist district and renting a car will, of course, cost you considerably more. Accommodations extend the usual range from inexpensive to extravagant depending on where you stay and how much you're willing to put up with. Food prices and dining out can both be economical, again especially away from the beach areas that only cater to tourists.

Language. Spanish is the official language, although Mayan is also widely spoken, particularly out in the countryside. People who cater to tourists can often speak English. Some knowledge of Spanish will serve you well when visiting out of the way places. Otherwise, take along a good phrase book. With few rules of pronunciation, Spanish is a very phonetical language, easy for the amateur to sort out.

Health. Treat both water and food with circumspection outside tourist areas. Use only bottled, filtered, or boiled water. Wash, peel, or cook all produce. Limit your eating out to places where the cooking premises look like something you wouldn't mind dealing with. Don't be afraid to indulge the local passion for fresh squeezed orange juice, sold on the streets. No immunizations are necessary. Children should wear sandals or shoes and wash before eating. Basic medical supplies are widely available, even in small towns where they're often sold in the one general store.

Food. Food in the Yucatán is inexpensive and delicious, both when eating out or cooking your own. Beans, cheese, and tortillas form the basis of the diet and are widely available. Tortillas can be bought fresh from small, local tortilla factories, or at the market. Bread is also delicious, baked in a French style (although not necessarily as filling). Other staples are sold in tiny, Third World-style shops in all sizeable villages. Local foods include excellent tropical fruits. Mérida, the state capital, has a Western-style supermarket, with a wide selection, including imported English products. Fresh produce is best bought at local open-air markets, located in almost every village each morning. Another inexpensive source of food are the many local women selling things from baskets. Oranges are the most common fruit, usually sold in the form of freshly squeezed juice from street. For an inexpensive meal out, eat the local staple of enchiladas and beans, very healthy and filling.

Clothes. Take lightweight clothing, plus something warm for overcast days during winter. Bathing gear, sunhats, and cotton clothing are paramount. Women can feel comfortable wearing T-shirts and shorts in touristed areas or while doing outdoor activities. Dress more conservatively when strolling around villages at night. Regular sandles are fine for the beaches and towns, while sport sandals or trail shoes are best when hiking or climbing up Mayan ruins. Expect to be tempted by locally made products, including lovely, colorful woven clothing made by Mayan women. Bargain if possible, usually the accepted practice at markets.

Laundry & Bathing. Many hotels offer laundry services, although these can be expensive. Tourist and urban areas like Cancún, Cozumel, and Mérida have laundromats where you can do your own laundry or have it done for you. Elsewhere, figure on mastering the art of handwashing yourself, or ask around for a local woman. Settle on a price first, something that seems fair to both of you. Remember, your clothes will be done by hand, not in a machine. They'll also come back cleaner than they've ever been. This type of laundry service usually takes two days to wash and dry. Bathing facilities are available at all types of accommodations, from modern hot showers to the basic cold variety. Keeping children clean is easy along coastal areas where they'll spend the majority of the time in the water. Give everyone a freshwater rinse at the end of the day to keep salt out of clothes and bedding.

Baby Needs. The usual assortment of sweetened baby cereals is available, plus jarred food in large towns. Better yet, do like the Indians and just improvise with what you're eating: mashed fruit, eggs, rice, potatoes, oatmeal, bread, powdered milk, cheese. Babies will even go for tortillas and beans, but don't overdo it with the beans. Take advantage of local women to provide you with a laundry service when staying in one place for a few days or longer. With a car, bring a bucket to soak diapers in so you can wash them yourself. They'll dry rapidly in the sun and heat. Include a baby carrier if you plan some Mayan explorations or bus travel. A stroller is fine if traveling by car. Good sun protection is essential, including cotton clothing, a sun hat, and an appropriate sunscreen.

TRANSPORTATION

Getting There. Flying to the Yucatán is easy. Charter flights to Cancún are frequent from North America and Europe, offering good round-trip fares. Regular commercial airlines all go through the United States, including Aviateca Airlines which has very affordable flights to the Yucatán from the southern United States. By car, the trip takes around three days from the Mexican border, only worth it if you plan to stay awhile. The Yucatán can also be easily reached via Belize on the well-paved Northern Highway. Buses leave regularly from Belize City.

Regional Transport. Public buses are frequent, not too crowded (except on weekends), and service just about everywhere. Prices are typically low and the experience always culturally entertaining. Fridays, Sundays and Monday mornings are the busiest on roads to and from Cancún, so try to avoid these times. Some buses have roof racks (useful for carrying bicycles), others do not. Cars can be rented in Cancún, but expect fuel and rental costs to be high. Bicycles can be an excellent alternative, depending on where you want to go and how much time you have.

Roads. Roads are narrow, usually ramrod straight, and among the flattest you'll ever see. Other than a couple of main roads, road conditions are mediocre at best, especially off the beaten track, where dirt and pot holes predominate. Traffic is light, mostly trucks and buses, except on the two main highways linking Cancún with Mérida and Tulum. Don't drive at night if possible, a hard and fast rule for all of Mexico.

ACCOMMODATIONS

Campgrounds. A number of official camping facilities are offered along the Caribbean coast, some with everything from hook-ups and hot showers to cabanas and restaurants. As always, this is certainly the most economical means of accommodation, although tent camping can be nothing more than a space on the beach. Free-camping safely is possible anywhere that seems appropriate. Ask first before stopping near someone's home. Locals usually are very open to people camping for the night, although in some spots you might find that you're regarded as the evening's entertainment. A number of places charge a nominal fee to let you pitch a tent or sling a hammock (a popular way to sleep in the Yucatán - hammocks can be bought locally). Beach areas outside the tourist meccas can be good places to camp provided you are near a village for water and provisions. Isla de Mujeres, for instance, permits it on any beach area. Frankly, we've found free-camping with children in a place like the Yucatán to be more trouble than it's worth unless you have your own vehicle and can load up on food and water. Even in tourist areas you're more likely to be neighbors with the Gringo Trail backpacking crowd than with other families. By all means take camping gear if you like the independence, but don't expect to totally rely on it. Fortunately, the Yucatán offers other affordable options.

Hotels and Cabanas. Accommodations run from elegant around Cancún to basic in small towns. Most villages have at least one simple place where you can stay, particularly along the coast. Larger towns and cities all have pleasant rooms for a reasonable cost. The longer you stay, the less you usually pay. Weekly rentals can always reduce costs. If you find a village or town that strikes your fancy, inquire about renting rooms or a house somewhere. Places tend to turn up. Arrangements can also be made for meals, maid, or laundry service, if you want. Check out the amenities first.

It's amazing what surprises can be sprung on you after you've settled in for the night. For inexpensive coastal accommodations, try the many places that rent cabanas, simple rooms with a mattress or hammock for sleeping. These have the advantage of easily enabling you to do your own cooking, a definite money saver with children.

Hammocks. One adventurous way to cut the cost of accommodations is by sleeping in a hammock. Many small hotels reduce nightly charges if you choose to sling a hammock instead of using the beds in a room. Hooks are provided on the wall for just this purpose. Paying a minimal fee to sling a hammock outside is also possible, best along the coast in beach areas. Hammocks are a tradition in the Yucatán, with local artisans creating the finest in the world. Forget bringing one with you. The market at Mérida offers the best selection and prices for

locally-made hammocks. Make sure someone demonstrates for you the proper way to lie in one. Hammocks come in single and double size.

POINTS OF INTEREST

Natural. The Yucatán has many areas of natural interest, including jungle and coastal parks, coral reefs and seabird nesting areas. Although the concept of preserved land is still a new one for this area, a number of preserves have been set aside, as well as natural areas of beauty around some of the Mayan sites.

• *K'an Biosphere Reserve.* Over a million acres of preserved land, including the lovely Boca Paila Peninsula, with 100 km of coast, barrier reefs, mangrove swamps, lagoons, and abundant birds and wildlife. Both camping and cabanas are available.

• *Parque Natural del Flamenco Mexicano.* A large river estuary area near Celestún on the north coast, with one of the largest flamingo colonies in North America. Includes mangroves, small islets, rocks, and a nice beach, as well as excellent bird-watching.

• *Isla Contoy National Park.* Wonderful bird-watching and snorkeling on this island park, located north of Isla de Mujeres. Sand dunes, mangroves, coconut palms, and coral reefs offer a lovely setting for a day outing or overnight camping trip.

• *Parque Nacional Submarino de Pakincar (Cozumel).* Located off a lovely, little-used beach, with spectacular snorkeling around the protected reef.

• *Xel-Ha.* A snorkeling park just north of Tulum, with natural saltwater pools.

Cultural. Getting away from tourist areas and out into the countryside is the best way to enjoy the culture. Begin by riding a few second class buses, always a fascinating procedure destined to produce some of your best travel stories. Local markets are equally interesting, with people from all over the countryside getting together to sell their wares. Mérida's is one of the best, with abundant wares from all over the state. Mérida itself makes a fascinating, lively destination, with its tree-lined streets, horse-drawn carriages, vibrant market, and streets vendors and musicians. Sunday is the busiest day to visit, with the downtown area closed to cars. For a quieter version of town life, visit Ticul, a veritable haven for bicyclers. Local taxi service is provided by three-wheeled bicycles, well worth a ride just for the experience.

Historic. By far the Yucatán's most famous historic sites are its Mayan ruins that virtually litter the landscape, many of them still buried under lush vegetation. Remnants of a great civilization that once encompassed what is now the Yucatán, Belize, and Guatemala, thousands of ruins remain, making this one of the richest archaeological areas in the world. To escape crowds (and heat), visit popular sites early or late in the day, or discover some of the lesser known ones, often equally impressive. The following are some of the Peninsula's key historic areas.

• *Chichén Itzá.* The Yucatán's most popular archaeological site, with extremely developed tourist facilities. Visit early or late to avoid busloads of tourists.

• *Uxmal.* Another popular ruin, also with tourist facilities. Fragments of ruins lie hidden in the surrounding jungle for adventurous visitors to explore. Includes an excellent "Sound and Light" evening show.

• *Cobá.* Situated in the jungle and part of a wildlife park, these ruins have mostly been left in their natural state (see the accompanying sidebar for more details).

• *Tulum.* Once a walled city, Tulum offers abundant exploration on foot through its ruined remains.

• *Sayil & Labna.* Two fascinating ruins, authentic in their jungle setting, with few tourists, abundant birds, and excellent walks.

• *Loftun.* An enormous system of caverns, with early Paleolithic rock paintings, signs of early habitation.

Nature Studies. The Yucatán offers excellent bird-watching, with tropical birds in the jungle interior and abundant seabirds along the coast. Two good areas for birdwatching are Río Largartos and Celestún, both with huge populations of flamingos. To see jungles birds, tread quietly while exploring less visited ruins inland.

OUTDOOR ACTIVITIES

Hiking. Hiking in the Yucatán is more a case of exploring areas on foot rather than following trails: up and down Mayan ruins, on jungle paths, along beaches, down dirt roads and paths that permeate the interior countryside. A number of areas around ruins have wooded footpaths, including Cobá, set in a wildlife park. The terrain is flat and blissfully easy throughout the Yucatán, with the biggest challenge being the heat, particularly inland where humidity can be intense. When hiking up ruins, be sure to start early to beat the midday heat. Wear sunhats and take plenty of water. Also remember that anything you hike up you also have to get down, an alarming experience for the vertiginous prone in some cases. Children usually have no problem with this; it's the adults that aren't too happy.

Bicycling. Bicycling on the Yucatán Peninsula is a mixed bag. While the predominantly level terrain guarantees easy bicycling, the intense inland heat and humidity can make even a level road seem like work. We invariably have conflicting feelings about biking in the heat, loving it sometimes, hating it others. Fall is the best time to plan any lengthy touring to avoid the worst of the hot weather. Traffic is sparse and road conditions mediocre. Make sure your bicycles have good durable tires. Plan a route that won't leave you out in the middle of nowhere with eight hours of bicycling before reaching a town with facilities. Also avoid the two main routes between Cancún and both Mérida and Tulum, taking to some backroads instead. Another option is to use bicycles for day outings, a great way to explore the countryside without the rigors of touring. Bicycles can be carried on the roofs of buses for covering long distances between places of interest. Even if you plan to stay in one place, consider bringing bicycles for local transport.

We always find them very liberating, as well as fun for the children. Day riding here is easy provided the itinerary is kept modest. Pulling a baby in a trailer would be possible. Use one that includes some type of sun cover.

Swimming. The swimming is unbeatable along most of the Yucatán's Caribbean coast, with long stretches of white sand beaches and warm water. Children will love the coastal areas, with the water to play in and plenty of tempting shells to find. For snorkeling, try Cozumel, best situated for trips to nearby reefs. Inland offers fascinating, unusual swimming in "cenotes", limestone pools filled with cool freshwater.

Cobá - Ruins of the Jungle

Hidden in the jungle of the Quintana Roo state lies the Yucatán's largest and perhaps most impressive Mayan ruin. Built over 2,500 years ago, the city of Cobá thrived until 900 A.D. when mysterious circumstances led to its abandonment. Today it sprawls an estimated 50 square kilometers across the thickly forested interior, its one-time grandeur now only recreated in the imagination of its visitors. Unlike some of the more popular and heavily visited ruins, Cobá has largely escaped the ravages of overtourism. Decidedly off the beaten track and only partially excavated, it remains mysteriously shrouded in jungle forest, the perfect location for outdoor enthusiasts, imaginative children, and those with a sense of adventure. Lying within a wildlife park, its natural setting not only complements the splendor of the ruins themselves, but provides frequent glimpses of jungle life.

Cobá is best reached from Tulum, making it a fairly easy target on a tour of the Caribbean coast. For families, the location is ideal. Booking into one of the many inexpensive beachside cabanas (or camping) south of Tulum, you can enjoy a visit to two contrasting ruins while based along the Yucatán's loveliest stretch of coast. Having explored the dramatically situated fortress of Tulum (go early to avoid Cancún-based crowds), take a bus, car, or taxi the 50 kilometers inland to Cobá. The ruins lie along the main route between Tulum and Valladolid, south of Nuevo X-Can. Only a few buses leave Tulum each day for Valladolid, so be sure to check the schedule. Be sure to tell the driver you want to get off at the Cobá junction, not normally a stop. The trip from Tulum takes about 90 minutes. The ruins are only three kilometers from the main road, easy to walk. As always, getting an early start is best in this hot, humid corner of the country. For optimum viewing pleasure, arrive early, do your pyramid climbing before the midday heat, then retreat to the jungle paths or a cafe to escape peak sun hours. For intrepid families traveling with bicycles, reaching Cobá by bike is a comfortable day's ride. Traffic is light and the road level. As always in the Yucatán, heat is the biggest factor. A side trip to Cobá can always provide a nice mini-tour into the interior, plus a pleasant alternative route north, away from the busy coastal road.

Even families with little previous knowledge of Mayan culture will find Cobá fascinating and exciting. Originally a trade center with a population of 50,000, Cobá was probably once the largest city in the Yucatán, with more ancient roads converging on it than any other ruin. Sacred causeways across the four lakes around Cobá connected it with outlying centers, an area of 50 sq. km that now lies buried under a mass of trees, vines and flowers.

It's easy to get lost or confused on the maze of dirt roads in the jungle, so take time to orient yourselves before beginning your explorations. Distances between groupings of ruins are about one to two km, with little pattern to their interconnecting paths. After entering the ruins, take the Grupo Cobá path to the right for the Temple of the Churches, an impressive pyramid with excellent views of the surrounding lakes, jungle, and neighboring ruins. Turning to the left, the path leads you to the Nohoch Mul group, with the tallest pyramid in the Yucatán. Architecturally similar to the ruins of Tikal in Guatemala, Cobá is believed to have been allied with it in some way, probably through marriage. Similar great pyramids rise from the jungle floor, their age-old grandeur a testimony to the architectural mastery of the Mayans.

With little that is excavated so far (more is being uncovered all the time), the bulk of the city still lies buried under lush vegetation.

To really discover the magic and natural wonders of Cobá, explore along the various paths, catching sight of overgrown structures and extensive avenues. Winding through the dense jungle, the paths also offer frequent sightings of toucans and herons, egrets and butterflies, with perhaps a glimpse of a monkey here and there. Be sure to arm yourselves with plenty of mosquito protection. Allow at least two days to really explore the ruins and surrounding lake and jungle area. In addition to the various rooms and hotels in the nearby village, it's usually possible to camp beside Lake Cobá. Don't leave anything of value behind at your campsite while touring the ruins. Freshwater swimming is possible in the lake if you don't mind wading in through the rather marshy and mucky shallows. The village itself is a small affair, devoid of the usual native presence in areas more frequented by tourists. For a taste of luxury, enjoy a pool-side drink at the Villa Arqueoligica Cobá, a Club Med facility. The accompanying library contains some wonderful information on the Mayan culture. Other facilities include a few small cafes and bakery, largely provided for the use of working archaeologists.

Even if you only take the time to visit one ruin during your visit to the Yucatán, make it Cobá. The combination of remote location, lack of tourists, mysterious jungle aura, and natural park setting will make your day or two there well worth the trip, something the whole family will long remember.

RESOURCES

TOURIST BUREAUS
Mexican Gov't Tourism Office, 405 Park Ave., Ste. 1002, New York, NY 10022 Tel: (212) 755-7261.
Mexican Gov't Tourism Office, 1 Place Villa Marie, Ste. 2409, Montreal, QUE H3B 3M9, Canada Tel: (514) 871-1052.
Other Mexican tourist offices located in Chicago, Houston, Los Angeles, and Washington, DC.

CONSULATES
Embassy of the United Mexican States, 2829 16th St. NW, Washington, DC Tel: (202) 234-6000.

NATIONAL AIRLINES
AeroMexico, 13405 Northwest Freeway, Ste. 140, Houston, TX 77040 Tel: (800) 237-6639.
Mexicana Airlines, 9841 Airport Blvd., Ste. 200, Los Angeles, CA 90045 Tel: (213) 646-9500.

SUGGESTED READING
Yucatán Handbook by C. Mallan. Moon Publications, Chico, CA.
Mexico & Central American Handbook by B. Box. Prentice Hall Travel, New York.
La Ruta Maya - Yucatán, Guatemala, & Belize: A Travel Survival Kit by T. Brosnahan. Lonely Planet Publications, Berkeley, CA.
Life in a Mexican Town by G. Peterson. National Text Book Co., Illinois.

SUGGESTED MAPS
Yucatán, H.F.E.T., Scale: N/A.
Yucatán, International Travel Maps, Scale: N/A.
Yucatán Peninsula, S.I.G.S.A., Scale: varies.

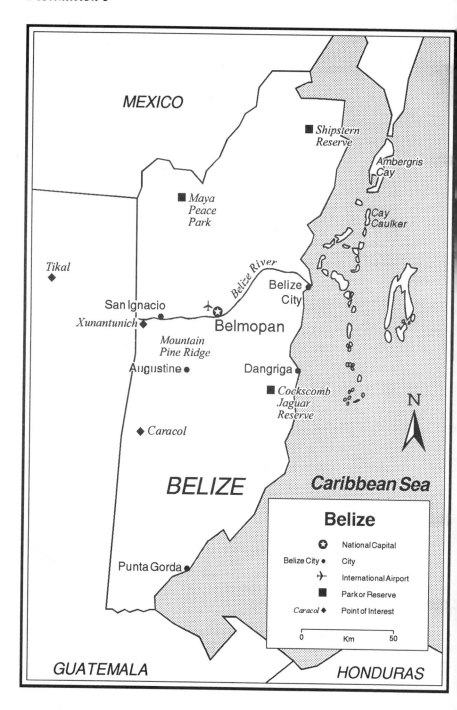

Central America & The Yucatán Peninsula

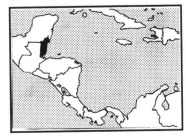

Belize

Small and ethnically diverse, Belize is a mixture of jungle and mountains, islands and coral reefs, forests and mangrove swamps. Renowned for its immense barrier reef, the country offers an ideal spot for a family adventure, with numerous islands, or cayes, to explore, warm water, and friendly, relaxed people. Recently, an element of eco-tourism has been developed along the western border where hiking, canoeing, and horseback riding all provide exciting ways to explore the interior. Adventuring in Belize can be as easy or strenuous as you want: weeks spent living on an island enjoying the sun and the laid-back Caribbean culture, or venturing into the interior by bicycle, bus, or car.

GENERAL DESCRIPTION

Location. Located south of the Yucatan and north of Guatemala, Belize clings to the edge of Central America, facing the Caribbean Sea. Tiny in size and isolated by location, the country retains its unusual Caribbean flavor among predominantly Latin neighbors.

Terrain. Belize is a country of surprising contrasts, given its miniature size. To the north and east lies the low mangrove coast. Offshore, the abundant cayes extend over miles of protected waters, their environment alive with coral reefs and marine life. The land is low and flat on the north, much of it marshland converted for agricultural production. Heading south, the terrain becomes increasingly impenetrable, with forest, rivers and mountains. Towards the west and the Guatemalan border, rivers and jungle harbor tropical vegetation and bird life.

Climate. Lying in the subtropics, the country experiences very warm weather year-round. The rainy season extends from June-September, with humidity highest at this time. Sea winds keep the islands and coast cooler than the interior. Jungle areas can be very hot. The best time to visit is during the dry season.

Culture & Lifestyle. The country's culture is a complete mixture of ethnic groups all living harmoniously together: Indian, African, European, and Mestize (a blending of Latin and Indian). Originally settled by Mayan Indians, the coastal area became a favorite hiding place for British privateers who subsequently settled there. Today, the coast and cayes are largely populated by their descendants and those of their slaves. The standard of living is low, with homes very basic and simple. Interior regions have only recently been opened for development with the coming of a few roads. An increasing number of Guatemalan refugees have resettled across the border, providing Belize with yet another ethnic community. One of the country's most unusual aspects is that so many different cultures and lifestyles can be experienced in such a small region, from the plantations of the north to the relaxed coastal villages and Indian mountain communities.

PRACTICAL CONCERNS

Political Update & Safety. Originally British Honduras, Belize gained independence in 1981. Since then it has made efforts to improve living conditions and recently begun to realize its potential for tourism. Despite the rather dubious reputation of Belize City, the country is perfectly safe and comfortable to travel around. The city itself is not nearly as intimidating as it's reputed to be, with no heavy drug scene or rampant theft. Normal precautions should be taken as with any relatively poor urban center.

Travel Documents. Citizens of the United States, Canada, England, Australia, and EC countries only need passports and either a return ticket or evidence of sufficient funds for visits up to 30 days. Other nationals require visas, available from local consulates.

Money. Currency is the Belize dollar. Use travelers checks for carrying money. Banks are open Monday-Friday and easy to find in most towns.

Travel Costs. By Central American standards, Belize is slightly expensive, though still a good budget destination if you're careful. On the coast, costs are highest in the tourist center of San Pedro on Ambergris Caye. Many areas in the west are best explored as part of an organized group, always a pricy option. How you travel will determine how much you spend. Food, accommodations, and public transportation are all relatively inexpensive.

Language. English is the official language, although both Spanish and Creole are also widely spoken. Despite the prevalence of English, don't count on understanding everything they say. The dialect can be a challenge.

Health. Employ the usual precautions with food. Water tends to be good, although bottled water is also widely available. Avoid street vendors that seem dubious in the cleanliness department. Cooking your own food is the easiest way to stay healthy. No immunizations are necessary, and taking malaria pills optional. This is probably only necessary if you plan to camp or spend a good portion of your time in jungle and marsh areas. If so, take Chloroquine, beginning one week before and continuing two weeks after your visit. Bring plenty of sunscreen to deal with the onslaught of tropical sun. Children should wear T-shirts in the water between 11 a.m. and 3 p.m., including while snorkeling.

Food. With little agriculture, food selection is somewhat limited, especially fresh produce. Best buys include seafood, coconuts, bananas, rice, beans, and bread. All the usual basics can be found in small, local shops. On the cayes, a cottage food industry thrives, with women selling delicious baked goods right out of their homes. An inexpensive, healthy meal can easily be planned around these small, delicious pastries stuffed with a variety of fillings. Beans and rice constitute the local diet throughout most of the country and are available everywhere. These make an excellent, filling, affordable meal the whole family can enjoy, both cooked on your own (easy on a camping stove - use canned beans) or at a restaurant. Shopping is done in small shops or open-air markets located in most towns.

Clothes. Bring lightweight clothing, ideally cotton. Include plenty of beachwear (bathing suit, sunhat, sandals). Children need only minimal clothes, particularly babies and toddlers who can go practically naked other than something for sun protection. Dress for women is casual.

Laundry & Bathing. The only formal laundry facilities are in Belize City and San Ignacio, so you might want to pass through just to get some clean clothes. Otherwise, count on having to do your own wash in a sink, or hiring a local woman. Ask around to find out who does laundry. Hotels and ranches can also always provide laundry service. Bathing isn't a problem, between swimming in the ocean and normal bathing facilities that come with any accommodations. Rinse children off at the end of the day to keep saltwater out of clothes and bedding.

Baby Needs. Disposable diapers, good powdered whole milk, and baby cereal (sweetened) are widely available. If using cloth diapers, finding a local woman to do laundry is usually easy. Bring a child carrier for walking and netting for naptime if you plan to have the baby sleep outside. Even if staying in one place on a caye, a stroller isn't too practical because of the dirt roads. Despite the lack of beaches on the cayes, little children can always find a place to paddle about in the shallow water.

Snorkeling Gear. By all means bring snorkeling gear. These are among the best waters in the world to explore. Children of all ages will love it, and the hot weather and warm water will keep them swimming for hours.

TRANSPORTATION

Getting There. Belize can be reached by air, car, or bus. The least expensive flights all leave from the southern United States, principally Miami, New Orleans, and Los Angeles. Try APEX (advanced purchase) for savings on short visits of three weeks or less. Charter flights also offer good savings. By road, the country can be entered via the Yucatan or Guatemala's Peten region. The Mexican route is by far the easiest on the paved, level Northern Highway. Buses leave frequently from Chetuzal in the Yucatan to Belize City. The Western Highway is also well-paved to the Guatemalan border, at which point things really break down. The road through the Guatemalan Peten (jungle region) is notorious, a dirt route that has been known to take hours longer than predicted because of mud and break-downs. Think twice before attempting this on a public bus with children (most of whom would die rather than spend 18 hours on the road). Driving on your own, of course, will ensure better success rate, but you should still plan on a difficult journey. It's also possible to reach Belize by ferry from Livingston, Guatemala to Punta Gorda. From there it's a long haul on the mountainous, dirt-surfaced Southern Highway, again not to be lightly undertaken when traveling with children. The last option is arriving on your own sailboat to what ranks as one of the best tropical cruising grounds in the world.

Regional Travel. Good public transportation is available by bus along both the Northern and Western Highways. Beyond that, things deteriorate rapidly heading south or into more remote regions. Car travel is easy along both main routes. Car rentals are available in Belize City and very expensive. If traveling by bicycle, bikes can be carried on the roofs of buses for long distances. Most of the cayes are still only accessible by boat. Ferries run frequently from Belize City to Caulker and Ambergris Cayes. Ambergris can also be reached by air from Belize City, a popular way to get there. To visit other cayes you'll need to hire a boat or bring your own. Cayes are small enough to easily walk around, usually on just a single dirt road.

Roads. Both the Northern and Western Highways are paved and in fairly good condition. Traffic is light, although fast-moving. Other roads are for the intrepid, with many in the interior hills requiring four-wheel drive. If bringing your own car, take your time when venturing south or inland, areas where the road conditions really deteriorate and your adventure has the potential of turning into a motorist's nightmare. Don't underestimate the time it will take you to cover a seemly miniscule distance in this pint-size country.

ACCOMMODATIONS

Campgrounds. Camping, at least part time, is a good way for families to cut the sometimes high cost of accommodations in Belize. Although camping possibilities are scattered throughout the country, only a few involve designated sites. These include Placentia, Caulker Caye, San Ignacio, Augustine, and Cockscomb Basin Jaguar Preserve. With a vehicle or on bicycles, you can safely camp most places, although lowlands will be buggy. Always ask first before assuming it's fine to camp. Both Ambergris and Caulker Cayes have official camping places, a very affordable option. This sort of thing is most popular with the young backpacking crowd. Caulker Caye in particular is still on what's popularly called the Gringo Trail, or one of the winter hangouts for young hippy types. If you find yourselves feeling a bit too old for this scene, preferring something more family-oriented, it's best to rent a bungalow or rooms. Other camping possibilities can be found in the west around San Ignacio, particularly on some of the ranches that rent cottages, or near some of the ruins. Again, always ask first.

Rooms & Bungalows. Accommodations are available all over the country, usually at higher prices than in neighboring Mexico or Guatemala. Tourist centers along the coast and on the cayes offer the best, from budget to luxurious. Small villages can get pretty basic. About 20 cayes have some type of tourist accommodations, from pricey resorts on private islands to inexpensive rentals. Caulker remains the best budget destination among the islands, with relatively inexpensive bungalows that are decent and clean. The western area near the Guatemalan border has recently developed as an eco-tourism center, with accommodation headquarters around San Ignacio. Most popular are cottage rooms on private ranches, a somewhat pricy option. These are all usually part of a package deal that includes interesting outdoor explorations into the surrounding countryside.

POINTS OF INTEREST

Natural. Belize is filled with areas of natural interest and beauty, many of them protected: coral reefs and atolls, rivers and jungle, mangroves and grasslands, mountains and valleys. The sheer number of parks and preserves in this small country is indicative of its increasing commitment to conservation and the environment.

• *Barrier Reef.* Most renowned of Belize's natural wonders is its barrier reef. Lying close offshore and extending over 150 km, it constitutes the longest barrier reef in the Western Hemisphere, second in the world. With atolls and cayes, coral and diverse marine life, the area has been proposed a World Heritage Site, thus ensuring its future preservation. Tourism in the cayes is low-key, offering a wonderful opportunity to explore the marine environment away from the destructive forces of over-exploitation. Even on a so-called "developed" island like Ambergris, development means a place with perhaps five bungalows and a thatched roof check-in. This is one area of Belize that shouldn't be missed. Consider spending at least a week on one of the cayes, enjoying the marine environment and exploring the mainland coastal river area by boat.

The following are a few of Belize's parks and preserves open to the public:

• *Hol Chan Marine Reserve.* An underwater preserve off the coast of Ambergris Caye offering excellent snorkeling.

• *Mountain Pine Forest Reserve.* Remote and beautiful, this park covers pine forest, grasslands, hills, rain forest and tropical valleys. Only accessible by private vehicle (4-wheel drive), horseback, or on foot. Guided tours are available. A trip here is most appropriate for the experienced adventuring family with older children. Augustine serves as the reserve headquarters, with accommodations (including camping).

• *Belize Zoo.* An open-air zoo with a collection of animals from different habitats in a natural setting. An important part of Belize's efforts to preserve the country's natural heritage.

• *Guanacaste Park.* A wildlife reserve in tropical forest. Good for even young children, with a handful of short hiking trails.

• *Society Hall Nature Reserve.* A privately owned park in rainforest.

- *Shipstern Reserve.* Has bird-watching (excellent), animal and marine life.

- *Crooked Tree Wildlife Reserve.* A park of inland waterways, lagoons and diverse marine and animal life.

- *Maya Peace Park.* Also called the Rio Bravo Conservation Area, this park was set up by the very active Belize Audubon Society and includes an abundance of animal and bird life.

- *Panti Medicinal Trail.* Although not a park, this trail provides a fascinating insight into the diverse plant life of this area and its medicinal capabilities.

Cultural. Most pronounced is the contrast between the Caribbean flavor of the coast and the Latin influences inland. For a sample of both, try a visit to one of the cayes, followed by a trip to the area around San Ignacio. Visitors with plenty of time and their own vehicle, as well as a strong sense of adventure, can explore the southern regions of the country, areas with yet more diverse cultures. Principal among them are the unique Garifuna, descendents of Carib Indians and African slaves living along the southern coast, and various Mayan Indian groups in the interior along the Guatemalan border.

- *Mayan Guest House.* An innovative program has been introduced in the southern region of Belize near Punta Gorda, offering temporary accommodations in a traditional Mayan village. In an attempt to combat the cultural exploitation that usually accompanies the development of tourism, Belize is implementing this pilot plan, along with others like it. Guests are housed in a traditional Mayan house of waddle, daub, and thatch (one guest house per village) and exposed to normal village life. All proceeds go towards improving living conditions and environmental preservation of the area. This is a unique opportunity to experience an aspect of the culture firsthand.

Historic. Mayan ruins lie scattered throughout Belize, some still buried in jungle and nearly inaccessible, others easily visited and offering a fascinating insight into the once great civilization that flourished throughout the Yucatan Peninsula area. Caracol, the most impressive ruin, lies far in the Mountain Pine Ridge Forest Reserve. All-day guided trips are possible out of San Ignacio, an adventurous, but strenuous trip. Other more accessible ruins include Cuello, Lamanai, and Altun Ha, all located in the northern portion of the country, and Xunantunich, west of San Ignacio. Belize is also a good jumping off spot for visiting Tikal, one of the most famous Mayan ruins of all, located across the border in Guatemala's Peten district (See sidebar).

OUTDOOR ACTIVITIES

Backcountry Camping. Backcountry camping is possible in some of the parks and preserves. This is strictly for experienced adventuring families with their own vehicle and older children. Try the Mountain Pine Ridge Forest Reserve in the western foothills or the Cockcomb Jaguar Conservation Reserve in the south. It's also possible, with permission, to camp at some of the remote ruins for the night.

Hiking. Walking potential varies from easy walks around low cayes to rigorous ventures into the mountains. Designated hiking trails are located at the following: Belize Zoo; Guanacaste Park; Community Baboon Sanctuary; Mountain Pine Ridge Reserve; Cockcomb Basin Jaguar Preserve; Shipstern Wildlife Reserve; and Panti Medicinal Trail (San Ignacio). Some of these, like the Belize Zoo, have trails that are even appropriate for very young children. As this is a hot country, keep the itinerary light and get an early morning start. Children should have plenty of water and wear a sunhat. No other special gear is necessary.

Bicycling. Bicycling is an excellent, adventurous way to tour this small country. A nice family tour would be a trip from the Yucatan border to Guatemala along the Northern and Western highways. These are Belize's two best roads, and while still possessed of their share of potholes and patched pavement, provide workable roads for riding without too much traffic. Bicycles can also be carried on the roofs of buses for covering long distances. Villages are well placed for easy accommodations and provisioning. Terrain is level in the east, becoming hillier as you head towards the border with Guatemala. Beyond the two highways, roads deteriorate, becoming appropriate only for the serious mountain biker. Heat is one factor that has to be taken seriously. If you have bicycle toured before in cooler climates, count on covering about half the distance you normally would in a day. Frequent drink stops will be another feature of tropical bicycling. Children will be particularly susceptible to the heat, so have them wear sunhats and carry plenty of water, at least two water flasks per bicycle. Spare bicycle parts are only available in Belize City, so come prepared.

Canoeing. Some of Belize's inland rivers offer superb opportunities for gentle canoeing in a tropical setting. The principal canoeing area lies in the central west, near San Ignacio along the Belize River. Here, canoe outings and rentals are available in a number of spots along the river, easy to find once you get there. Canoes can also be rented out of Placencia for explorations up the Monkey River.

Boating. This is an exciting way to explore the coastal jungle region along the eastern shore on organized boat trips. Day outings can be arranged while staying on Ambergris or Caulker Caye, a fascinating, fun experience for all ages.

Sailing. Cruising is without a doubt the best way to explore the coast, with its vast system of islands, most of them only accessible by private boat. Belize offers one of the best cruising grounds in the world: protected, rich in marine life, with hundreds of places to explore in a small area. Like the Bahamas or South Pacific island groups, it is an area where you could literally spend months poking about in a sailboat, enjoying quiet anchorages, warm water, small villages, and the relaxed lifestyle. Sailing families will find it irresistible. So far, chartering is undeveloped, so bringing your own boat is a must. Include snorkeling gear for children, plus plenty of cotton clothing for protection from the sun. Things like laundry and bathing are easy in this climate on a boat. Provisions are mostly available at Belize City, with limited variety on inhabited cayes.

Swimming. Out on the cayes, Belize offers wonderful swimming, with warm water and fascinating marine life. This is not for beach lovers, however, as much of the coast is lined with swamps and deep water mostly accessible by long jetties. The coral reefs and marine life here are among the best in the world. A hired boat will be needed to reach most of the good snorkeling areas. Scuba diving is also popular, with some operations offering exciting day outings to complete amateurs. One of the best places to dive is Hol Chan Marine Reserve, off Ambergris Caye.

Nature Studies. Nature studies abound in this country committed to the preservation of its natural areas and wildlife. Each park has something to offer as a learning experience for children, from the animal life at the Belize Zoo to the tropical rainforest of Cockscomb Jaguar Reserve. With a rich bird life and active Audubon society, many areas are good for bird-watching, including Shipstern Preserve and Crooked Tree Wildlife Reserve. A hike on the Panti Medicinal Trail makes an unusual outing as it teaches about the medicinal capabilities of tropical plants.

Following the Western Highway

While famous for its fascinating offshore waters, many scattered cayes, and impressive barrier reef, Belize has an equally lovely interior, including the varied splendors of the northwestern region. Unlike the south, where travel is arduous at best and the rewards questionable for families traveling with children, the west is easily accessible. Heading inland from Belize City, the well-paved Western Highway penetrates the interior, passing through a series of terrains, cultures and communities. Following its narrow ribbon of road will expose you to a whole new facet of this miniature country, one that belies its diminutive size and seems far removed from the Caribbean flavor of the coast. For families traveling on their own, the trip can be an easy one, savoring each scenic area, town, park, preserve, and historic site that lie scattered like gems along the route. It is here that the country's ecotourism movement is mainly afoot, cultivating a new type of tourist development that strives to promote cultural and ecological sensitivity. For adventuring families, opportunities abound for enjoyable outdoor activities, nature studies, and historic explorations.

Heading west from Belize City, the humid mangrove coast is left behind as you pass through grasslands dotted with pines. The Belize Zoo is the first point of interest reached, containing 100 species of indigenous animals. Originally started to provide a home for partially tamed animals used in a film, the park now seeks to promote the preservation of Belizean wildlife. Beyond the zoo is Guanacaste Park, containing a sole survivor of the huge tree for which it is named. Walk the handful of trails through lush tropical vegetation, enjoying the chance to experience the largely impenetrable forest that dominates much of the country's interior. All walking paths are short and easy for even young children.

At Belmopan, the country's capitol, consider a visit to the Archaeological Vault, the nearest thing Belize has to a national museum. The array of Mayan treasures is impressive, potentially fascinating to children who are studying Mayan culture to enhance their trip. Visits are possible most weekdays, but must be arranged in advance (two days before) through the Archaeological Department. A short distance west of Belmopan lies San Ignacio, the main town servicing the west, and Belize's ecotourism center. Located at the convergence of two rivers, it marks a transition point between the lowlands and the forested foothills of central Belize. An ethnically diverse town, it makes an easy, interesting place to linger awhile, with numerous tourist facilities and opportunities to enjoy the outdoors. Accommodations are plentiful, from rustic camping and simple rooms to elegant, high-priced cabanas on scenically situated ranches. For those doing their own housekeeping, San Ignacio has one of the best markets in Belize, with more than the usual limited variety of fresh produce. Outdoor activities, including hiking, backpacking, canoeing and horseback riding, are primarily group-oriented, with many ranches in the outlying area offering package deals. Although beyond the means of most budget-minded families, their services can often be enjoyed on a short-term basis. Inquire about camping, sometimes possible on the grounds of various ranches. Day trips down the Belize River by canoe, into the interior on horseback, or off to the remote Mountain Pine Forest Reserve are always possible.

Just south of San Ignacio lies the Mountain Pine Forest Reserve, one of the country's most spectacular parks. A short distance as the crow flies, the route is rigorous in actuality, with travel within the park only possible on foot, horseback, or by four-wheel drive. Experienced backcountry families can camp at Augustine, site of the park headquarters, and explore

on their own. Others should arrange a guided outing from San Ignacio (most appropriate for families with older children). Natural and cultural splendors within the park include the Hidden Valley Falls (a spectacular chute of water falling one thousand feet), abundant streams, a variety of landscapes, caves, and Belize's largest Mayan ruin, Caracol.

Continuing west, don't miss a visit to Ix Chel Farm and Tropical Research Center, reached by boat or vehicle from San Ignacio. A guided tour through this privately-run botanical wonderland along the Panti Medicinal Trail will teach you much about the fascinating ancient Mayan art of herbal healing. Recognized today as a valuable source of medicine, numerous tropical forest plants and traditional practices are being preserved by its owner, aided by the renowned Mayan bushdoctor Don Eligio Panti, for whom the trail is named.

Lying within the ancient territory of the Mayan culture, the area accessed by the Western Highway contains various impressive ruins.

Given Caracol's present inaccessibility and unexcavated state, Belize's best ruin remains Xunantunich, lying just west of San Ignacio. Left much as it was found, lying enshrouded in jungle and reached via river ferry, the place contains an element of magic and mystery. Walking the deserted paths, peering at ruins through lush vegetation, one finds it almost impossible to visualize the grandeur that once reigned here. Beyond Xunantunich, you may be tempted to continue across the border into Guatemala for a visit to Tikal. The Western Highway offers an excellent backdoor approach to these ruins, among the most impressive of all excavated Mayan ruins. Lying in the northern Peten region of Guatemala, Tikal is most easily visited by vehicle from Belize. Although a rugged 50 km separate the border from the ruins, the route is infinitely preferable to the notorious road through the Peten that accesses the ruins from southern Guatemala. As travel along the Western Highway is easy and comfortable, covering the remaining short distance on dirt should seem more entertaining and adventurous that anything else. Allow a couple of days to fully enjoy the ruins, either staying in nearby Flores, at one of the hotels beside the park, or camping at the park entrance (an acceptable, if rustic, practice).

Travel along the Western Highway is easy by private car or public bus. Adventurous families might consider a bicycle tour the length of the highway, returning by bus at the end. Terrain is manageable, traffic light, and facilities well spaced. Although a visit to the coastal waters of Belize should not be missed, don't overlook the charm of a visit to this lovely country's fascinating western interior.

RESOURCES

TOURIST BUREAUS
Belize Tourist Board, P.O. Box 325, Belize City, Central America   Tel: (501) 2-77213.
Belize Tourist Board, 15 Penn Plaza, 415 Seventh Ave., New York, NY 10001   Tel: (800) 624-0686.

CONSULATES
Belize Honorary Consul, 8354 NW 68th St., Miami, FL 33166   Tel: (305) 628-4077.
Belize Mission to the U.N., 820 2nd. Ave., Ste. 922, New York, NY 10017   Tel: (212) 599-0233.

NATIONAL AIRLINE
Taca International Airlines, Tel U.S.: (800) 535-8780, Quebec (800) 263-4063, Ontario (800) 263-4039, Other Provinces (800) 387-6209.

SUGGESTED READING
Belize Handbook by C. Mallan. Chico, CA: Moon Publications.
Belize, A Natural Destination by R. Mahler & S. Wotkyns. New Mexico: John Muir Publications.
Adventure Guide to Belize by H. Pariser. Edison, NJ: Hunter.
Belize Guide by P. Glassman. Champlain, NY: Passport Press.

SUGGESTED MAPS
Belize, Belize City, John P. King, Scale: 769,000:1.
Belize, Map Link, Scale: 250,000:1.
Belize, International Travel Maps, Scale: 350,000:1.

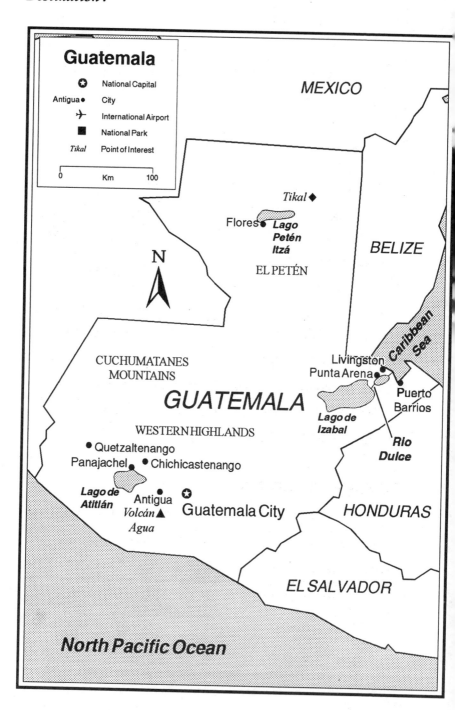

Central America & The Yucatán Peninsula

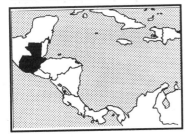

Guatemala

Mountainous and rugged, extending from steamy jungle to cold volcanic peaks, populated with an array of Mayan Indian tribes, Guatemala is perhaps Central America's most fascinating, awe-inspiring country. With a history of political unrest and native oppression that have done much to dissuade visitors, the country is lightly touristed, a situation it hopes to rectify. For those who venture there, it is a surprise, a discovery of a beautiful, friendly place. Travel here should be slow and relaxed as you delve into life in this welcoming land.

GENERAL DESCRIPTION

Location. As Central America's most northern country, Guatemala lies south of Mexico, reaching from the Caribbean Sea to the Pacific Ocean. To the south, the country borders Honduras and El Salvador.

Terrain. Guatemala is made up of two distinct areas, El Peten in the northeast and the mountains to the west, part of the Great Continental Divide that extends the length of the Americas. Comprising a third of the country's land area, but only a fraction of its population, the Peten is still mostly impenetrable jungle. To the south and west, the rest of the country unfolds in a series of jagged mountain ranges, ending at a narrow plain bordering the Pacific Ocean. Divided into two principal mountain areas, the Eastern and Western Highlands (located on either side of Guatemala City), it is the fertile valleys of the west that contain most of the country's population.

Climate. Much of Guatemala's climate is dictated by altitude. Located in the subtropics, the coast enjoys hot weather year round, with steamy conditions in jungle areas. Inland, the climate is temperate, ranging from cool nights to hot days. The rainy season extends from May through September, mostly in the form of daily afternoon showers. Travel is pleasant throughout the year, with peak season being December through April, during the dry months.

Culture & Lifestyle. Originally populated by a variety of Mayan Indian tribes, the country now has two distinct groups, indigenous Indians and Ladinos, descendents of Spanish invaders. While Ladinos hold political power and control the country's wealth, it is the Indians who lure and fascinate visitors. Living in a subsistence, agriculture based economy, they live much as they always have, resisting efforts to integrate them culturally. Native costume is frequently worn, particularly in the Western Highlands where local weaving and embroidery attract a worldwide market. Homes are often simple mud huts, the land tilled by hand, babies worn on backs, and baskets carried on heads. Sixty-five percent of the population is indiginous and still lives in poverty, in marked contrast to the affluent, American-style standard of living enjoyed by city-dwelling Ladinos. It is the indigenous population that sets Guatemala apart from its Central American neighbors, making it culturally fascinating, yet politically disruptive. Fortunately, the past few years have seen an increased interest in improving conditions for the Indians, as well as growing respect for their culture.

PRACTICAL CONCERNS

Political Update & Safety. Guatemala is one of those countries where political reputation and news coverage have done much to deter tourists, particularly Americans. The U.S. State Department issues a warning against travel there, based on incidents that periodically take place between the army and guerilla forces. As long as political insecurity prevails, isolated pockets of the country will remain relatively unsafe. Non-political crime occurs principally in sections of Guatemala City. Nervous visitors should remember, however, that what occurs in Guatemala City is considered as normal in New York City, Chicago, and Los Angeles, and is infinitesimal compared to the total amount of violence that occurs yearly in the United States.

Don't let the highly visible military bother you. Machine-gun toting guards outside places like banks are the norm and hardly indicative that war is about to break out. Under the present civilian government, guerilla activities are down to almost nothing. Avoid Guatemala City as much as possible, skip hiking Pacaya Volcano (a favorite target for petty theft), and take normal travel precautions elsewhere. You'll find this country a delightful place to visit.

Travel Documents. Visitors must have a passport and visa or tourist card. The matter of tourist cards seems somewhat vague. Airlines usually issue them at your departure point. You might, like us, find yourselves faced with a ticket counter that claims they are out of tourist cards, in which case you'll be sent onward with promises that the situation will be rectified upon arrival. The whole business seems fairly casual, with someone finally issuing the required document. Tourist cards are usually good for ninety days. Both your tourist card and passport should be with you at all times while traveling. Police checkpoints can be frequent.

Money. Currency is the quetzal, made up of 100 centavos. Money should be carried as travelers checks. These can be changed at banks or hotels. Exchange rates vary little. Banks are open Monday through Friday, although Fridays are best avoided since they tend to be very busy.

Travel Costs. At the present, Guatemala is a true budget destination and the least expensive country in Central America. Food, lodging, and public transportation are all inexpensive, as is most craft work. You can live very nicely while visiting and still pay little, even in touristed areas. This is one place where finding the cheapest room or meal in town won't be your main objective.

Language. The official language is Spanish, with a variety of secondary Indian dialects spoken at the local level. Some knowledge of Spanish is definitely helpful if you don't want to rely on sign language your whole visit. Practically no one speaks English, including in tourist areas. The charming historic town of Antigua specializes in Spanish language schools, with a total of over twenty where foreigners can spend a few weeks doing intensive study before traveling around the country. This is a wonderful opportunity for the whole family to get a quick smattering of rudimentary Spanish. Like everything else in the country, the cost is low and all classes are done one-on-one with the teacher. Very reasonable accommodations (including all meals) are offered in homes, providing another opportunity to practice the language (see sidebar for more details).

Health. All the usual precautions need to be exercised here. No immunizations are required. Wash, then peel or cook all produce. Drink only bottled, boiled, chlorinated, or filtered water. If using a filter, make sure it's one that removes bacteria and viruses. Have children wash well before eating. Malaria pills are advisable when visiting low coastal areas or the Peten. Be aware that cholera is present in certain areas, as throughout Central America. Avoid eating from open stalls. When buying something homemade from the market such as tortillas, heat before eating. Hepatitis is definitely a risk as well, but can be avoided by careful handling of food. Preparing your own meals is the best prevention against both hepatitis and cholera, or only eating out in obviously clean conditions.

Food. Don't bother to bring a thing beyond your first few days, even when traveling by car. Food is excellent and easy to find, with small food stores in every village. Basic items include bread, powdered whole milk, oatmeal, cold cereals, cheese, beans, tuna, eggs, rice, pasta. For fresh produce, Guatemala is like heaven. Fruits and vegetables are sold in amazing variety and abundance at local markets for rock-bottom prices. This, plus tortillas and beans, forms the basis of the local diet. Tortillas are available fresh at the market. In touristed places like Antigua, Panajachel, and Quetzaltenango, it's possible even to find items like peanut butter, yogurt, granola, and other natural foods. Restaurants are reasonably priced, especially small, local ones.

Clothes. Warm weather clothing is all you'll need unless traveling to really high areas like the Cuchematas Mountains. Nights are cool to cold in the highlands, so bring one sweater or light jacket. Otherwise, you'll spend most of the time in shorts and T-shirts. Along the coast and in the Peten, the weather is steamy and tropical, so dress accordingly. Bring bathing gear if venturing to Lake Atitlán in the Western Highlands or either coast. Count on buying some clothing in Guatemala for the whole family (not to mention all your relatives at home). It's impossible to resist. Material is woven, embroidered, and sewn into bright, striking clothing. Items for sale include dresses, shirts, shorts, pants, belts, skirts, and shawls. Prices are excellent and bargaining the norm.

Laundry & Bathing. Although Guatemala has few laundromats, laundry is never a problem. Women frequently offer their services. Just mention you're interested and someone will show up. Remember when bargaining on a price that laundry is done by hand in cold water. Clothes will be returned looking cleaner than you would have believed possible. The only drawback seems to be the somewhat battered condition they rapidly acquire after all that beating on the rocks, bleaching, or whatever. Hot water showers are the norm in hotels and pensions, sometimes at extra cost.

Baby Needs. Powdered whole milk and baby cereal (sweetened) are available everywhere. Better than the baby cereal, try the ubiquitous instant oatmeal, called "Mosh". Count on using cloth diapers and getting someone to do laundry for you (easy to find and economical). Bring a good child carrier unless you want to do like the natives with a shawl (not nearly as comfortable). Skip the stroller. Roads are either dusty dirt or paved with bumps and potholes. Include sun protection (hat, cotton clothing). Netting for sleeping is only necessary in the Peten.

TRANSPORTATION

Getting There. Guatemala can be reached by air, land, or boat. A number of airlines fly into Guatemala City, mostly from the southern United States and Europe. Guatemala's national airline, Aviateca, offers daily flights out of Miami, a highly recommended route, as prices are among the lowest available and the whole experience offers an early introduction into the local culture. By road, Guatemala can be reached via Mexico on the Pan American Highway. The only reason to subject your children to this epic drive is if you want your own car and have plenty of time on your hands. Overland, the trip takes about 5-7 days from the U.S. border, two weeks if you want to enjoy yourselves. The trip can also be done by bus, or a combination of bus and train, but again, we strongly recommend another option unless you plan to take your time and want to explore Mexico on the way. It's a rare child who doesn't balk at endless travel hours cooped up on a bus (not to mention what it does to adults as well). Coming from Belize, it's possible to take a boat from Punta Gorda to Puerto Barrios/Livingston on the east coast. This option really only makes sense if you're already in southern Belize. Boats leave twice weekly.

Regional Travel. Buses go everywhere in Guatemala with amazing frequency. The trick is not catching one (they stop anywhere along the road), but finding a seat. No matter how many leave a town in rapid succession, they all appear to be filled to bursting point. Standing up or sitting five and six to a seat isn't uncommon, something the local inhabitants accept with equanimity. With the exception of a handful of pullman express buses, all are recycled American school buses, their seats built to

the proportions of the average American school child (also the average adult Mayan). Prices are very low, and luggage is carried on the roof.

Roads. For those who plan to bring their own vehicle or rent a car, roads can be quite a work-out. The Pan American, the main highway running the length of the country, is well-surfaced and smooth, with two lanes and light traffic. Beyond that, roads are in various states deterioration. Whether paved or dirt, the ride is usually a rough one. Getting to Tikal, the renowned Mayan ruins in the Peten, is an infamous test of endurance.

ACCOMMODATIONS

Campgrounds. Guatemala has little in the way of official camping. With a vehicle, you could find somewhere to camp in most places, and still get a degree of privacy. When camping on private land, always ask first. Camping is also possible at a number of popular tourist spots, among them Antigua, Tikal, and Lake Atitlán. Don't expect designated sites and picnic tables. Privacy and scenic surroundings are in short order, but the price is definitely right. Because of the the number of other attractive, affordable options, we would recommend leaving the camping gear at home unless you are traveling with your own vehicle.

Rooms & Rentals. Guatemala is an easy place to find a nice, affordable room to spend the night. Prices range from rock-bottom to extravagant, with a reasonable amount of money getting you practically luxury conditions. Check out the premises first before committing yourself. This is one instance where renting and staying in one place is a wonderful way to experience the country. Rentals are easy to find and always less expensive overall. Houses, cottages, and rooms are all available. Prices are best off-season, or any time other than Christmas and Easter, when urban Guatemalans take their vacation.

POINTS OF INTEREST

Natural. There are a number of areas of natural interest, some of them easily accessible, others remote and largely untouristed. So far, little has been done in the way of parks and preserves, although much of the country still retains its wild, natural appearance.

• *Tikal National Park.* The country's only national park, this is the site of the famous Mayan ruins of Tikal. An area of dense jungle and rainforest, the abundant wildlife includes a variety of tropical birds, mammals and fish.

• *Western Highlands.* Guatemala's highlands extend the length of the country and contain a number of volcanos, two of them active (Fuego and Pacaya). From the remote, impenetrable Cuchumatanes in the north to the fertile valleys of the south, the highlands are the country's most beautiful area.

• *Lake Atitlán.* Lake Atitlán is unquestionably one of Central America's most beautiful spots, if not one of the loveliest lakes in the world. Ringed with mountains and edged with tiny Indian settlements, it makes a fascinating destination, one you definitely should not miss.

• *Monterrico Reserve.* A coastal area of mangrove swamps along the Pacific, this reserve has retained the beauty and diverse birdlife that once spread over the bulk of this region. An excellent spot for birdwatching or catching a glimpse of the protected sea turtle.

Cultural. Guatemala's greatest source of cultural interest is its indigenous population. Centered in the Western Highlands, the Indian culture is very much intact today, with people retaining their native ways, wearing traditional dress, and living much as they always have. Women sit in the shade weaving with backstrap looms. Men till the steep corn fields by hand. Fishing is done by dugout canoe. Take a walk through the countryside or visit a village on market day to experience the pace of life and see the details of daily living. The Indian culture will fascinate the whole family as you expose yourselves to these quiet, friendly people.

Historic. With its rich heritage as part of the once-great Mayan empire and early Spanish settlement, the country has a number of historic spots.

• *Mayan.* Mayan ruins dot the landscape, some of them crumbling and overgrown, others preserved and well worth a visit. Most famous is Tikal, with over 3,000 buildings set in the rain forest of Peten. A family could easily spend a week here, camped in the park or staying at one of the local hotels in nearby Flores. If driving or traveling by bus, remember that getting there is an infamous test of endurance. Inexpensive flights are available from Guatemala City to Flores, definitely the least painful option. Other interesting ruins in the Peten include Seibal, and Uaxactún. Western Guatemala features ruins at Zaculeu (rather poorly reconstructed), Iximché (near Antigua), and various sites around Santa Lucia Cotzumalguapa on the coast.

• *Antigua.* Once the capital of Guatemala, this is the country's most historic town. Scenically located in a fertile valley at the base of three towering volcanos, the town is lovely and peaceful, with cobblestone streets, crumbling ruins (the result of repeated earthquakes), and a prevailing Old World flavor.

• *Museums.* There are a number of museums, principally located in main cities like Guatemala, Antigua and Quetzaltenango. Perhaps more interesting is visiting the ancient Mayan ruins and exploring the highland Indian culture.

OUTDOOR ACTIVITIES

Backcountry Camping. There are no designated areas for this. Very experienced, adventurous families could do some cross-country travel on dirt paths and roads with camping gear, finding places to spend the night along the way. Water would be the main difficulty during the dry season. Villages always have a source, although carrying some means of water purification is a must.

Hiking. Hiking in Guatemala is mostly a matter of exploring the countryside on foot: down dirt roads, along footpaths, through cultivated fields, up volcanos. Hiking is hot, so what might look like an easy day's trek can turn into a major test of endurance unless you keep distances modest. Trails offer little shade in most cases. Altitude can also be a factor, particularly when climbing volcanos. The rewards of the unique exposure that hiking affords you, however, well outweighs the occasional discomforts. Choose modest distances, take plenty of water and food, wear sunhats, and enjoy this intimate view of Guatemala's countryside and culture. Good areas to hike include the Lake Atitlán district, around Antigua, and the Cuchumatanes (best for experienced families, due to its remote location).

Bicycling. Although touring would definitely be a strenuous affair (mountainous terrain coupled with abysmal road surfaces), daily outings are a fun way to explore an area. Bicycles can be carried on the roofs of buses for a small fee. If bringing your own, make sure your bikes have a good set of gears (15-18 speeds) and heavy-duty tires that can cope with rough surfaces and dirt. This is the kind of country where it's even nice to have bicycles just for daily errands like runs to the market or visiting friends. Bicycling is a popular mode of travel and shops can be found in all large towns.

Boating. Boating is possible on the Rio Dulce, a lovely, tropical river area on the east coast. Rentals are available out of Livingston, a small Caribbean community, or El Relleno, a resort. The 30 km of navigable river pass through an area of rainforest, including a gorge, a lake, and a wildlife preserve. Camping is possible along the route, although all provisions will have to be brought with you.

Swimming. Guatemala isn't really a country of beaches, despite borders along two oceans. Some of the best swimming is on Lake Atitlán, where beaches dot much of this cool, clear, very deep lake set in the center of the country. The Pacific coast offers the best ocean swimming, although the black sand can get too hot to touch just when you want to be out enjoying the sun.

Spanish School in Antigua

One of the best ways to introduce your family to travel in Guatemala, or anywhere in Latin America, is spending a week or two attending a Spanish school in Antigua. Once the country's capital, until a series of earthquakes forced a relocation to Guatemala City, Antigua remains a lovely, historic town, renowned for its many small Spanish schools. Located in a fertile valley at the base of three volcanos (one of them active), the town is quiet and sedate, providing a gentle introduction to the local culture, and a lovely setting for language studies.

With a total of about 25 schools, finding one to suit you is never a problem. They're easily found around town, their small signs mounted atop simple doors in the walls that line the streets. Ask at the centrally located tourist bureau for suggestions if you want, or talk to students milling about the central square in the sun. All the schools offer accommodations in private homes at unbeatable prices. This includes room and full board (three meals a day, except Sunday). Even if you're the type that shies away from this kind of thing, preferring your own privacy, it's worth the experience. Antiguans who open their homes to students are educated, interesting people, families who enjoy cross-cultural interaction and whose friendship will greatly increase your enjoyment. Facilities in homes are very comfortable, and privacy respected. You'll also get to sample some excellent local food and triple your opportunities to learn and practice the language as you find yourself conversing at mealtime. Mothers will especially enjoy the break from cooking, allowing more time to study and to explore the area. When choosing a school, it's worth noting that schools located in quiet parts of town will provide quiet accommodations, and vise versa. Schools and rooms around the marketplace are the noisiest.

Classes are all private, with one student per teacher, ensuring quick results. Day sessions can run anywhere from two to six hours, five days a week. Like the accommodations, weekly rates for classes are excellent and very budget oriented. A family with two children might consider splitting a morning session, with each member receiving two hours of instruction a day. This is just about right for children, especially as they will need to do some studying later in the day to prepare for the next lesson. We found it worked well this way, with each child doing two hours of Spanish and two hours of regular school work before lunch. Afternoons were free for outings and explorations, with a final collapse at a cafe for drinks and an hour of Spanish study. Our children enjoyed the whole thing immensely. Teachers enjoy working with children and do a nice job of keeping them interested and inspired. The atmosphere is also conducive to study for children, an idyllic school situation. Not only do they have the full attention of the teacher (no room for boredom here), but classes often take place outside around an open courtyard. The whole experience is wildly different from a conventional classroom, one they won't soon forget.

As an added bonus, Antigua offers much more than just a language and homestay experience. The town itself is fascinating, with magnificent, crumbling ruins, museums, cobblestone streets, a lovely central square, fascinating markets, natives in traditional Indian clothing, cafes, and a mixture of cultures, from cosmopolitan to indigenous. With bicycles (bring your own or rent for the day), you can explore the surrounding countryside, discovering interesting villages and enjoying the scenery. Take the dirt road to San Antonio Aguas Calientes, with its open market, beautiful handcrafts, and terraced countryside. Three volcanos tower above Antigua , all of them possible to hike. Agua, the nearest, is the easiest for families to undertake. Catch an early morning bus to Santa Maria de Jesus and hike the spectacular, strenuous route from there. Bring plenty of water. With experienced children (age ten and over), the trip should take about four and a half hours to the summit. With younger ones, don't bother trying to get to the top. Lower regions of the trail are easier and shadier, with equally impressive views. For an easy afternoon hike, take the paved trail up Cerro de la Cruz, marked by a cross at the top. The view across Antigua to Volcan Agua is magnificent.

RESOURCE SECTION

TOURIST BUREAUS
Guatemala Tourist Commision, 7a Avenida 1-17, Centro Civico, Zona 4, Guatemala City, Guatemala   Tel: 311333.

CONSULATES
Guatemala Consulate, 50 Park Ave., New York, NY 10016   Tel: 212-686-3837.
Consulates are also located in Miami, Los Angeles, New Orleans, Chicago, and other major North American cities.

NATIONAL AIRLINE
Aviateca, P.O. Box 20027, New Orleans, LA 70141.

SUGGESTED READING
Guatemala Guide by Paul Glassman. Champlain, NY: Passport Press.
Real Guide: Guatemala & Belize by M. Whatmore. New York: Prentice Hall.

SUGGESTED MAPS
Guatemala, John P. King, Scale: 1,800, 000:1
Guatemala, Guatemala City, Latin American Publishers, Scale: 1,000,000:1
The tourist bureau sends out a serviceable map with their literature package.

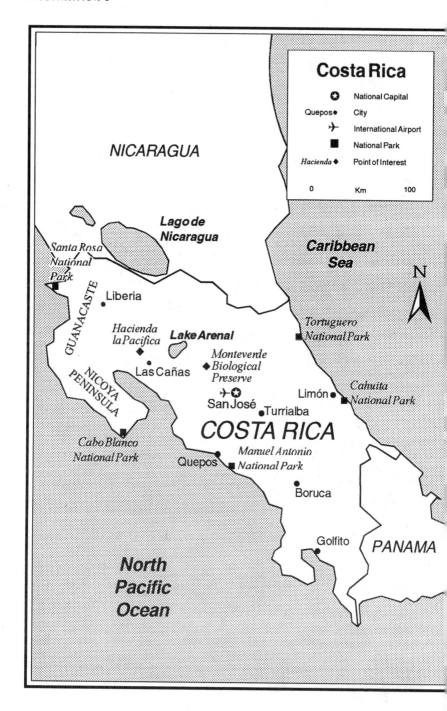

Central America &
The Yucatán Peninsula

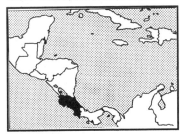

Costa Rica

Tiny and diverse, Costa Rica lies at the heart of Central America, its small size belying its far-reaching influence. Long renowned for its disarmament policies, a marked contrast to the political instabilities of neighboring Latin American countries, Costa Rica has recently emerged as a leader in the growing commitment to environmental protection. With numerous parks and preserves, a peaceful, friendly people, and some of the best beaches in the world, families both new and old to adventure travel can feel comfortable visiting here. To experience the best of Costa Rica, divide your time between coastal relaxation and exploration of the country's vast ecological wonders.

GENERAL DESCRIPTION

Location. Located in the south of the Central American isthmus, Costa Rica reaches from the Caribbean Sea to the Pacific Ocean. To the north lies Nicaragua, to the south Panama.

Terrain. Costa Rica enjoys a varied terrain. The central portion is dominated by a volcanic mountain chain, its fertile valleys the home of over half the country's inhabitants. Descending towards either coast, mountains and valleys give way to hot, tropical lowlands, with mangroves and coral reefs along the Caribbean and grassy savannah in the west. The south remains mostly uninhabited, a land of arid, rugged mountains and dense coastal swamps.

Climate. Lying in the tropics, the country's climate is hot year-round. Altitude differences between the coastal lowlands and the interior mountains cause the air to be slightly cooler inland, but, for the most part, the entire country experiences very warm weather throughout the year, with little seasonal temperature change. The rainy season, called winter, extends from May-November in the form of torrential afternoon showers. The best time to travel is the dry season, or summer, although it's wise to avoid peak vacation time for Costa Ricans, when San José residents descend on the beaches. This includes the month of December (their summer vacation) and Easter Week (Costa Rica's biggest holiday).

Culture & Lifestyle. Costa Rica's largely peaceful history has done much to shape the culture and lifestyle of its people. Only sparsely settled by native Indians at the time of Spanish colonization, the country was passed over in favor of more profitable territories. With little indigenous population to offer resistance, eventual European settlement met with little opposition. Led by a stable democracy for over 100 years, the country has put its efforts into economic development, establishing a non-military position and abolishing its army. Today, Costa Rica is a country straddling two worlds, that of its Third World neighbors, and the developed nations it seeks to join. Expensive four-wheel drive vehicles share the countryside with ox carts and horseback riders. While the affluent lifestyle enjoyed by San José "Ticos" is patterned after the U.S., country "camposinos" continue to live modestly. Overall, Costa Rica is rapidly bridging the gap that separates it from the developed world. Education is widespread and its health care is among the best in the world. People live simply, yet a major step above poverty. Costa Ricans are immensely proud of their country's accomplishments: its pacifist policies, political stability, economic growth, soaring tourism, and environmental commitment. They are happy to share this pride with visitors to this small, peaceful country.

PRACTICAL CONCERNS

Political Background & Safety. Since abolishing its army in 1948, Costa Rica has enjoyed years of peaceful democracy. The stable core at the heart of Central America, the country has come to represent a powerful symbol of Latin American stability, winning its leader the Nobel Peace Prize. Consequently, the country is completely safe for travel, with virtually no violent crime. Theft is the only concern for visitors, and certain areas definitely experience this in epic proportions. Most notable is San José, followed by certain beach areas. The importance of watching your possessions at the beach cannot be stressed enough. Extra precautions should be taken on Christmas and Easter vacations, when, as the locals put it, all the thieves of San José come to the beaches, following in the wake of city holiday seekers.

Travel Documents. Passports are the only requirement for citizens of North American, Commonwealth, EC, and most Latin countries. Visits up to ninety days are permitted without visas.

Money. Currency is the colon, comprising 100 centimos. Tourists should carry money in travelers checks, which can easily be exchanged at all banks. Be prepared to wait a while. The exchange process is a laborious exercise in officialdom. Credit cards are also widely accepted. Banks have normal weekday hours and are in all main towns. Exchanging money with black marketeers at the airport (typically cab drivers) is standard procedure.

Travel Costs. Travel costs in Costa Rica are higher than in many Latin American countries. With its higher standard of living and well-developed tourism industry, the country can't really be considered a budget destination, although there are some ways to keep costs down. Accommodations and the probable need of a rental car for some of your visit will be your highest costs. Most rooms cost about what you would pay for a night in an American motel. Staying a week or longer should give you a better rate. Figure on having to rent a car while visiting the national parks and preserves, most of which are located somewhat off the beaten path. Camping in the parks will help cut costs. Food bought in local shops and markets is inexpensive, as is dining out at small, local restaurants. Public transportation on buses is also fairly low cost.

Language. Spanish is the official language. The large number of expatriate North American and Europeans who have settled here, coupled with the abundant tourism, have helped English to become widely used as a second language. Some knowledge of Spanish, however, is always useful and welcomed in the countryside.

Health. Costa Rica has few health concerns. Food and water are almost always safe, although you might experience some stomach upsets at the beginning of your trip as your system adjusts. Fresh produce should be carefully washed to remove pesticides. With the recent arrival of a few cases of cholera in the country, people are being urged to boil unchlorinated water, and peel or cook all produce. Malaria pills should be taken if visiting the Caribbean coast. Use chloroquine, beginning one week before and continuing two weeks after your visit. Chloroquine is reputedly safe for pregnant women and children.

Food. Like so much about Costa Rica, food runs the gamut from tradi-tional fare to modern fast food, from rice and beans to hamburgers and french fries. Just about everything you might want can be found in main towns, including natural foods like peanut butter, granola, whole wheat bread, and fruit juice. Tortillas are sold packaged and make a good bread substitute. Fresh produce is excellent and sold at markets in large towns or produce shops in smaller villages. Variety is good, including a broad range of tropical fruits. Food shops are easy to find, with at least two or three, even in the smaller towns. For an inexpensive meal out, find a small restaurant frequented by locals. Gallos (tortilla style sandwiches) and gallo pinto (the national rice and bean dish) are both excellent, affordable, and filling.

Clothes. Only lightweight clothing is needed throughout the country, with the exception of something warmer for a visit to the cloud forest and higher elevations. Bring lightweight rain gear during the rainy season. During the dry season, temperatures get very hot, particularly during March and April. Coastal areas can be steamy at this time. Include plenty of bathing gear, light cotton clothing, and a sunhat for everyone. This is serious tropical weather, where even the ocean feels hot. Clothes can be bought in Costa Rica, but aren't terribly alluring.

Laundry & Bathing. Most people do their own laundry or hire some-one. Finding a woman to do your washing is easy and economical. Hotels often offer a service, but this tends to be pricey. It's much better to ask around town and find the local home service. Negotiate a price first and expect it to take two days for your laundry to be done. Clothes will come back impeccably clean. Good bathing facilities are always provided at any type of hotel. Water is usually hot, although you'll probably find yourself using the cold just to cool off. This is one climate where you won't have any trouble convincing your children that a cool shower is more fun than a warm one.

Baby Needs. Costa Rica is an easy place to travel with a baby. All baby foods are available (many sweetened). Try substituting instant oatmeal, mashed fruit, or whatever regular foods your child likes. Bring plenty of sun protection (hat, sunscreen, cotton clothing). Leave the stroller at home unless you don't mind struggling over dirt and gravel roads. Include a child carrier instead for hikes around the countryside or through the parks. There are no bugs or health hazards to worry about, other than malaria on the east coast. Chloroquine is reputedly safe for babies. Give your baby plenty of fluids to avoid dehydration from tropical heat.

TRANSPORTATION

Getting There. Flying is the easiest way to visit Costa Rica. The national airline LACSA has daily flights from the United States, as does the Guatemalan airlines Aviateca and other international airlines. Most flights from Europe connect with the U.S., except KLM and Iberia. By bus or car, the trip is possible from the United States or other Central American countries on the Pan American Highway, although this is only for the diehard adventuring family with plenty of time on their hands.

Regional Transport. Costa Rica has an excellent public bus service, serving nearly every corner of the country. Buses are frequent and rarely crowded, other than early morning and late afternoon "rush hour". Most are comfortable, although a few retain that Third World school bus aura that makes bus riding in some countries such an intensely cultural experience. Luggage is usually carried underneath rather than on the roof. Bus stops are clearly indicated along the road with roofed benches. Destinations are affixed to the front of buses. Not all buses stop everywhere and available seating can be limited en route. For long distance travel, it's best to make inqüiries and try to board buses at their point of origin. We once went 50 km in the wrong direction to get the bus to San José we needed. Children over the age of two pay full fare on all buses.

Roads. Roads come in all guises, from dual highways around San José to some memorable gravel teeth shakers. The emphasis throughout the country is still on dirt roads. The main highway, the Pan American, is a paved two-lane affair running the length of the country, with little traffic. Count on spending most of your time on dirt roads, some of which can be rigorous, to put it mildly, especially on the Nicoya Peninsula. Traffic is very light outside the immediate San José area, although the state of the roads can make distances seem deceptive.

ACCOMMODATIONS

Campgrounds. The camping situation in Costa Rica is something of a mixed bag. Technically, it's possible to camp your way around the country, either in designated areas or by finding a spot yourselves. Facilities, however, are definitely on the unorthodox side. Little yet exists on the order of formal campgrounds. Instead, you're much more likely to stop at a campground sign and find yourselves inches from an outdoor cafe or camped on a public beach. Privacy is in short supply and theft a valid concern, particularly on the beach. On the other hand, a camping trip can expose you to the culture in a way more conventional accommodations rarely do, as you find yourselves negotiating for a night in someone's backyard or tenting beside their restaurant. Camping is also permitted in a number of national parks and reserves, an excellent way to visit, as many are located some distance from the nearest town and invariably down a formidable gravel road. A car, however, would be necessary for bringing in enough supplies. Water, and usually picnic tables, are provided, and the surroundings peaceful and private. If for no other reason, bring camping gear just to enjoy a week or two of exploring Costa Rica's parks, the highlight of any trip to this country.

Pensions & Hotels. Finding a pension or hotel is rarely a problem. Expect to pay more than in most developing countries. Costa Rica has a well-developed tourism industry, something reflected by the cost of its accommodations in all tourist areas. With children, you'll often find it's worth paying a little extra money for that special place that will make the difference between just staying somewhere and staying somewhere you really enjoy. Don't be afraid to try some negotiating to reduce the price. Staying a week will always help. Another cost cutting technique is seeing if you can cook your own meals with a camp stove. We had great success with this, allowing us to stay in some very nice places without the added cost of dining out. Make sure there's a working fan in the room before paying!

POINTS OF INTEREST

Natural. With 27% of its land set aside in parks (the greatest percentage of any country in the world), Costa Rica is making an effort to preserve areas of natural beauty, interest, and importance. One park might be the breeding ground for giant sea turtles, another a piece of the magical cloud forest, a third the site of an active volcano. Visiting some of these should be a major focus of any trip to Costa Rica. Count on needing a car, as many are quite inaccessible by public transportation. The following are a few of the many areas worth seeing.

• *Santa Rosa National Park.* A lovely park in the northwest that protects the remaining tropical dry forest that once covered Guanacaste. Includes some lovely coastal beach area, accessible only on foot. Efforts for forest regeneration are underway. Varied animal life, including monkeys and peccaries.

• *Cabo Blanco National Park.* A coastal park at the tip of the Nicoya Peninsula. Located within easy reach of Montezuma, an attractive beach area. Excellent hiking, beaches, monkeys, plant and animal life. No camping.

• *Cahuita National Park.* Caribbean coastal area south of Limon. Beautiful, unspoiled surroundings with little tourism. Includes Costa Rica's only coral reef. Camping, swimming, snorkeling, hiking. A quiet, undeveloped part of the country.

• *Monteverde Biological Reserve.* The most famous park in Costa Rica. Located next to a Quaker community in a remote part of the mountainous interior. Dense tropical cloud forest, with diverse bird, plant,and insect life. Excellent hiking and birdwatching. Not to be missed.

• *Tortuguero National Park.* Site of the largest nesting area of the green sea turtle in the Caribbean, this park is a vast waterway through luxuriant vegetation. Travel is all by boat. To really explore and experience the park, rent a dugout canoe.

• *Manuel Antonio National Park.* Considered one of Costa Rica's most beautiful stretches of coast, Manuel Antonio has felt the full effects of overtourism. Located just beyond the town of Quepos (which is at the end of a truly ghastly stretch of gravel road), the park is best enjoyed by those who don't mind company. Includes some lovely beaches and swimming.

Cultural. Culturally, much of Costa Rica feels like a modern country, its lifestyle almost a scaled-down version of the United States. If your children are the kind that crave hamburgers and french fries, or insist on wearing the latest in popular clothing, they'll feel right at home. One doesn't go to Costa Rica to experience an alien culture or marvel at the lifestyle differences. Instead, a trip here should make even the most timid adventurer feel at home. Fortunately, what the country perhaps lacks in cultural interest it more than makes up for with its environmental focus. Two contrasting areas worth noting are the Caribbean coast and the interior "camposino" regions. The people here take a gentle approach to life that can't help but seduce you. Cultural differences are pronounced and each is fascinating in its own way. The following offer insights into unusual pockets of culture.

• *Monteverde Quaker Community.* A unique village founded by Alabama Quakers in the 1950's. Bordered by the famous Biological Reserve of the same name, the community remains an unusual blend of two cultures, commited to a basic communal principal. Points of interest include the surrounding countryside, village layout, dairy industry, communal cheese factory, and handicrafts.

• *Boruca.* A town in Costa Rica's one Indian reservation, a visit here offers a view of the country's tiny pocket of indigenous people. Similar to Mayans throughout Central America, the people live very much as they always have. Interesting craft work includes beautiful weaving and carving.

Historic. Costa Rica has a smattering of areas of historic interest, including the following:

• *Guayabo National Monument.* Located on the slopes of a volcano in Turrialba, this is the most impressive archaeological site in the country, the remains of a large city that existed 3000 years ago.

• *Casona, Hacienda Santa Rosa.* The site of several military defeats of invading forces. Now a museum in Santa Rosa National Park with historical and environmental exhibits, plus a natural history hiking trail.

OUTDOOR ACTIVITIES

Backcountry camping. This is possible in a handful of parks and preserves. Among the best opportunities are Santa Rosa National Park, where camping is permitted at a lovely, isolated ocean campsite, and the cloud forest of Monteverde (at shelters). Backcountry camping in Costa Rica is definitely best for families with experience and older children capable of carrying a large load.

Hiking. There are plenty of opportunities for hiking, mainly in the parks. The biggest issue is not the availability of places to hike or trail conditions, but the heat, particularly during the dry season. Hiking in the topics is hot and should be undertaken carefully and modestly. Children will need lots of water, even on short hikes. The following are a few of the many exciting places to explore on foot.

• *Monteverde.* Wonderful, magical hikes through the cloud forest. There's no problem with the heat here, as temperatures are always cool.

• *Cahuita National Park.* Caribbean coastal hiking through easy, level terrain.

• *Cabo Blanco Nature Preserve.* Easy day hikes through open woods, with plenty of monkeys to keep children excited.

Bicycling. Costa Rica is definitely not a bicycler's paradise. On the other hand, we biked a portion of it, an experience that led to a number of memorable adventures. This is not for the uninitiated. As an introduction to bicycle touring, it would be a nightmare, but for experienced families it can be a real adventure. Heat and road conditions are the two main issues. Costa Rica is hot, which means bicycling is going to be very hot. Carry plenty of water bottles and expect to stop at every cafe along the route for cold drinks (something the children will love). Between the heat and rugged road conditions in many areas, covering 20 km with children can be a major day's accomplishment.

If bicycling is your passion and real adventure is something you crave, pick a few small areas to explore in depth. Both provisions and accommodations are always easy to find. Possible routes include around Lake Arenal, a small portion of the Nicoya Peninsula, and a tour of the east coast. Bicycles are difficult to carry on buses (no roof racks, except on some local routes). Try hitching a ride in pick-ups instead for covering long distances. Traffic is light and considerate, even on highways.

Whitewater rafting. Although not an outdoor activity we normally include, some mention of Costa Rica's immense potential for this sport is necessary. With the largest whitewater rafting company in Latin America (Rios Tropicales), the country offers a variety of opportunities for exploring its many scenic rivers. Children ten and older are usually eligible. A day outing will expose you to an exciting view of some of the country's loveliest natural areas. Whitewater rafting outfitters often offer sea kayaking opportunites along the coast as well.

Canal Travel. Consider doing some canal exploration along the country's east coast, an area still accessed only by water. Travel is by ferry or private boat along the public waterways that service the communities north of Limon. Unlike whitewater rafting, boating here is not a sport or tourist attraction, but the main source of transportation, making this type of travel an unusual, cultural experience. Dugout canoes can be rented from local inhabitants for exploring the many waterways of Tortuga National Park.

Swimming. The swimming is excellent throughout Costa Rica's coastal regions, with many tourists making this the focal point of their visit. Beaches are plentiful and lovely, with gorgeous sand, palm trees, and warm water. In fact, the water is so warm it's almost impossible to get children out of it. Some of the best beaches are on the Nicoya Peninsula, the west coast of Guanacaste, and the Caribbean coast. Some are near deserted, others surrounded by tourist facilities. Chances are the harder it is to get there, the less developed the area. Stay away from beach areas during the week of Christmas and Easter, the traditional holiday seasons when all of San José goes to the beach. Swimming can be dangerous on the Pacific coast due to the strong currents, so check with the locals before plunging in. There's plenty of surf if you want it (body-surfing is excellent) as well as places appropriate for little children.

Nature Studies. With 27% of the land set aside in parks and preserves and 5% of the world's biodiversity, Costa Rica offers numerous opportunities for nature studies. Monteverde has one excellent self-guided nature trail through the cloud forest that children will enjoy and learn from. National parks and preserves usually include some type of information about the nature and wildlife found within the park, including informative signs, leaflets, and guided walks. The country is particularly rich in bird, insect and plant life, with more bird species than on the entire North American continent.

Hacienda La Pacifica

Lying in the plains of Guanacaste, against a magnificent backdrop of mountains, the Hacienda La Pacifica represents a true ecological destination. In a country renowned for its environmental commitment, a reputation that has spilled over into the tourist industry, it's inevitable that some exploitations of the concept have taken take place. At one so-called "eco-adventure" tourist lodge we visited, the only "adventuring" being done was shooting pool and imbibing liquor. Conversely, places like Monteverde Biological Reserve enjoy a well deserved worldwide reputation. La Pacifica is similarly authentic, committed to the preservation of native species and the development of environmentally sound agricultural practices.

Hidden in the countryside, unknown and bypassed by many, the Hacienda is combination ranch, dairy farm, research center, and low-impact resort. Here a family can easily experience Costa Rica's outdoors and many of its natural wonders, while gaining a sense of how a developing country confronts the dual needs of economic development and environmental commitment. While many national parks still remain difficult to reach and minimally serviced, La Pacifica offers the ideal combination of outdoor activities, ecological focus, and comfortable accommodations. Everything about the place is wonderful. There's a large dairy herd, irrigated fields, experimental agriculture, and research center. Various nature studies are conducted by outside sources each year, using the Hacienda as their base. Even the resort makes an effort to maintain the environmental focus. Guests find their rooms stocked with natural soaps and shampoos.

Located two hours north of San José, beside the Interamerican Highway, La Pacifica is easy to reach on the Liberia bus. Despite its proximity to the so-called highway, the atmosphere is quiet and rural, the highway little more than a two-lane road with light traffic. Set in the semi-arid region of inland Guanacaste, La Pacifica appears like an oasis of greenery, its lush fields and woods in marked contrast to the surrounding, wind-swept plains. Once the summer retreat of a Costa Rican president and named for his wife, the Hacienda became the property of a Swiss immigrant family. Environmentally committed, they gave the hacienda its present focus, although the property is now owned by a corporation.

There's a bit of everything here for the adventuring family: the lovely, small resort set beside a river and sheep farm (children will love "helping" on the farm), with bungalows, a swimming pool, and abundant trees and flowers; hiking or bicycle riding (rentals available) along dirt roads through the Hacienda's 4,000 acres; nature or bird-watching walks (guided or otherwise) along riverside trails through lush, tropical growth frequented by birds and howler monkeys; guided raft trips on the Rincon River; day bike rides into the surrounding countryside (transportation uphill is provided—all you have to do is bike back downhill to the Hacienda). There's a lovely, quiet restaurant, an informed staff, daily maid service, and a library with English-language books (including some for children). With its large dairy herd, morning milkings provide a fun outing for children. Accommodations are in small bungalows with porches, set under shady trees. Weekly rates are lowest, as is off-season travel.

Although prices here are slightly higher than many budget destinations, it's worth every penny. The whole place is bliss for families with a love of the outdoors. If traveling on a shoestring budget, consider doing your own meals at your bungalow with a camp stove. Nearby Cañas has an excellent market with very affordable food. Another option is to camp for free beside the Rincon Restaurant, adjacent to and affiliated with La Pacifica. We did a combination of both, camping first for a few days, then basking in the luxury of a bungalow for a week.

RESOURCE SECTION

TOURIST BUREAUS
Instituto Costarricense de Turismo, Box 777-1000, San José, Costa Rica   Tel: 23-17-13.
Costa Rica National Tourist Bureau, 1101 Brickell Ave., BIV Tower, Ste. 801, Miami, FL 33131   Tel: (800) 327-7033.

CONSULATES & EMBASSIES
Costa Rica Consulate, 80 Wall St., Ste. 1117, New York, NY 10005.
Consulates are located in Chicago, Miami, Los Angeles, San Francisco, and other major North American cities.
Embassy of the Republic of Costa Rica, 1825 Connecticut Ave. NW, Washington, DC 20009   Tel: (202) 234-2945.

NATIONAL AIRLINES
LACSA Airlines, 1600 NW Lejeune Rd., Ste. 200, Miami, FL 33126   Tel: (800) 225-2272.

SUGGESTED READING
New Key to Costa Rica by B. Blake & A. Becher. Costa Rica: Publications in English.
Costa Rica Guide by Paul Glassman. Champlain, NY: Passport Press.
Costa Rica: A Travel Survival Kit by R. Rachowiecki. Berkeley: Lonely Planet Publications.
Costa Rica: A Natural Destination by R. Sheck. New Mexico: John Muir Publications.

SUGGESTED MAPS
Costa Rica National Parks, Scale: 500,000:1.
Costa Rica, International Travel Maps, Scale: 500,000:1.
Costa Rica, John P. King, Scale:1,100,000:1.

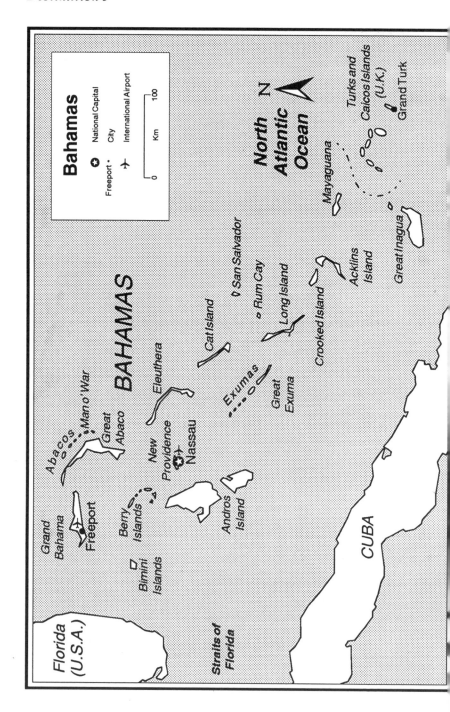

The Bahamas

Made up of over 700 islands, like the scattered pearls of a necklace, the Bahamas offers a wealth of tropical adventure at America's doorstep. White sand beaches, coconut palms, warm waters, coral reefs, and sleepy villages typify this offshore paradise. Outside of Nassau and a handful of tourist resorts, the islands remain untouched by the pressures of tourism, the ideal destination for families escaping winter's cold. Unquestionably one of the world's prime cruising grounds, there's also plenty of scope for hiking, bicycling, swimming, and underwater explorations.

GENERAL DESCRIPTION

Location. Lying off the southeast coast of the United States, the Bahamas is separated from its neighbor by the Gulf Stream, a veritable river in the sea that warms the landmass around it and strikes trepidation in the heart of sailors who must cross it. Made up of islands strung together like stepping stones to the tropics, the country extends 970 km (600 miles) south, from central Florida to the Greater Antilles.

Terrain. Natural and unspoiled throughout the islands, the Bahamas is reminiscent of what coastal Florida must have once been. Tropical growth is abundant, with tall pines gracing the shore, and exotic flowers adorning village streets. Approaching by boat, it is the graceful coconut palms that one first sees, long before catching a glimpse of these low islands. Lying in shallow water, the islands are actually part of two giant offshore shoals, vestiges of land rising just above the level of the ocean. Lacking in the taller grandeur of their Caribbean neighbors, the Bahamian islands have a charm of their own, one that suits the gentle, friendly, unexploited pace of this country. Surrounded by coral reefs teeming with sea life, the Bahamas' underwater world is one of the richest on Earth.

Climate. Located in the subtropics,the country experiences minor seasonal changes. Similar to Florida, the islands have their own version of winter, dictated by northers that sweep through from December to April. Never really cold, it is more a question of wind. With such a broad latitudinal range, winter weather can be noticeably cooler in the northern Abacos, for instance, than the Exumas. From April-November, all the islands enjoy hot temperatures. Summer is typified by light winds and afternoon thunderstorms. The best time to visit is spring (March-May).

Culture & Lifestyle. Originally populated by peaceful Lucayan Indians, the Bahamas is now inhabited by a mixture of ethnic groups, all of which play a part in today's culture. The Abacos and Spanish Wells are principally populated by white Anglos, descendents of Loyalists who fled to the islands following the American Revolution. Today, the architecture of island homes and villages here reflects its New England origins. The remainder of the islands are populated mainly by Blacks, descended from slaves of island cotton plantations as well as unruly slaves shipped to the Bahamas from Bermuda. Years of British colonial rule have also left their mark, as have the early years of Loyalist settlement and the brief plantation era. Outside Nassau, the one heavily populated and touristed island, the lifestyle is simple and relaxed, in a manner typical of Caribbean cultures. Towns are small, roads quiet. Water is a constant presence, providing both a livelihood for island people and a means of transportation. Each island group has its own distinctive flavor, from the industrious Abacos to the laid-back Exumas.

PRACTICAL CONCERNS

Political Update & Safety. Once a British colony, the Bahamas has adjusted well to self-rule since gaining independence in 1973. Today it is one of the wealthiest countries in the Caribbean. There are no safety concerns for visitors to the islands. The Bahamas does have a history of involvement with drug trafficking from South America, which has caused nervousness among some sailors. Recently the government has made a push to eradicate this trend. Other than avoiding anchoring in isolated spots along the coast of Andros Island, there's really no cause for concern.

Travel Documents. Citizens of the United States need only some form of identification for visits of up to 8 months. Canadian citizens need the same for visits no longer than 3 weeks. Visas are required for all others except most Commonwealth and EC countries, as well as most South American nationals, depending on the length of stay. Contact the local consulate for particulars.

Money. Currency is the Bahamian dollar, comprised of 100 cents. Bahamian money is currently given the equivalent value of the American Dollar. Money is best carried in travelers' checks. A variety of credit cards are also accepted. Banks are located in all major towns.

Travel Costs. Travel to the Bahamas is a bargain compared to the Caribbean Islands. Sailing there on your own boat is certainly the least expensive way to visit. By stocking up on food in the U.S. before making the crossing, you can cruise for months at minimal cost. Although fuel is expensive, you really won't need much as good sailing breezes predominate. Chartering or staying on land is, of course, more expensive, although here again it can be a much less costly tropical holiday than what you can usually find further south. Flying to the Bahamas, rather than the Caribbean, can alone be a big savings. Once on the islands, travel can be inexpensive, with accommodations probably your biggest cost. Most islands are small enough to walk or bicycle around, so no car is necessary. Food prices are about 50% higher than in the U.S. Best buys include locally-grown products and British imports.

Language. English is the national language of the Bahamas, although you might find yourself struggling to understand it from time to time, due to the strong regional accent.

Health. Sun is really the only thing to worry about. Cover up during peak sun hours and use a sunscreen of #15 or higher. Children (including babies) should wear sunhats during the heat of the day. To avoid sunburns while snorkeling, use a waterproof sunscreen or a cotton T-shirt. Fresh produce should be washed well before using. Water is fine, although a precious commodity on these dry islands. Many islands rely on raincatching devices.

Food. Most food in the Bahamas is imported due to the thin topsoil and lack of water. Aside from a few basic vegetables and fruit, almost everything else comes from the United States. As part of the British Commonwealth, the Bahamas also receive a number of English food imports at reasonable prices. Best fresh produce buys include potatoes, onions, cabbage, tomatoes, bananas, and pineapple. Islands with good, locally grown produce include Cat Island, Great and Little Exuma, Long Island,

Eleuthera, and Harbour Island. Chicken is easy to find, as is fresh seafood, a staple of the islands. There's little fresh milk, but powdered whole milk, condensed milk, and cartons of longlife milk are all available. Oranges grow wild and look good, but don't be misled; they're sour. Coconuts grow along the shores, an excellent source of free food that children will enjoy. Food shops are easy to find on all the populated islands, from tiny corner stores to bigger groceries. Prices are best in main towns like Marsh Harbor, Nassau, and Georgetown. If you're coming for a short visit of one or two weeks, stuff your bags with goodies and bring it all with you. This is popular procedure with boaters. Our children have never forgotten the veritable larder of gourmet delights that emerged from my parent's luggage when they came to cruise on our sailboat.

Clothes. Few clothes are needed, no matter when you visit. Lightweight clothing is the norm except in the Abacos in mid-winter, when you'll need a warm jacket and long pants for the occasional spell of bad weather. Beach and bathing gear is most important. Bahamians are easy-going in

attitude, although immodest clothing and beachwear are not considered appropriate in town, particularly in the Abacos. The topless boat-code of the Caribbean is not an accepted practice here. Bring cotton clothing, especially for children to cover up from the sun and keep them cool. Wonderful handmade straw hats for the whole family can be bought in the Bahamas.

Laundry & Bathing. Laundromats are in large towns like Marsh Harbor, Nassau, and Georgetown. If staying in a hotel, cottage, or rental, ask about having your laundry done locally. People on sailboats usually do theirs by hand after a rain. On a boat with a baby, do diapers in saltwater with a saltwater detergent (available through boating catalogs or retail stores), giving them a final freshwater rinse. Bathing is a simple affair, between the endless swimming and sufficient facilites. Hotels and rooms always provide bathing facilites, while boaters should be sure to bring a sun shower. Charter boats always have some means of freshwater showering. Be aware that freshwater is in short supply throughout the Bahamas, mostly in the form of rainwater (you'll see raincatching devices all over the islands), so use it sparingly. All freshwater for boats must be bought.

Baby Needs. Baby food can be bought in most food shops, as well as disposable diapers. Bring some cover-up beachwear, an appropriate sunscreen (like Johnson & Johnson), and a cotton sunhat. On a sailboat, include a harness for toddlers and mobile babies. Include a good baby carrier for hikes around the islands on dirt paths.

TRANSPORTATION

Getting There. There are two ways to get to the Bahamas, by boat and by plane. Cruise ships visit Nassau and the Berry Islands regularly on quick hops over from Florida and New York. We don't recommend spending much time in Nassau as it is quite unlike the rest of the country, being both overpopulated and overtouristed.

Freeport and Nassau have international airports with flights from North America and Europe. Marsh Harbor, Georgetown, and Eleuthera also have daily flights from Florida. Linking up with a charter flight from Canada, the United States, or Europe is one way to fly inexpensively to the Bahamas.

Sailboats crossing to the Bahamas usually make for West End in the Abacos or the Bimini Islands off Miami. The trip takes approximately 12-15 hours, depending on weather and the chosen route. Expect delays up to a week or more while waiting for the right weather conditions to cross during winter. Prevailing headwinds and the presence of the Gulf Stream make crossing a matter of precision timing, with whole convoys of boats leaving an anchorage at once, given the right conditions.

Regional Travel. Inter-island travel is principally by boat, anything from ferries to small freighters to hired craft. Just ask around when the urge strikes to visit a new island. To travel to more remote islands south of the Exumas, you can either fly (twice weekly flights from Nassau) or travel by mailboat, also from Nassau. Renting an outboard boat is another way to get around. This can be well worth the money if you plan to explore coral reefs or discover deserted beaches. Many islands are small enough to explore comfortably on foot. Car rental shouldn't be necessary, even on the larger ones. Bicycles are another popular and convenient way to get around, with the sound of locals ringing their bicycle bells in passing a common one in places like the Abacos. Both bicycles and mopeds are often available for rent on a daily basis or longer. Larger islands do sometimes provide bus service, running on a schedule that remains a mystery to all except local inhabitants, so ask around for information. As a last resort, taxis are always available for hire, expensive, but entertaining, with informed drivers who often double as guides.

Roads. Traffic drives on the left in the Bahamas, similar to Great Britain. Roads are level and good, with little traffic. Many island roads are dirt, and pleasant for walking or bicycling.

ACCOMMODATIONS

Just about any type of accommodation (other than camping) is available on the islands, from luxury hotels to cottage rentals. Most towns have a choice of places to stay, often in lovely, Old World hotels that take you back in time. Intended solely for the tourist industry, they can be expensive, certainly your highest cost on a trip there. One option for longer stays is to find a local house to rent. Friends of ours did this for a few months on Man O' War. Not only was the cost considerably less than a tourist cottage or apartment, but they experienced life in the local community, with their children attending the village school. Unfortunately, camping is not permitted in the Bahamas, thus eliminating this inexpensive source of accommodation. Contact the Bahamas Hotel Association for a list of tourist accommodations, or just trust your luck to find something when you get there (often the best and least expensive option). Bareboat chartering is another wonderful means of accommodation, one the whole family will enjoy. Although pricy, as chartering always is, there's no better way to experience travel on a sailboat than in the lovely Bahamas islands.

POINTS OF INTEREST

Natural. Like a piece of the South Pacific scattered off the coast of North America, the Bahamas are lovely and unspoiled, with many areas of natural interest. If you've already been to Nassau, don't be misled. Throughout the other islands, with few exceptions, nature reigns. Gorgeous beaches line the shores in many areas, with privacy easy to come by. Children will love exploring the shallow, warm waters filled with sea life or collecting colorful shells along the water's edge. Some of the best coral reefs in the world are here, a number of them protected in sea parks. Sea life is abundant, from a variety of tropical fish and colorful starfish to large manta rays, barricudas, sharks, and dolphins. The following are some of the Bahamas' protected areas of natural interest.

• *Lucayan National Park (Grand Bahama).* The site of the world's largest underwater cave system. Much of this lovely coastal area can be explored on foot or by canoe. Paths lead through the park, passing high dunes, deserted beaches, mangroves, and two caves. Includes an excellent, magical canoe excursion down a three km creek.

• *Peterson's Cay National Park (Grand Bahama).* An underwater sea park with a designated snorkeling trail along a barrier reef.

• *Rand Nature Center (Freeport).* Exhibits depicting the history of the island, including geological features, early Indian culture, and piracy era.

• *Alder Cay (Berry Islands).* Accessible by private sailboat. A bird-watcher's paradise, with an interior lagoon and footpaths. Although privately owned, boaters and birders are welcomed to the quiet, remote anchorage.

- *Exuma Cays Land & Sea Park.* 500 sq. km of the Exuma Island chain, set aside to protect the habitat of the rare Bahamian iguana. Includes spectacular coral reefs with rich marine life.

- *Inagua Nation Park (Great Inagua).* Comprising almost half the island, this preserve is the breeding ground of the Bahamas flamingo, containing up to 30,000 birds at one time. Camping is possible on the edge of the park, a wilderness experience Bahamas-style.

Cultural. The Bahamas' easy pace of life and Caribbean flavor make this an interesting place to explore. All over the Bahamas it is the villages that are the main source of interest, providing an insight into a lifestyle that is resourceful and modest, unhurried yet hardworking. Notice the fascinating difference between the architecture and lifestyle of the different islands, reflecting their cultural heritage. Life in the Abacos, Harbour Island, and Spanish Wells is reminiscent of a tropical version of New England, with small wooden homes, colorful flowers, quiet streets, and hardworking people. The shabby, but elegant, Dunmore Town on Harbour Island reflects its heritage as one of the oldest settlements in the Bahamas. The spacious, grand buildings of the once-prosperous Governor's Harbour on Eleuthera form a marked contrast to the thatched-roofed, stone houses of Cat Island where life has always been simple. Scattered through Great and Little Exuma, and to a lesser degree other southern islands, lie the remains of original cotton plantations, now evolved into picturesque towns, their inhabitants descendents of freed slaves.

Historic. With its fairly recent history of settlement, the Bahamas has only a smattering of places of historical interest. With the extermination of the local Lucayan Indians by Spanish invaders, the island remained uninhabited for years until the coming of the Loyalists and British. The following are some of the historic points of interest scattered throughout the island chain that reflect the country's diverse past.

- *Grand Bahama Museum (Freeport).* Exhibits depicting the history of Grand Bahama Island, including early Indian culture and piracy era.

- *Wyannie Malone Historical Museum (Hopetown).* A fascinating collection of local artifacts and period furniture from the town's early settlement days, housed in an old island house.

- *Lighthouses.* Both Hopetown and Dixon Hill (San Salvador) lighthouses are well worth a vist, among the few manually operated ones still in existence and well worth the climb to the top. Lighthouse keepers, or their children, will happily give you a guided tour.

• *New World Museum (San Salvador).* Artifacts excavated from Indian settlements around the island.

• *The Hermitage (Cat Island).* Tiny hermitage built by John Hawes, religious convert and architect who built a number of lovely churches in the Bahamas. Impressively located on the highest point in the country, Mount Alvernia.

• *Cotton House (Little Exuma).* Plantation manor house and slaves cottages, dating from the early 1800s.

OUTDOOR ACTIVITIES

Hiking. Most people come to the Bahamas for the beaches, sailing, and snorkeling, but few discover the wealth of places to hike. Many places can only be reached by boat or on foot. Footpaths criss-cross islands, linking homes, villages, beaches, and lighthouses. As most are short and level, the hiking is easy for children of all ages, even very young ones. This is hiking at its most informal, with trails used for everyday use. Even roads supply good areas to walk due to the scarcity of cars. Good places to hike include Man O'War, Hopetown, Green Turtle, Little Harbor, and Eleuthera. Getting out and walking anywhere that looks enticing will expose you to the island pace of life as you explore areas most tourists never see.

Bicycling. Exploring by bicycle is fun and easy, both on day outings, or longer tours on the larger islands. Main roads are paved, traffic light, and the bicycling level and easy. While staying in one place, bicycles can be used for quick local transport, a popular mode of travel on some islands. Heat can be the biggest factor, but the easy terrain, short distances, and abundance of places to swim should alleviate most of problem.

Sailing. There's no denying that this is the best way to explore the Bahamas. The islands were made for cruising, with a seemingly endless selection of tropical anchorages, coves, beaches, harbors, and deserted spots. Sailing is completely sheltered inside each island group and passages between them are no more than short day hops. For people who like to get away from it all, the Bahamas offers uncrowded sailing in idyllic surroundings, with none of the boat crush that prevails in much of the Caribbean. Sailing is particularly well-suited to families with young children, as there's always a beach to play on, shallow water for swimming, and easy snorkeling near-by. Places to explore by rowboat abound, as do villages where children can safely roam. Popular cruising areas include the Abacos, Berry

Islands, Eleuthera and the Exumas. Boats can be chartered out of Marsh Harbor and Hopetown in the Abacos and Georgetown in the Exumas.

Swimming. It could eaily be argued that the Bahamas offers the best swimming in the world, expecially for families. Endless stretches of white sand beach, calm, warm water, and almost no one around typifies swimming in this glorious island nation. With a boat to take you places, you rarely need to share a beach with anyone else. Outside heavily touristed areas like Nassau, Treasure Cay, and West End, even local town beaches remain blissfully quiet and sparsely

used. While many of the tropical beach areas of the world have succombed to the pressures of overdevelopment, the Bahamas remains completely natural, with beach areas a delight for outdoor enthusiasts. Children of all ages will spend almost their entire time in the water. Even infants can comfortably play in the shallows, and older ones can develop their swimming skills in record-breaking time. Beach areas offer no hazards or dangerous marine life, but stay away from grassy bottoms where spiny urchins like to live. The Bahamas is one of the best places to learn to snorkel, with numerous accessible reefs and some of the richest marine life in the world. Bring snorkeling gear for any child old enough to swim.

Nature Studies. Bring along a book about tropical sea life and vegetation for children. There's no better place to get comfortable with the underwater environment than in these shallow, inviting, warm waters, destined to turn any child into an addicted swimmer. Children can learn much about the fragile ecology of these coral islands and reefs that have escaped the ravages of man.

Man O' War Cay

One of the loveliest islands in the Bahamas, Man O' War Cay is easily accessible, rich in history, and ripe for outdoor exploration. Whether you arrive by sailboat or ferry, stay a week or a month, have young children or old, a visit here can be fun and adventurous. Part of the Abaco island group in the northern Bahamas, Man O' War was principally settled in the 1780's by a group of New England Loyalists, following the American Revolution. Hardworking and enterprising, they created a boat building industry for themselves that remains renowned and active to this day. Each year, traditional island-built crafts journey to Georgetown, Exuma for the Family Island Regatta, often returning with winning boats.

Even today, the people retain a strong sense of their cultural identity, living a modest yet comfortable lifestyle on this small, prosperous island. Extending an authentic welcome to visitors, they remain unaffected by the trappings of tourism, committed to the work ethic and integrity that is their trademark. No hotels or resorts mar the island's natural beauty. No alcohol is sold, nor do island women wear shorts or immodest clothing. A walk around the village reveals its true character, past harborside boatyards, a handful of small, interesting shops, along narrow streets lined with pastel colored, New England-style homes. Flowers spill out of every corner, their abundance in keeping with the natural beauty of this island. Protected to the west by Great Abaco Island, Man O' War enjoys shallow, warm water, ideal for boating.

To the east, white sand beaches line the coast, broken by outcroppings of the sharp coral rock that forms the bedrock of the Bahamian islands. Offshore, a long series of barrier reefs provide protection from the sea, leaving the beaches gently washed by small waves. Even small children can safely swim here, although they may have to get used to being watched by a cluster of curious barricuda. Despite their fierce appearance, these large fish remain harmless in their seemingly endless fascination with swimmers. Experienced snorkelers can rent a boat and venture out into the underwater world of coral and sea life around the outer reefs.

A sailboat is the best way to visit the cay, approaching through the narrow opening that services both island harbors. Once through, an experience destined to get any sailor's heart palpitating should he meet a boat coming the other way, there are two choices: North or South Harbor. While South Harbor lies peacefully surrounded by private homes, most of them hidden amid the lush island growth, North Harbor is in the heart of the town, teaming with nautical activity. Each offers an excellent, all-weather anchorage. Landing is only permitted in the village, so you'll need an engine with your dinghy if you plan to anchor in South Harbor. Provisions and ice are available, although prices and selection in food are better in Marsh Harbor, an easy sail away.

Chartering is possible out of either Marsh Harbor, Great Abaco, or Hopetown, Elbow Cay. Although a pricy option and one that hardly qualifies as budget oriented, the experience of sailing here and in the surrounding Abaco area is unbeatable and worth the money. Accommodations on land are available either in small cottages or housekeeping apartments. Off-season travel (late fall) will get you the best rates. Another option is to try renting a local village house, particularly for families who want to stay and savour the experience of living on a Bahamian island. Ferries run frequently between Man O' War and some of the other islands, providing transportation for those without a boat. Small motor boats can also be rented by the day or longer. No vehicle is needed while staying on the island, as everything is within easy walking distance, even for very young children. Take a child carrier for walking with babies or toddlers. A stroller would work fine in the village.

Man O' War has some of the best walking in the Abacos, with a footpath that runs the length of the island. With no roads beyond the village itself (and most of these are too narrow for vehicles), the island is best explored on foot. Islanders with homes beyond the village rely more on boats for transportation, leaving the interior unspoiled and filled with lush, tropical growth. The presence of houses along the coast can only be gleaned by the appearance of narrow footpaths winding off into the trees, their entrance marked by a charming bell for approaching visitors to ring. Even three and four-year-olds will find the going easy along this level route, perfect for walking in a hot climate under cool, shady trees. At the northern end of the island, the path crosses a narrow strip of land, with views towards water on both sides. Walking either direction from the village makes a nice, easy hike.

No matter how you visit the island, don't hesitate to stay a while. With its distinctive culture, physical beauty, small town community spirit and outdoor potential, Man O' War has far more to offer families than any playground resort.

RESOURCE SECTION

TOURIST BUREAUS

Ministry of Tourism, P.O. Box N3701, Nassau, Bahamas   Tel: (809) 322-7500.
Tourist Information Office, 150 E. 52nd St., New York, NY 10022   Tel: (212) 758-2777.

CONSULATES & EMBASSIES

Bahamas Mission to the U.S., 767 Third Ave., 9th Fl., New York, NY 10017.
Bahamas Consulate, 360 Albert St., Ste. 1020, Ottawa, ON K1R 7X7, Canada   Tel: (613) 232-1724.

NATIONAL AIRLINES

Bahamas Air, P.O. Box 4881, Nassau, Bahamas   Tel: (809) 327-8451.

SUGGESTED READING

Birnbaum's Bahamas by S. & A. Birnbaum. New York: Harper Perrenial.
Fielding's Bermuda & The Bahamas by Christmas & Christmas. New York: Fielding Travel Books.
Insight Bahamas by S. Whittier. Eaglewood Cliffs, NJ: Prentice-Hall.
Outdoor Travel Guide to the Caribbean by K. Showker. New York: Stuart, Tabor, & Chang.

SUGGESTED MAPS

Bahamas, Berndtson & Berndtson, Scale 2, 250,000:1.
Bahamas, north & Bahamas, south, Berndtson & Berndtson, Scale N/A.
Caribbean 1, Nelles Verlag, Scale 2,500,000:1. Large-scale map showing Bermuda, Bahamas, and the Greater Antilles.

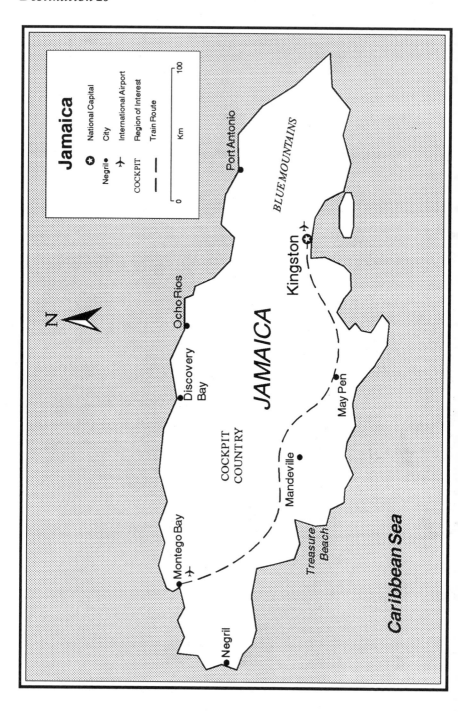

The West Indies

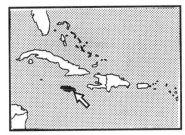

Jamaica

Jamaica rises from the Caribbean Sea, its diverse landscape some of the most spectacular in the world. Long stretches of white sand beach, densely forested mountains, abundant rivers and waterfalls, a profusion of flowers, and moist, tropical vegetation spread across much of the land, seductive in its vivid beauty. The culture is distinctive and proud, the pace of life relaxed, the climate perfection. Jamaica has evolved and matured into an exciting, safe destination, a place where families can feel comfortable. Prices are lower than on many neighboring islands, enabling even budget-minded families to enjoy the Caribbean experience.

GENERAL DESCRIPTION

Location. The third largest island in the West Indies, Jamaica is located in the island group known as the Greater Antilles. Surrounded by the Caribbean Sea, its nearest neighbors are Cuba to the north and Hispaniola (Haiti and the Dominican Republic) to the east.

Terrain. Predominantly mountainous, Jamaica's terrain is surprisingly diverse, from the tall, forested Blue Mountains to the remote, limestone regions of the Cockpit Country. Plains line a variety of coastal areas, rich, fertile regions where agriculture flourishes. Inland areas are densely tropical, while gorgeous sand beaches alternate with rocky headlands and luxuriant growth along the shore. Due to abundant rain, over 100 rivers course down the mountainsides, spilling over into a variety of spectacular waterfalls, rapids and streams. Combined with the aquamarine sea, the dramatic landscape is overwhelmingly beautiful.

Climate. Jamaica enjoys a perfect climate, with year round temperatures averaging in the 80s. Rain is most common in May and October, although quick showers can occur any time, helping to keep the island lush and beautiful. Inland mountain regions can be cooler in the higher altitudes, especially at night. Along the coast is rarely too hot, due to cooling sea breezes. Peak season runs from the middle of December through March, when tourists flock to the island to escape winter. Off-season is equally pleasant, uncrowded, and definitely cheaper.

Culture & Lifestyle. Once the home of gentle, peace-loving Arawak Indians, Jamaica has evolved into the ethnic meltingpot that typifies the country today. Most prevalent are those of African origin, descendents of slaves once imported to work the extensive sugar plantations during British colonial days. Like most Caribbean islands, Jamaica experiences a wide discrepancy between the prevailing low standard of living and the affluent lifestyle exhibited by its resort areas. Very much a Third World country, Jamaica's lifestyle is simple, with modest homes, running water a rare commodity, and education scant. Traditional village life prevails throughout the countryside, while coastal resort areas project a completely different image. To discover the quiet pace of Jamaican life, the traditional close-knit rural values, and the true Caribbean flavor, explore the less touristed areas.

PRACTICAL CONCERNS

Political Background & Safety. Following over 300 years of British colonial rule, Jamaica became independent in 1962. Periodic upheavals have marked Jamaican politics from time to time since, although never at the cost of democratic rule. Since the turbulent 70s, things have settled down, with the country's growing maturity and sense of identity. Predominantly a safe, enjoyable place to travel, tourists are well-received and made to feel comfortable. Apart from avoiding the poorer sections of cities like Kingston and Montego Bay, there's little cause for concern. Both hustling by street vendors and the visible drug scene can seem a bit intense, although rarely intimidating. The government is currently taking steps to improve the quality of its tourist industry and deter persistent hustling. In the meantime, try to be tolerant. Most street vendors are simply attempting to make a living however they can.

Travel Documents. Citizens of the United States and Canada need only a valid I.D. for visits up to six months. EC and Commonwealth nationals require a passport, while most other national must have a visa.

Money. Currency is the Jamaican dollar, consisting of 100 cents. Travelers checks are safe and widely accepted, while credit cards are useful in tourist resorts. Banks are easy to find in any sizeable town, with regular weekday hours for the most part (exact times can change from town to town).

Travel Costs. Jamaica lies in the middle expense bracket for traveling families. Much less expensive than most Caribbean islands, it allows you to economize without jeopardizing your enjoyment or comfort. Public transportation, food and lodging are all fairly inexpensive. Where camping exists, the price of accommodations can be kept to a reasonable amount. A great number of cabins and cottages are available that offer nice rooms with cooking facilities at modest cost. Cooking your own meals and shopping at local markets will help keep costs down. Despite their sometimes attractive price tag, package deals to places like Montego Bay are best avoided. The experience is anything but adventurous or culturally sensitive.

Language. The official language is English, frequently spoken in a local patois that will leave you groping for a familiar word.

Health. Jamaica has no major health concerns, despite being a predominantly poor country. Water and all foods are safe, and general hygiene is good. Eating from street vendors or in local homes is fine. It's always a good precaution to keep children's hands clean when eating. Sun protection is a must, with a good #15 or higher sunscreen. Bring plenty with you, including lipscreen. With little children, make sure they get plenty of fluids when exercising. Even breastfeeding babies will probably need a water supplement.

Food. Local food is wonderful, diverse, spicy, fresh and healthy. Fresh fruit and vegetables abound, some of them familiar, others delightful tropical fare that are fun to experiment with. Rice, beans and fresh produce form the basis of the diet, liberally flavored with spices. Whether eating out, snacking at a food stall, or cooking your own, meals are a delight and very economical. With the country's wonderful climate for growing, fresh produce is easy to come by, sold at local markets or small roadside stands. Modest-sized grocery stores are prolific and well-supplied, particularly in larger towns and tourist areas, where you'll find good variety. Both seafood and chicken are readily available. Fresh fruit juice can be purchased at local stands. Local cuisine features rice and bean dishes, meat-filled pastries, fritters, soup, and jerk, a kind of dried meat grilled with spices. Check to see how spicy things are before offering them to a fussy child.

Clothes. With an average temperature of 85 degrees, lightweight clothing is all you'll need. Sea breezes keep the air cooler along the coast, while higher interior regions also experience a slight drop in temperature. Include a light sweater or sweatshirt just in case. Rain jackets are helpful, although short, tropical showers are more often greeted as a welcome opportunity to cool off, and everything dries quickly in the intense sun. Beachwear, of course, is of prime importance. Bring sandals and a sunhat for everyone (or buy them there). Dress is casual, although bathingsuits should be limited to the beach. Good local products include sandals, straw hats and cotton clothing, all available at reasonable cost. Try buying from vendors around hotels (bargaining is the norm).

Laundry & Bathing. Jamaica has next to nothing in the laundromat department. You'll either have to launder your own clothes (bring a piece of clothesline, pins, and scrub brush), or hire someone. With children, you might find it worth the money to have a local woman do it, although you should agree on a price first. Hotel laundry rates are typically very high. Ask around to find out who does clothes. Bathing facilities range from communal cold water showers to private baths, depending on price. In this heat you'll probably find yourselves prefering the cold water anyway. Keeping children clean won't be a problem, particularly with all the swimming they'll invariably be doing. Be sure to rinse everyone off with fresh water at the end of the day to keep salt out of bedding.

Baby Needs. Like all tropical areas, Jamaica is a wonderfully easy place to travel with a baby. The climate is perfect, the people welcoming, food plentiful and healthy,and the atmosphere laid-back and relaxed. As always, the presence of a baby will open doors for you, bridging the gap between your family and local ones. Clothes can be kept to a minimum, just enough to provide sun protection. Bring cotton clothing, a sunhat, and appropriate sunscreen. Cloth diapers can easily be laundered, with local women offering their services. Baby food and wonderful fresh produce are easy to find. Bring a good child carrier, perhaps a stroller if you plan to stay in one place. One important thing to remember is to give your baby plenty of water, even if breastfeeding.

TRANSPORTATION

Getting There. Jamaica is easy to reach by air, with frequent flights from the United States. Most flights from other parts of the world make a connection in the U.S. International airports are at Montego Bay and Kingston, with most flights from the United States using the former. Fares are significantly lower off-season, or from April-November. Both APEX and various charter companies offer good savings on short-term visits.

Regional Transport. With few inhabitants owning their own vehicles, public transport is prolific, albeit somewhat freewheeling. The one railroad line connects Montego Bay with Kingston, a wonderfully scenic five-hour ride through the heart of the country. Making the trip is worth it just for the images and insight it offers into rural Jamaican life. Assorted buses and privately run mini-vans provide island transport at reasonable cost. Mini-vans operate on the premise that they'll leave when filled, something you won't have to wait long for. Prepare yourselves for some hair-raising transport, as Jamaicans love to drive fast, an interesting procedure on their winding, narrow roads. Car, moped and bicycle rentals are available in tourist areas, with the best rates for cars in Montego Bay and Kingston. Renting a moped for a few days is a nice way to enjoy some independent travel without the exorbitant cost of a car (children five years and up can sit in front or back).

Roads. Roads tend to be narrow, twisting, and colorful. What looks like an innocent 59 km or so on the map can translate into hours of driving as you wind your way around endless corners and through villages, scattering chickens, goats, pigs and children in your wake. All main routes are paved, including the coastal road and a number of north-south routes across the interior. Driving is on the left. Jamaicans rely on liberal use of their horns to warn anything lurking around the inevitable next corner. Try to avoid driving at night if possible.

ACCOMMODATIONS

Campgrounds. So far, camping in Jamaica is still in its infancy. Jamaica Alternative Tourism Camping and Hiking Association (JATCHA) is currently the prime mover behind developing camping facilities around the island. Along the coast, Negril and Ocho Rios both offer some camping possibilities associated with hotels. Prices are a bit high as campgrounds go, but considerably less than hotel costs. Camping is also possible in the Blue Mountains, principally at Maya Lodge, or various Forestry Department bases such as Whitfield Hall. Other good camping options include those at Crystal Springs, Treasure Beach, Yallahs, and Maggotty, all run by members of JATCHA. Camping on private land is possible, but choose where you stay with care and always ask first. Free camping in an isolated spot is not recommended, and prohibited on beaches or public land. The main problem with camping in Jamaica at the moment is not the availability of facilites, but security. This includes most designated campgrounds, where theft is still unfortunately always a possibility.

Cabins, Cabanas, & Bungalows. These are plentiful in all tourist areas, offering the best accommodations for the least money. Facilities range from communal baths and basic rooms to kitchens and hot water. Be sure to inspect the premises and the clientele thoroughly before checking in. Some places are definitely more oriented to the backpacking singles crowd than to a family with children (even an "adventuring" family). By Caribbean standards, cottage accommodations in Jamaica are very reasonably priced. Finding something with cooking possibilities, or bringing a camp stove and cookset with you will help keep daily costs down. Accommodation prices are usually significantly lower off-season.

Rentals. Over 800 cottages and apartments are available around the island for rent to tourists. Ranging from basic to luxurious, they offer independence, comfort, and a sense of home, things that can be important when traveling with children. Contact the Tourist Board, or look around when you get there. Because renting means you'll be spending most of your time in one place, it's often best to make your own arrangements after you've discovered an area you like. Again, prices are much lower off-season.

POINTS OF INTEREST

Natural. Blessed with an exquisite landscape and a rich diversity of plant and bird life, Jamaicans are awakening to the natural wonders of their island. Recent tourist development is more oriented towards preserving the cultural and environmental integrity of the country than creating the mass resort development that characterizes the Montego Bay area. Although Jamaica's national park system is still developing, a number of natural areas have been set aside for protection, including part of the Blue Mountains and the reef areas off Montego Bay. Jamaican Alternative Tourism Camping and Hiking Association (JATCHA), a private enterprise, is helping encourage a new orientation towards low-impact tourism through environmental sensitivity. Any of their contacts around the island are excellent sources of information on local sights, undeveloped areas, and outdoor activities. (For more information on this organization, refer to the sidebar). Take to the countryside, the interior mountain regions, the quiet coastal areas, to enjoy the natural beauty of this lovely island.

• *Blue Mountains.* Jamaica's highest mountain range, this can be enjoyed a number of ways: hiking the logging tracks and backcountry roads, watching the dawn from Blue Mountain peak, camping, relaxing at a mountainside lodge, or exploring by car.

• *Treasure Beach.* One of the island's most unspoiled beach areas, development here has been kept to a minimum. Drier than the north coast, the vegetation is more arid, set against a backdrop of mountains. Explore footpaths that line the coast. An excellent spot for families to base themselves.

• *Montego River Valley.* Lovely and untouristed, this scenic, lush interior region is largely ignored by the tourists that throng to nearby Montego Bay. There's walking, swimming, and plenty of opportunities for nature studies.

• *Marshall's Pen Nature Reserve.* Privately owned, this beautiful reserve in the interior is open to the pubic for hiking, birdwatching, and touring the extensive gardens of trees, flowers and ferns. Call ahead. Camping can be arranged.

• *Fern Gully.* Most notable of the local flora are Jamaica's ferns, with over 550 species found throughout the island, some growing up to 50 meters high. Take a drive along Fern Gully, five km of road through a dense forest of ferns near Ocho Rios.

• *Waterfalls.* Jamaica has a number of waterfalls, some of them popular tourist spots, others only seen when hiking with a guide. Among the best known are Dunn's River Falls and Y.S. Falls.

Cultural. Jamaica has a very vibrant, distinctive culture, an amalgamation of strong African roots, ethnic diversity, British colonial influences, Caribbean flavor, and unique religious affinities.

• *Rastifarianism.* Both a cultural and religious sect, Rastafarianism evolved from a need for Jamaican self-identity. Frequently identified with reggae music and the popular dreadlock hairstyle, it has also been traditionally linked to the striving of Jamaica's young for self-expression.

• *Reggae.* Unquestionably Jamaica's most renowned cultural attribute, reggae music evolved during the 60s, growing in popularity that remains worldwide. Created in part by the legendary Bob Marley, reggae developed a new sound, different from the calypso rhythm that had dominated Caribbean music for so long. Almost a cult in itself, reggae, along with Rastafarianism, helped young, black Jamaicans form a cultural foundation for themselves. Reggae music is celebrated all over the island, culminating in the Reggae Sunsplash in mid-summer, one of the country's largest festivals.

• *Crafts.* Most distinguished of Jamaican craftwork is wood-carving, a reflection of cultural artistry rather than a catering to tourism. Roadside stands and markets frequently exhibit works by local artisans. Other local crafts feature straw, wicker, beads and shells.

Historic. Historic sites and museums around the country reflect Jamaica's varied history, including its native Arawak Indians, the plantation years of British occupancy, and its quest for freedom.

• *Rose Hall (Discovery Bay).* A restored mansion, or Great House, on what was once a prosperous sugar plantation. Famed for its mistress, who was reputed to have killed a succession of husbands, Rose Hall is a popular tourist destination.

• *Columbus Park (Discovery Bay).* A park commemorating the arrival of Columbus in Jamaica. Includes a museum, park, and exhibits depicting Jamaica's history.

• *White Marl Arawak Museum (Kingston).* Built on the site of an original Arawak settlement, this depicts aspects of the Native Indian culture that once thrived throughout the Caribbean islands.

• *Fort George (Port Antonio).* For children who thrive on forts, this one has numerous cannons and original 18th century fortifications, built overlooking impressive Port Antonio Harbor.

• *Plantations.* Take a tour of Brimmer Hall, Friendship Plantation, or Prospect Plantation, all working farms that continue agricultural practices begun centuries ago. All are located outside Ocho Rios.

OUTDOOR ACTIVITIES

Hiking. Jamaica has numerous places to hike, most of them unofficial and waiting to be discovered on your own: down dirt roads, along beaches, through forests on logging roads, among flowers, trees and ferns. Exploring on foot is a wonderful way to enjoy the beauty and pace of island life, as well as to escape the tourist infrastructure that can be intense in certain spots. Bring good hiking shoes if you plan anything extensive in the mountains. Sunhats, sunscreen and water bottles are all a must. Don't expect to cover your usual distance when hiking in this heat.

• *Blue Mountains.* Hiking possibilities here are the best in the country, principally on the south side of the mountain range, along logging tracks and backcountry roads. Take a good topographical map (available at the Land & Survey Dept. in Kingston) if not hiking with a guide. A copy of "A Hiker's Guide to the Blue Mountains" is a very helpful reference. Extensive hiking is possible around Jack's Hill, Catherine's Peak, Holywell National Forest, Clydesdale National Park, and Blue Mt. Peak (the most popular hike).

• *Marshall's Pen Nature Reserve (Mandeville).* A 300 acre private property, with hiking trails that offer excellent birdwatching and explorations through cultivated gardens.

• *Montego River Valley.* Hiking here is excellent, with few tourists and plenty of dirt roads and tracks to follow through quiet, scenic countryside.

• *Treasure Beach.* One of the best coastal areas to explore on foot, try hiking along the coastal footpaths, used by local farmers and fishermen.

Bicycling. Bicycling is possible throughout much of the island, particularly along coastal areas where the terrain is less strenuous and the roads paved. Bicycles can be rented in a number of resort areas, including Negril Beach, Port Antonio and Ocho Rios. If you plan any extensive biking, however, it's definitely cheaper to bring your own. The narrow, twisting nature of the roads and the locals' daredevil driving techniques can be a bit unnerving, but Jamaicans are well versed in looking out for things on the road, and bicycling is subsequently quite safe. Mountain biking enthusiasts can always take to the backroads and logging tracks that permeate the interior. Bicycling the coastal route makes an ideal tour, with easy distances between accommodations and provisions. Bicycles can also be carried on the train between Montego Bay and Kingston, making it easy to hop from coast to coast. Heat can be a factor, so carry plenty of water bottles and avoid bicycling during midday.

Canoeing. An unusual activity to find on a Caribbean island, canoeing has nevertheless come to Jamaica. A number of guided trips are offered by Maya Lodge outside Kingston, with scenic expeditions along a variety of rivers, most of them appropriate for children. Although canoeing is not really possible independently, a day outing with a group can be a thrilling experience, showing you some of the interior's loveliest areas.

Swimming. Not surprisingly, Jamaica abounds with places to swim: gorgeous seaside beaches, rivers, waterfall pools, blue holes, and hot springs. Water is everywhere, most of it good for swimming. The best beaches are principally on the north and west coasts, although lovely Treasure Beach on the south offers some of the most unspoiled surroundings. Those around resort areas, such as Negril's 7-mile beach, are lovely, but can get crowded during peak season. To discover private beach areas along the north coast, explore along the shore road until you find something that looks enticing.

Nature Studies. With its abundant plant and birdlife, coral reefs and diverse landscapes, Jamaica offers numerous opportunities for nature studies. Tropical birds fill the mountain areas, often glimpsed on quiet hikes. Visit the Rocklands Bird Feeding Station (Montego Bay) for a closer look at up to 150 species. Marshall's Pen Nature Reserve also offers excellent birdwatching (51 species) as well as a variety of butterflies, ferns, trees and flowers. Bird-watching is also good along the shore by Treasure Beach. Visit the Hellshire Hills region to see indigenous iguanas, once thought to be extinct. As always, JATCHA is an excellent resource for learning about the environmental aspects of each area.

ALTERNATIVE TOURISM

Although Jamaica has long been a popular resort destination, a new type of tourist development has recently evolved, one that reflects the growing interest and popularity of alternative tourism. While traditional tourist development has too often had a negative impact on a country, alternative tourism stresses the need for environmental and cultural sensitivity. No group better reflects this philosophy than Jamaica's grass roots organization Jamaica Alternative Tourism Camping and Hiking Association, or JATCHA. Founded by native Peter Benchley, JATCHA has grown to include an increasing number of concerned local people,

committed to offering a new tourist experience. Not only is the experience more rewarding and exciting than the typical resort stay, but far better for the country, both culturally and ecologically. Instead of isolating tourists in an artificial resort, most of which are interchangeable the world over, JATCHA encourages them to learn about the country's natural surroundings, participate in outdoor activities, and interact with local inhabitants. A visit to one of their information centers can serve as a wonderful resource for finding places to hike, camp, canoe, learn about nature, meet local families, and generally avoid the more touristed spots.

Most well known is Maya Lodge, run by Peter Benchley, the founder of both JATCHA and Sense Adventures, an adventure travel outfitter. Located a short distance outside Kingston in the Blue Mountains, it offers camping, hiking, backpacking and river canoeing in lush, tropical surroundings. Facilities at the lodge are simple, comfortable and congenial, either in cabins, a hostel, or tents. Delicious meals are available at the Maya Cafe, or you can cook your own. With camping gear, this is an excellent, low-cost place for a family to base themselves while exploring the Blue Mountain region. Hiking is possible right from the lodge grounds, or at numerous other nearby locations. Guided outings (both alone or with a group) are also easily arranged, with a number of personable guides affiliated with the lodge. Sense Adventures runs a variety of day trips, including river canoeing, rafting, swimming, snorkeling and cultural outings. Or you can just relax in peaceful inactivity, ideal for families with young children.

Another enticing area founded by a JATCHA member is Crystal Springs, located inland from Port Antonio on the north coast. Equally low-key and ecologically sensitive, Crystal Springs features camping and cabin accommodations, swimming, gardens, a lovely stream, and a bird sanctuary. This is an excellent place to learn something about the flora, fauna, culture, and history of Jamaica. For more information on this and other alternative tourism attractions on the north coast, visit Stuart's Travel Service in Port Antonio, a JATCHA information center. Other centers around the country can be found at Montego Bay, Negril, Ocho Rios and Yallahs.

On the cultural side of things, JATCHA is also promoting contact with local people through homestays. A far cry from the insulation of a room in a hotel or week at a resort, even a couple of nights spent in a local home will give you tremendous insight into the lives of people in Jamaica. Appropriate homes have been selected carefully and recommended for nightly stays all over the country. Contact one of the members, or visit an information center to learn more or make arrangements. Along the same lines, a program called "Community Tourism" has been adopted by communities on the south coast and central area to counteract the ill-effects of tourist development. Seeking to preserve their cultural integrity, they've developed a program oriented towards bringing visitors into private homes. Some offer bed & breakfast type accommodations, others a chance to share a meal or outing with local families. Children of all ages are always welcome. The program offers a rare opportunity for visiting families to mingle with local ones on an intimate level. Not only is "Community Tourism" an ideal antidote to the artificiality of resort development, but in this case it exposes visitors to the often overlooked, laid-back charms of the central and southern areas of the country. To learn more about the program or participate, contact or visit Mrs. Diana McIntyre-Pike at the Astra Hotel in Mandeville, a lovely mountain town well worth a visit of its own.

RESOURCE SECTION

TOURIST BUREAUS
Tourist Information Office, 21 Dominica Dr., P.O. Box 360, Kingston 5, JA W.I.
Jamaica Tourist Board, 866 2nd. Ave., New York, NY 10017 Tel: (800) 223-5225.
Jamaica Tourist Board, 1 Eglinton E., Ste. 616, Toronto, ON M4P 3A1 Tel: (416) 482-7850.
Other Jamaican tourist offices located in Chicago, Miami, Los Angeles, Dallas, & Montreal.

CONSULATES
Jamaican Consulate General, 866 2nd. Ave., New York, NY 10017 Tel: (212) 935-9000.

NATIONAL AIRLINE
Air Jamaica, 72-76 Harbour St., Kingston, Jamaica, W.I.
Air Jamaica, 444 Brickell Ave., Ste. P-55, Rivergate Plaza, Miami, FL 33131 Tel: (305) 358-3222.

SUGGESTED READING
Jamaica Handbook by K. Lunnta. Moon Publications, Chico, CA. This is a very complete, well-written guide to the island.
Adventure Guide to Jamaica by S. Cohen. Hunter, Edison, NJ.

SUGGESTED MAPS
Jamaica, International Travel Maps, Scale: 1:250,000. A detailed, colorful map with a complete street map of Kingston on the reverse side.
Jamaica, Berndtson & Berndtson, Scale: N/A.

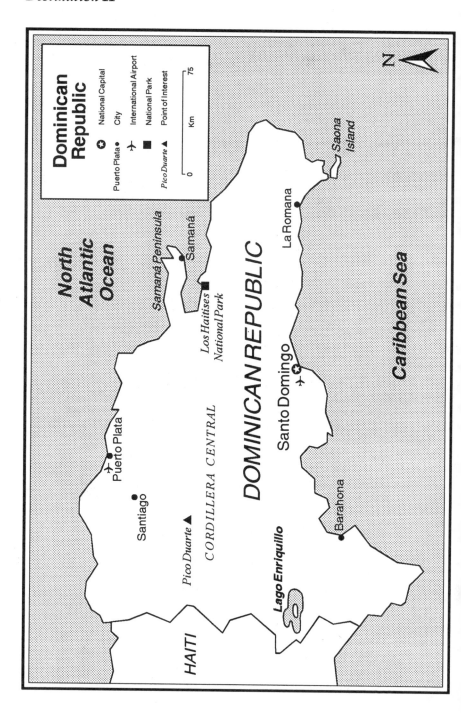

Dominican Republic

Lovely and tropical, lush and exotic, the Dominican Republic seems made for adventuring novices and families with young children. Blessed with exquisite scenery, beaches, and perennial warm weather, the atmosphere here is friendly and relaxed. With a tourist industry that is still in its infancy, the feeling is of cultural integrity, of a country little changed over the years. The best way to experience it is to find a spot and stay a while, enjoying the flavor of this lovely island and its attractive people.

GENERAL DESCRIPTION

Location. Located in the West Indies, the Dominican Republic shares the island of Hispaniola with Haiti, occupying its eastern portion. Surrounded by the Caribbean Sea, it lies in the island group known as the Greater Antilles. The nearest countries (other than Haiti) are Cuba and Jamaica to the west, the Bahamas and Turks & Caicos to the north, and Puerto Rico to the east.

Terrain. Occupying the eastern two-thirds of Hispaniola, the Dominican Republic epitomizes all one hopes to find on a tropical island. Mountains rise in the rugged interior, among them Pico Duarte, the highest peak in the Caribbean. Conversely, the country also boasts the lowest place in the Caribbean, the saltwater Lago Enriquillo, 27 meters below sea level. The landscape is predominantly tropical jungle, a lush, forested growth that appears almost impenetrable. The land is fertile, supporting a variety of crops in cultivated valleys and plains. Much of the coast is lined with exquisite sand beaches, so far largely spared the mega-tourism that has permeated much of the West Indies. The sense of physical grandeur and opulence is intense, with dense tropical forests, tall, graceful palms, hidden waterfalls, wilderness mountain regions, and deserted stretches of coast.

Climate. The country enjoys hot, tropical temperatures year round, with little change other than during the rainy season. Rain is most common June - October, although short hard showers can occur throughout the year. Peak season runs mid-December-April, with the habitual influx of Northerners escaping winter. The island, however, is lovely and comfortable at any time of year. Fortunately, even peak season is still far from crowded, other than in the few obvious resort areas.

Culture & Lifestyle. Culturally, the country is a fascinating mix. Colonized by the Spanish, developed into a plantation society by the French, populated by imported African slaves, it evolved into an amalgamation of cultural factors, much like the rest of the West Indies. What makes the country so unusual is its almost complete Spanish - African mix, its predominantly mulatto ethnic identity. Tall, lean, and graceful, the people are strikingly handsome. While parts of Santo Domingo seem very chic and Latin, the country as a whole exudes a quietly friendly atmosphere, with little of the noisy exuberance that typifies the Latin culture. The lifestyle is poor, the country very much a Third World economy. Agriculture and fishing are widespread, much of it still practiced on a subsistence scale. Homes are basic, often little more than four wooden walls and a handful of furniture. Cooking is done outside under a thatched shelter. This is a simple, yet welcoming society, one where tourists are treated with interest and cordiality.

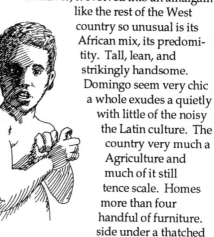

PRACTICAL CONCERNS

Political Background & Safety. Once inhabited by peaceful Taino Indians, the Dominican Republic suffered all the usual cultural devastations, upheavals, and transitions experienced throughout the West Indies.

Following the arrival of Columbus and European settlement, it changed hands a number of times between Spain and France before gaining independence in 1844. Since then, the political situation has varied, ranging from the dictator years of Trujillo to American intervention to democracy. Aside from some gun-toting guards on the streets of Santo Domingo, there's little evidence of any political stress, despite repeated government corruption that has contributed to the country's economic woes. Ever cheerful, the Dominicans themselves go on about their business. Tourists can feel very safe here.

Travel Documents. Citizens of Canada, the United States, Australia, most EC countries, plus a variety of Latin American and Caribbean nations, need only a passport for visits up to 60 days. A tourist card is issued upon arrival for a small fee.

Money. Local currency is the peso, comprised of 100 centavos. Travelers checks are the best and safest way to carry money, preferably in American dollars. Getting them cashed can be an interesting business. Banks, on the whole, are a shaky enterprise in the Dominican Republic, even non-existent in some towns where you'd expect to find them. On the other hand, the black market business in American dollars is widespread and while not openly acceptable, is often the only way to change money. Local, reliable black marketeers are easy to find. If using a bank, note that they are usually only open mornings. Armed guards are the norm and no cause for alarm (you'll find the same thing outside places like telephone offices).

Travel Costs. A Caribbean bargain destination, the Dominican Republic can make your money go a long way. With little outside the Santo Domingo and Puerto Plata areas in the way of tourist infrastructure, prices have stayed low, oriented more towards the modest traveler than the resort enthusiast. The result is an excellent place for families, with comfortable, yet modestly-priced accommodations, inexpensive public transportation, and fabulous, inexpensive food, both at markets and restaurants. Few places in the West Indies can match the Dominican Republic for bargain family travel.

Language. The official language is Spanish. Don't expect much English outside the tourist industry. A number of coastal areas have ex-patriate North Americans living there who can be helpful. There's often also at least one opportunistic entrepreneur with a sufficient command of English, a young, educated man willing to find you whatever it is you want. Some knowledge of Spanish is helpful if heading into the interior mountain regions.

Health. Overall, there are no major health concerns. Malaria does occur, particularly in the region near the Haitian border, but no medication should be necessary unless planning extensive inland travel. Take chloroquine, if necessary. Coastal areas are completely safe. Both water and food are usually fine in tourist areas. Bottled water is widely available, although tap water is often also safe to drink. Ask at the local tourist bureau to make sure. Market food should be washed well before eating. Restaurants and food stalls are all safe to eat at unless they seem particularly unhygienic. There is no particular risk of hepatitis. Include plenty of good #15 (or higher) sunscreen, plus sunhats for everyone. Pharmacies and health clinics are widespread.

Food. Food is wonderful, both bought and cooked on your own, or eaten at local restaurants, markets, or stalls. Fresh produce is abundant and locally grown, sold at open-air markets and off the streets. Saturday is usually the main market day, plus often one other day a week. Prices are very inexpensive. Bargaining for food is not the norm. Fruit fanatics will be in heaven, what with the pineapples, bananas, melons, citrus, papayas, and mangoes, all at rockbottom prices. For basics, look around for small, discreet grocery shops. Most towns have numerous ones, each with its tiny interior and jam-packed shelves. Learning the Spanish words for things is helpful, as the proprietor usually gets you what you need (pointing at things can get old). All the basics are available, including flour, rice, pasta, oatmeal, canned goods, corn flakes, crackers, and often peanut butter(!).

Powdered whole milk is readily available. Sweets are in noticeably short supply. Instead, oranges, sold fresh from street vendors, are the popular snack food (one of the reasons the people are so lean). Rice, beans, a smattering of meat, and fresh vegetables form the basis for the local diet, with often the same dish served for lunch and supper. Dominican women bake their own bread, so ask around to see if you can buy some. Due to the distribution problems that plague the country, certain foods can disappear for weeks on end. If possible, stock up when you find something vital.

Clothes. Lightweight, warm weather clothing is all you'll need unless venturing into the mountains where nights can be cold. Even a sweater will probably be superfluous. Cotton clothing is best in this tropical climate. Include sandals, sunhat, and bathing gear for everyone. Visiting during the rainy season will warrant including some kind of lightweight rain jacket. Otherwise, leave it at home. Western-style cotton clothing at reasonable prices can be bought locally. Try the marketplace for the best prices.

Laundry & Bathing. Laundry will either have to be done by you or a local woman. Hotels also usually offer a service, but at a higher price. Ask around who does laundry if you don't fancy doing it yourselves. Clothes hung on a line dry rapidly in this hot climate. Bathing usually means tepid showers. In this heat, hot water is hardly missed.

Baby Needs. As with many tropical places, the Dominican Republic is an easy country to visit with a baby. The warm climate and lovely weather are ideal for babies, with little need to include much beyond some light-weight cotton clothing. Bring a sunhat and appropriate sunscreen. Disposable diapers are available, although cloth ones can always be washed by a local woman. Baby food is available, plus plenty of regular foods good for little children. A good child carrier is helpful for traveling around, shopping, walking to the beach, or whatever. Dominicans are very relaxed with their babies, and will treat yours the same.

TRANSPORTATION

Getting There. The Dominican Republic has two international airports, at Santo Domingo and Puerto Plata. Charter flights from North America frequently use Puerto Plata, a popular resort destination, while most other international traffic goes through Santo Domingo. For a short visit of a week or two, try to land on the side of the island you plan to visit. Travel between the two involves a long bus ride. Various reduced fare and charter options are available from the United States, so shop around before booking a flight. Off-season rates are always lower.

Regional Transport. With few people owning private vehicles, the Dominican Republic has plenty of low cost public transportation. Technically, buses cover all the major routes between population centers. Whether they're all functioning at the same time is another matter. Publicos are also plentiful, privately run vehicles that will take you (and as many others as can possible be squeezed in) to your destination. To obtain additional breathing space, simply pay for a few extra seats. Special trips to wherever it is you want to go can always be arranged. Bargain for the best price. Local town transport around Samaná features the ubiquitous moto-concho, a kind of motorized rickshaw, ridden at minimal cost. Rates are preset and per person, so find out in advance what you should be paying.

Roads. Roads vary from good to abysmal. Main roads are all paved (in a manor of speaking), narrow, and usually empty of traffic other than the main north/south route linking Santo Domingo, Santiago, and Puerto Plata. Dominicans like to drive fast, but not so as to be suicidal. The convoluted nature of the roads is enough to keep most of them at a reasonable speed. Driving is on the right.

ACCOMMODATIONS

Campgrounds. So far, the Dominican Republic offers little in the way of camping potential, and no official campgrounds. Camping is permissible in park land, and is the only option when traveling in the mountains, but everything will have to be brought with you.

Rooms, Bungalows, & Rentals. Inexpensive rooms are easy to come by just about anywhere. Bungalows on the beach, rooms in a private home, and housekeeping apartments can all be found without much difficulty. Prices are low and affordable for families. There's always the problem that the electricity will get turned off, in which case any enterprising landlord will have his own generator. Water is another thing that comes and goes with regularity. Find out what to expect and act accordingly. If the whole town habitually loses electricity every night, there's no point in getting upset. For a stay of a week or more, check out the rental possibilities. An apartment with kitchen facilities can give you the most for your money, plus some room to move around in. Check out all the amenities carefully beforehand, although be forewarned that malfunctioning apparatus is a Dominican way of life. Fortunately, the people themselves are infinitely resourceful. Tourist offices or freelance entrepreneurs are good resources for finding a rental.

POINTS OF INTEREST

Natural. With its lush, tropical setting and lack of development, the country has numerous natural points of interest. As always, the combination of mountains and sea, thick forests and sparkling water is irresistible. A hike or drive inland reveals an amazing vista of jungle growth and deep valleys, small patches of cultivated fields set against a wilderness backdrop. A number of national parks have already been set aside, helping to establish a respect for the natural wonders of this island. Facilities are virtually non-existent in most parks, but a visit is always worthwhile.

• *Parque Nacional del Este.* This encompasses a portion of the southeastern corner of the country, including the island of Saona. There are opportunities for hiking, exploring caves (complete with bats and owls), and visiting wonderful beaches, accessible by boat. Trips to the island can be arranged through the National Park Headquarters. Come prepared for mosquitoes.

• *Lago Enriquillo and Isla Cabritos National Park.* An inland saltwater lake that at 27 meters below sea level is the lowest place in the Caribbean. Isolated and surrounded by forested mountains and hills. Vegetation is arid, with a rich bird life. Isla Cabritos, in the center of the lake, protects the habitat of numerous alligators and iguanas. Exploration is possible by road around the lake or by boat to the island. Contact the National Park Headquarters to arrange a boat ride.

• *Valle Nuevo Scientific Reserve.* A lovely interior region of densely wooded mountains, with hiking on logging roads. Includes some tropical cloud forest and unusual species of indigenous trees. Best for people who love remote areas.

• *Los Haitises National Park.* A coastal park, accessible only by water (private yacht, or arranged boat from Samaná). A spectacular, magical region of "karsts", limestone hills covered with lush, tropical vegetation and penetrated by creeks lined with mangroves. Rich with bird life, small sand beaches, and caves. Particularly exciting to explore by small rowboat, venturing up into the mangrove creeks.

• *Waterfalls.* The Dominican Republic has plenty of these, usually well advertised by word of mouth in a given area. Visit Jimenoa or Aguas Blancas, near Costanza, or Limón, located in isolated splendor near Samaná. Local guides (plus assorted other family members) are always available to lead the way.

• *Cordillera Central.* With two national parks (Bermudez and Ramirez) and the country's highest peaks, this interior region makes a spectacular destination. Includes the lovely Constanza valley area. Mountains, dense forests, waterfalls and birdlife. Serves as a center for hiking, including up Pico Duarte, the highest mountain in the West Indies.

• *Botanical Gardens.* The country has two of these, one in Santo Domingo and the other in Puerto Plata. Carriage, boat, and train rides are offered through the gardens in Santo Domingo, while the ones in Puerto Plata can only be reached via cable car up towering Isabella de Torres Peak.

Cultural. A melange of Latin and African cultures, the Dominicans possess their own unique blend, distinctive among Caribbean cultures. More than anything, it is a culture of contrasts. Exuberant yet quiet, carefree yet hardworking, friendly yet reserved, efficient yet laid-back, they can't fail to enchant you. As always, the best way to experience the culture is by getting out into the countryside, away from the few tourist centers.

Small, wooden homes peak out from the lush growth, an elegantly carved rocking-chair glimpsed through the open door. Cooking is done outside over a fire, a clay oven sitting to one side like some obsolete beehive . The people seem healthy, their cleanliness and grace notable against a subsistence backdrop. Men gather under a shade tree to indulge their passion for Dominoes, slapping the chips down with a practiced snap. Markets, as always, are colorful and fascinating, a comfortable place to mingle with the local inhabitants. A relaxing people to be around, Dominicans seem to accept life with complacency and a notable degree of pleasure.

• *Crafts.* Local craftwork features leatherwork, embroidery, baskets and attractive jewelry, made with locally-mined amber and a blue sea stone the color of turquoise. Buying from street vendors is easy and pleasant, with bargaining the norm.

• *Costanza.* A high mountain valley with small, prosperous farms, founded by a colony of Japanese immigrants. A fascinating, scenic region with a completely different culture from the rest of the country.

Historic. Historic points of interest range from evidence of early Indian inhabitants to the remnants of years of Spanish settlement.

• *Santo Domingo.* The country's capitol is also the oldest permanent European settlement in the West Indies. The town was originally founded by Christopher Columbus, and for many years served as the Spanish seat of power in the Caribbean. Santo Domingo has a wealth of museums, historic buildings, parks and military con-

structions: The Casa de Colon, a fortress-like house built by Columbus' son; the Cathedral; the Royal Houses Museum; and the impressive Forteleza (fort). For some insight into the pre-Columbian culture of the indigenous Taino Indians, visit the Museo del Hombre Dominicano, filled with artifacts and fascinating dioramas.

• *Ingenio de Enngombe.* Located outside the city, these ruins of a 16th century sugar plantation include the Great House and various outbuildings.

• *Puerto Plata.* An interesting town, with a decided colonial air: Victorian architecture, central square, narrow streets, and fort overlooking the snug harbor.

OUTDOOR ACTIVITIES

Backcountry Camping. This is the only way to camp in the Cordillera Mountains. Travel is almost always done with a guide and pack mules. A true wilderness experience, everything will need to be taken with you in this remote region. Unless you are very experienced, forget doing this with young children. Guides can be hired in the vicinity of Costanza and Jarabacoa.

Hiking. Hiking potential in this lovely country has barely been tapped. Among the few places you will find real trails are those leading to popular waterfalls like Limón (Samaná Peninsula), Jimenoa and Aguas Blancas (Costanza). The high mountain valley by Costanza offers some of the best hiking. For the most part you'll have to freelance, exploring the countryside on footpaths when you find them. The hike up Pico Duarte, the highest mountain, takes two rigorous days, with a guide necessary. Trail hiking is also possible in El Morro National Park (along goat paths), Valle Nuevo Scientific Reserve (along logging roads), Parque Nacional del Este (trail begins at the eastern end by Boca del Yuma), and Saona Island.

Bicycling. Bicycling definitely has its limitations. More a country where you find a niche and stay awhile, the Dominican Republic is probably not destined to become a popular touring destination. Even local transport rarely warrants the need for bicycles. If bicycling is your passion, the easiest place to explore is along the coasts, with fairly level roads, frequent facilities, and not too much traffic. Come prepared for hot temperatures, although the north and east experiences a steady onshore breeze most of the time.

Sailing. Although the Dominican Republic has a limited potential for cruising, sailboats are a common sight along the north and east coasts due to the country's location along one of the major boat migratory routes linking North America with the Caribbean. Popular harbors lie scattered from Puerto Plata in the northwest to Samaná Bay in the east. Due to the prevailing easterly winds, sailing in this direction is best done at night or early in the morning before the wind picks up for the day. Heading west is almost always easier since the wind is behind you. With so little to offer in the way of coastal cruising, chartering has so far not been developed. Provisions are plentiful at scattered harbors and the boating atmosphere convivial among an international group of world cruisers. Boats must be officially cleared upon arrival and before departure at each harbor. Don't miss a visit to Los Haitises National Park on Samaná Bay, a truly unique experience by sailboat (for more information on this area, see the accompanying sidebar).

Swimming. Swimming is plentiful, with beaches along much of the coast. Those in the immediate vicinity of Puerto Plata and Santo Domingo are the most developed. The further afield you go, the better it becomes. Many areas are still quiet and nearly deserted. Try Las Terranas on the Samaná Peninsula, a low-key place with good swimming for children. All beaches in the Dominican Republic are open to the public.

Nature Studies. The Dominican Republic has abundant bird life, tropical flora, and some unusual opportunities for nature studies.

• *Whale-watching.* January - March is the time to see humpback whales off the east coast of Hispaniola, where up to 3,000 congregate to give birth on the Silver Bank. Whale-watch craft leave regularly from Samaná, but investigate carefully before boarding just any boat. Some are decidedly more seaworthy than others.

• *Alligators & Iguanas.* Isla Cabritos, an island national park in the center of Lago Enriquill, protects the habitat of numerous alligators and iguanas. Private boat trips can be arranged through the National Parks Headquarters in Santo Domingo.

• *Bird-watching.* This is possible all over the country. Principal birding areas include Los Haitises National Park, El Morro National Park, Valle Nuevo Scientific Reserve, and near Lago Enriquillo in the surrounding hills of the Neibo and Bahoruco Mountains.

The Samaná Peninsula

Of all the fascinating, lovely regions in the Dominican Republic, the Samaná Peninsula emerges as one of the best. Thrusting out into the Caribbean Sea, it forms a slendor, rugged finger of land nearly surrounded by water. The vegetation is lush, fed by the frequent tropical showers that form in the tradewind-driven clouds. Dense stands of palms and banana trees, ferns and vines grow to the water's edge, a compelling tribute to the fertility of the land. Like a distant, almost forgotten relative, it bears only a slight resemblance to the chic Latin tempo of Santo Domingo or studied tourist development of Puerto Plata. A visit here offers a truer picture of this attractive, rural country.

No matter where you are coming from, the Samaná Peninsula seems unnaturally hard to get to. Geographically closer to Puerto Plata, it is nevertheless usually easier to reach via Santo Domingo. Although public buses technically service the main peninsula town of Samaná from both cities, reality can be a different story. Upon occasion, a search for the appropriate bus in Puerto Plata can produce nothing better than verified information that the driver has totalled it. The alternatives, in that case, are a four hour taxi ride (settle on a price before hand) or a bus to Santiago and connection with the Santo Domingo/Samaná bus. If all this seems daunting, don't let it be. Once reached, the destination more than makes up for the inconveniences of getting there. Like all difficult places to reach, most tourists don't bother to go, thus enabling them to remain the most desirable destinations of all. A rental car, of course, would minimize the difficulties except for the fact that rental cars in the Dominican Republic are notorious for malfunctioning. Nor do you actually need one once you've arrived. Samaná is the kind of place to relax in and let the laid-back Caribbean culture ease you into a slower pace—perfect for families with young children.

The peninsula has three places where you can base yourselves: Samaná, Las Galeras, and Playa Las Terranas. Samaná, the main town in the region, is culturally the most interesting, while the other two cater more to the budding tourist trade. Having happily spent over two months living in Samaná, we can highly recommend it to families. Admittedly, we were living on a sailboat, the ideal way to visit the area, but friends with three young children enjoyed an equally wonderful two weeks renting an apartment. Situated on a scenic natural harbor, the town perches on the edge of the wide Bahia de Samaná. A village of fishermen and farmers, it was once slated for tourist development and given a half-hearted facelift along the waterfront. The result is a paradox of styles: modern architecture juxtaposed with the traditional; a handful of spacious streets beside narrow alleyways, open-air cafes adjacent to hole-in-the-wall shops.

For visitors, the town has all the necessities: an excellent selection of small cafes and restaurants, modest rooms and rentals, a colorful market, sufficient food stores, and friendly people. The tourist trade is minimal, almost forgotten issue away from the waterfront. The combination of low-key tourist facilities and cultural authenticity is ideal for families, making a stay here interesting and colorful without being too rigorous or demanding. Local transport around town is provided by numerous "moto-conchos", ridden for a pittance. For expeditions beyond town, publicos can be hired on a daily basis to take you wherever you want.

One reason Samaná has so far been neglected by the tourist trade is its lack of easily accessible beaches. Not that there aren't beaches, but the town has none of those mile long stretches of pristine white sand that personify the West Indies in most peoples' minds. The town itself has a couple of small sand beaches with excellent, safe swimming. Located on the outer side of the islands across from the waterfront, they can be reached via a concrete footbridge. Try the small one halfway out to the end, hidden down a dirt footpath. Good swimming is also possible next to the wharf on the last island, beside the sailboat anchorage. Although the inner harbor, in true Third World style, doubles as the local town dump, the outer areas are fine and attractive for swimming. The best beaches of all are on Cayo de Levantado, a lovely, small island a mile offshore ringed with white sand. Numerous passenger boats make the trip back and forth daily, so getting there is no problem. Choose your craft wisely, as some are in serious jeopardy of sinking. Fortunately, the trip is quickly over and the waters calm. Excellent swimming is also possible at Playa Las Terrenas, a relaxed resort area on the north coast of the peninsula, easily reached from Samaná for a day outing.

Despite its small size, the Samaná environs offer some wonderful areas of natural beauty, from palm-studded Levantado to the unusual beauty of Los Haitises National Park. The hour-long hike to Limón Waterfall is well worth the effort, affording an intimate glimpse into the lush interior. Winding through dense jungle vegetation, the dirt path follows the contours of the hills, crossing streams, and ending at the impressive, isolated waterfall. Bring bathingsuits, as the swimming in the large pool at its base is refreshing. A guide (and probably most of his relatives) can be picked up at the entrance to the trail. Another wonderful, albeit difficult to get to, destina- tion is Los Haitises National Park, a spectacular region of "karsts", limestone hills that look like lush, tropical humps rising from the sea. Only accessible by water, the best way to visit is in your own boat, sailing from nearby Samaná. Explorations can be done via dinghy up the numerous mangrove and cliff-lined creeks. This is really a magical place, not to be missed if you travel to the Dominican Republic on a sailboat. Boat trips can also be arranged in Samaná for day outings.

Lying on the "Thorny Path" sailing route to the Caribbean, Samaná harbor serves as a jumping off spot across the Mona Passage to Puerto Rico and the beyond. Consequently, you'll find numerous sailboats anchored off the town, many lingering for weeks on end as they succumb to the lure of the area. Coming from either the Bahamas or Puerto Rico, it offers a congenial, protected anchorage. Whether arriving by land or by boat, staying for a week or a month, exploring the area or just basking in the relaxed atmosphere of its towns, the Samaná Peninsula offers some of the best of the Dominican Republic.

RESOURCE SECTION

TOURIST BUREAUS
At the time of publication the tourist office activites for the Dominican Republic are being handled by:
Kahn Travel Communications, 4 Park Ave., New York, NY 10016   Tel: (212) 679-3200.

CONSULATES
Consulate General of the Dominican Republic, 1 Times Sq. Plaza, 11th Fl., New York, NY 10020   Tel: (212) 768-2480.

NATIONAL AIRLINE
Dominicana Airlines, 1200 NW 78th Ave., Ste. 108, Miami, FL 33126   Tel: (800) 327-7240.

SUGGESTED READING
Caribbean Island Handbook by B. Box & S. Cameron. Prentice Hall Travel, New York.
Cadogan Guide to the Caribbean by J. Henderson. Globe Pequot Press, Chester, CT.
Outdoor Traveler's Guide: Caribbean by K Showker. Stuart, Tabor, & Chang, New York.

SUGGESTED MAPS
Hispaniola, Berndtson & Berndtson, Scale: N/A.
Hispaniola, Hildebrand, Scale: 1:816,000.

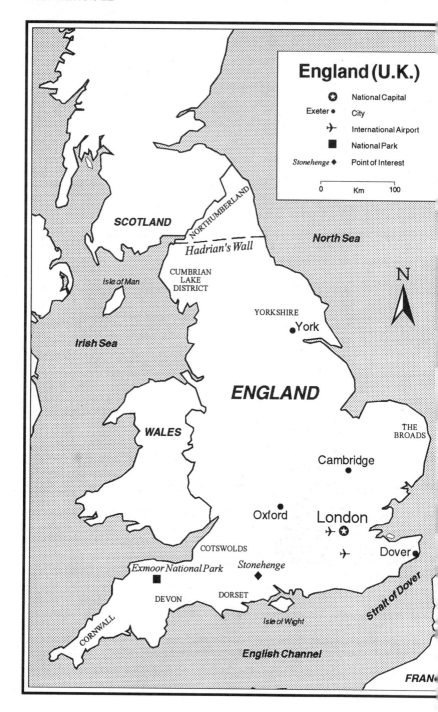

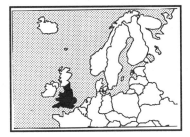

England

Pastoral countryside and rural villages, windswept coastline and fields of grazing sheep, ancient manor houses and crumbling ruins, all beckon you to England with the promise of adventure. This is one of those countries that seems made for families, one that newcomers will feel comfortable with and experienced travelers long to return to. Like a haven away from home, England combines the familiar with the excitement of the unknown. Nearly every aspect of the country is appropriate for children, from the thrill of

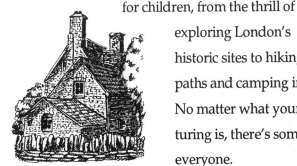

exploring London's historic sites to hiking coastal footpaths and camping in rural settings. No matter what your level of adventuring is, there's something here for everyone.

GENERAL DESCRIPTION

Location. Lying off the northwest coast of mainland Europe, England forms part of the United Kingdom. Sharing its island setting are the tiny country of Wales to the west and larger Scotland in the north. Separated from France by as little as 50 miles across the English Channel, England is set apart, dominated by its island status. To the west across the Irish Sea lies Ireland, to the north the notorious North Sea.

Terrain. England's terrain is delightfully varied, from the mountains, moors and lakes in the north, to the gentle, rolling hills and valleys of the south. The fells, an expanse of marsh and inland waters, permeate the east coast, while the southwest shore lies rocky and wind-swept, facing the Atlantic. It is a country typified by rural countryside, with farms and villages spreading across the land in an endless tapestry of pastoral imagery.

Climate. Despite lying at an extreme northern latitude, one equal to Labrador in northeast Canada, England enjoys a surprisingly mild climate due to the warming influences of the Gulf Stream. As an island, the weather is quickly changeable, and the sight of families picnicking in the sun with umbrellas parked nearby a common one. Despite a well-deserved reputation for rain, endless downpours are unusual and weather during summer and fall far better than one might expect. Summer weather can range anywhere from high 80s (F) inland to low 40s during a bad spell, all in a matter of 24 hours. Southwest England enjoys the warmest weather, with beach days during peak summer season. Winters are damp and gray everywhere. The best time to visit is definitely summer and fall.

Culture & Lifestyle. England's culture is distinctive, the product of an ancient, impressive history. Once the ruler of the world's largest empire, present day England reflects a heritage that harks back to the days of unprecedented world power. Despite decades of colonialism, immense exposure to foreign influences, and the recent influx of large numbers of immigrants, the English remain firmly entrenched in their own cultural identity. Proud of their civilized behavior, they appear quiet and controlled, soft-spoken and self-contained. A country built on the foundation of class distinction, the English possess a unique blending of Old World values with modern liberalism. Even small villages contain a mix of classes, from farmers and laborers to professional people and landed gentry, all intermingling comfortably. The lifestyle is predominantly modest, despite an abundance of elegant estates, relics of a once widespread, wealthy aristocracy. Today, most remain in private use, although many are also properties of the National Trust and open to the public. Village life continues to thrive, with a small town flavor that has survived generations of change. It is a lifestyle reminiscent of another age, a welcome respite from the usual modern trends of industrialized nations.

PRACTICAL CONCERNS

Political Background & Safety. Once the domain of powerful monarchs, England long ago managed a non-revolutionary conversion to democracy. Today the royal family remains highly visible and active, the result of a typical English blending of tradition with modern needs. Despite an on-going conflict over the independence of Northern Ireland, plus occasional racial difficulties, England is a very safe place to visit, the people honest and peaceful. In a country that made politeness a national characteristic, there's not much to worry about.

Travel Documents. Passports are all that's required for citizens of the United States, Canada, and Commonwealth countries. EC members need only an identification card. All others will need a visa. Passports are stamped for visits up to 6 months.

Money. Currency is the British pound, comprising 100 pence. Travelers checks and most credit cards are widely accepted. Banks are easy to find and are open Monday-Friday.

Travel Costs. England lies somewhere in the middle bracket of budget destinations. As with all northern European countries, prices are fairly steep, although still better than places such as Switzerland or Scandinavia. Camping and B&Bs both offer inexpensive accommodations. Public transportation costs can be cut by traveling with a tourist pass or on one of the many rate-reducing plans. Car rentals and fuel costs are high, as is food. Fortunately, England is filled with exciting, adventurous activities that cost almost nothing: exploring ruins, hiking footpaths, bicycling backroads, exploring villages.

Language. English is the national language, spoken with a variety of accents that can leave North Americans in a state of confusion. Nationals can usually pinpoint where someone is from just by the way he speaks.

Health. England has absolutely no health concerns. There's not even rabies. The National Health Service provides excellent facilities and care all over the country, free for visitors in an emergency. Children's medicine is also free at drugstores.

Food. English food reflects its climate, hearty and filling, the kind of thing you feel like eating on a cool, crisp day. Food shops are everywhere, even in small villages where daily shopping is a national pastime. Typically, bread is sold at the

bakery, meat at the butcher, basics at the grocer, etc. Many town have market day once a week, when prices are best for fresh produce. With plenty of farms, it's easy to buy locally grown foods. Milk is delivered daily by the milkman, even to campgrounds where you can order yours the day before. Food shopping here can be a delightful step backward in time, with people taking the time to chat and no one in a hurry. English foods to try include meat pies, any baked goods, cheddar cheese, sweetmeal biscuits (a kind of cookie), and muesli.

All the usual western foods are easy to find. For a real cultural experience the whole family will enjoy, go out for tea at a teahouse. Traditional English breakfast, served at B&Bs, includes toast, eggs, bacon, and cereal. Also fried bread and tomato, something some of you might want to skip. Pubs, a national institution, are good places to get inexpensive supper food (meat pies, sandwiches, etc.). Families with children must sit outside in the garden.

Clothes. Bringing warm clothing and rain gear is a must. Include at least one sweater, jacket, and long pants per person. Cool weather here can be like a crisp fall day in North America, not really cold, but cold enough (no wool hat or mittens necessary). Also include lightweight summer clothes, especially for visiting the south. We found ourselves wearing everything from skimpy outfits to heavy clothes, all in one brief visit. Beach wear will be needed if visiting the south coast in summer. Make sure everyone has a good pair of walking shoes or boots, equipped with hiking type soles and able to cope with wet conditions. England has so many excellent places to hike it would be a shame to miss them. Nice cotton and wool clothing can be bought in England at good prices. Try a place like Marks & Spencers, a popular, affordable department store with just about everything. Weekly town markets also sell clothing at terrific prices, a good place to stock up on children's clothing.

Laundry & Bathing. Laundromats can easily be found in numerous towns. The English have some intriguing washing machines, including ones so small they fit into a kitchen cabinet like a trash bin. Good bathing facilities are always included with any type of accommodation, sometimes bathtubs, sometimes showers, and frequently a combination of both, or a bathtub with a handheld shower attachment (children love these). Water gets heated in a variety of ways, often by a heater mounted on the wall that must be turned on before using hot water.

Baby Needs. Traveling with a baby is simple in England, although the English are not noticeably tolerant of children. Bring a child carrier to use when walking the many wonderful footpaths. A stroller is fine for walking around villages or cities, although only practical if traveling by car. Baby food, diapers, clothing, and assorted paraphernalia are available everywhere. With frequent laundry services, it's easy to use cloth diapers. Familiar foods are easy to find, so feeding fussy babies or toddlers won't be a problem.

TRANSPORTATION

Getting There. England can be easily reached by air from all over the world. Coming from North America, this is the least expensive place in

Europe to fly to, making it a good budget destination, with generally excellent fares offered year round. The two principal international airports are Gatwick and Heathrow, both located just outside London. Ferries also service the island from the Continent (France, Belgium, Holland, and Germany), Norway, and Ireland. Crossing times vary according to distance covered. Upon completion, the tunnel under the English Channel from France will allow quick transit via the car train.

Regional Travel. England has an excellent public transportation system, with buses and trains reaching all corners of the country. Rail passes are available to tourists to help cut costs. The Rail Europe Family Card (available all over Europe), for instance, has one adult pay full fare, while the other and children receive a one-third discount. Children under five ride free. Other discounts are offered on a variety of short-term travel deals, so be sure to make inquiries. Public buses are a bit cheaper, but not nearly as fun for children. You might want to try a combination of both. All public transportation is extremely well run and comfortable.

Roads. Roads vary from dual highways (called trunk roads) to single rural lanes with turnouts should two cars meet. England has some of the most enjoyable, scenic roads in the world, twisting and turning endlessly across the lovely countryside. Traffic is very light on country roads. Contrary to what you might expect, the English tend to drive with a suicidal flair at variance with their habitual controlled behavior. Don't be alarmed when you suddenly find yourself confronted with three parallel cars on a two lane road. Expanding the road to accommodate an overabundance of passing cars is common practise on country roads. Don't forget - driving is on the left, something that can get a bit confusing on a rotary (which way do we go around this circle?).

Car rentals are expensive, with prices highest at airports. If exploring backroads, hiking public footpaths, and camping in out of the way places is what you want to do, you'll probably want a car for some of your trip. Consider using public transportation for covering long distances, then perhaps renting a car for a few days or a week to really delve into an area. Better yet, travel by bicycle, a really perfect way to enjoy the freedom of a car without the other drawbacks (cost, boredom, etc.).

ACCOMMODATIONS

Campgrounds. Camping is undoubtedly the best way for families to travel in England. Not only is the price right, but children can have the freedom to run around and play. A night here or there in a B&B can always be substituted for a taste of luxury or in the event of bad weather. Campgrounds are located all over the country, from downtown London to remote sheep farms. Most are both conveniently and beautifully situated near areas of interest. Unlike the campgrounds in North America, the emphasis here in on inexpensive lodgings rather than communing with nature. Don't expect to find designated sites or spacious layouts. Privately owned, a campground here is more likely to be someone's backyard or farm field. Self-contained and privacy oriented, the English make easy camping neighbors, no matter how crowded the conditions. Facilities are usually basic: pay showers, bathrooms, running water, and often a small food canteen, but no picnic tables. Bring beach mats for sitting on the ground, or a small folding table and chairs if traveling by car (that's what the English do). The British Tourist Bureau publishes a comprehensive list of campgrounds located throughout the country.

Bed & Breakfast. These are another good option for families, although more confining for children than camping. Located in private homes, B&Bs are oriented to budget travelers. Rooms are simple, but clean, the breakfast traditional English fare (see **Food**). Most welcome children. Staying at one allows some cultural interaction with local inhabitants, although the English tend to maintain a somewhat formal air between owner and guest.

Youth & Family Hostels. Unlike many hostels, these are intended for people of all ages, including families with children. Prices are always low and facilities provided for cooking your own meals. Accommodations are comfortable, usually in bunk rooms (a family can pay for an entire room). Prepared meals are often also available, as well as a small shop with provisions. Membership in the Youth Hostel Organization is required in order to stay at any hostels.

POINTS OF INTEREST

Natural. England is filled with areas of natural interest. Some are places of wild, haunting beauty, others a peaceful blending of man and nature in rural splendor. This is a country where you can feel comfortable visiting just a small corner and still enjoy many of its natural wonders.

• *National Parks.* These operate very differently from their North American counterparts. All are almost entirely privately owned and dedicated to the preservation of each area's natural beauty. Public access is available throughout the parks, with visitors respecting the property of private owners. The result is not only a conservation of the land itself, but of the way of life that exists within each park. All national parks offer extensive hiking.

• *Coast of Cornwall.* Rocky and rugged, this is a magnificent area to explore along its coastal footpath.

- *Western Dorset.* Coastal and inland areas of unsurpassed beauty, easy to explore on foot or by bicycle. Beaches, cliffs, valleys, rolling hills, streams. Lovely and unspoiled.

- *The Broads.* An unusual eastern coastal area of marsh, rivers, and navigable waterways. Best explored by boat or bicycle, with plenty of bird-watching and small wildlife. A marked contrast to the Cornwall coast.

- *Dartmoor and Exmoor National Parks.* Both incorporate the two largest moors in southern England. Mysterious and wild, with wonderful walking opportunities. Inhabited by wild ponies.

- *Peak District National Park.* Unusual geological formations: limestone valleys and caverns, topped by vast moors. An area of dramatic beauty.

- *Cumbria National Park.* Site of the famous Lake District. England's largest park, located within one of the wildest, least populated areas of the country. Mountains and lakes combine to make a place of pronounced beauty.

- *Yorkshire Dales National Park.* Starkly beautiful northern countryside, with hills, rivers, woods, and caves.

- *North York Moors National Park.* Another area of remote, northern beauty, with barren moors and deep, fertile populated valleys.

Cultural. Areas of cultural interest are hard to miss—they're everywhere: small, picturesque villages, twisting country lanes between high hedge rows, miniature shops along a village street, a landscape dotted with family farms. Despite a high population density, England preserves a rural flavor reminiscent of bygone days, something that permeates its entire lifestyle. With its small town ambience, even the city of London seems like nothing more than a string of villages grouped together, with each inhabitant identifying with his own area. Walk around the villages along country lanes, noticing how the English like to grow things, even on the tiniest postage stamp of a front garden. Shops are still specialized, and milkmen make their daily rounds. Like the English country lane, no one seems in a hurry to get where he's going.

Try a visit to a teahouse, particularly in Devon where you can savour the local speciality, clotted cream. Children will never forget their first encounter with a cream tea, served with casual elegance in a teahouse garden filled with flowers. A pub visit is another must, with pubs a social institution throughout the country, integral to each community as a social gathering place. A far cry from American-type bars, they possess an

Old World charm. Children can play outside in the gardens that are now provided at many. Attend one of the many country fairs, festivals, or animal shows that take place year-round. A day trip to London can be a real highlight of the trip, even for families who don't like cities. With its spacious parks, double decker buses, historic sites, and attractive streets and shops, London can teach much about what makes a city livable.

Historic. With an impressive history that goes back thousands of years, England is filled with historic sites and areas of interest. It's difficult to know where to begin. Everywhere you turn seem to be crumbling abbeys and ancient castles, impressive churches and elegant manor houses, Roman remains and religious relics. Children will find England's history particularly exciting, with its heritage of knights, kings and battles.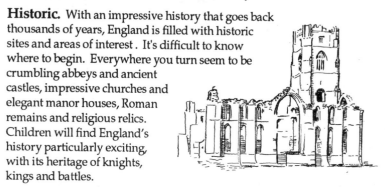

• *Tintagel.* Believed to be the remains of the castle where King Arthur was born. Impressively located on the rocky coast of southwest Cornwall. Very exciting for children.

• *Stonehenge.* 4,000-year-old religious circle of huge stones, their purpose and construction remain a mystery to this day. Guaranteed to awe the whole family with the feats of early man.

• *National Trust Properties.* Dedicated to the preservation of England's heritage, the National Trust maintains historic points of interest located all over the country. These include historic houses (many still occupied by the original families), castles, abbeys, famous gardens and parks, historic industrial sites, and archaeological ruins. Admission is always reasonable. The local tourist bureau can always point you to those in the vicinity. Many include lovely walks through neighboring grounds, often at no cost.

• *Cambridge.* An historic university town with many historic buildings of different architectural styles.

• *York.* Probably England's most renowned historic town. Includes a medieval city wall, historic buildings, a famous cathedral, and museums.

• *Hadrian's Wall.* Remains of a Roman defensive wall built along England's north border. Spectacular, isolated setting.

• *Tower of London.* Another exciting place for children, with just the kind of gory, dramatic history they invariably like. Includes guards in period dress. Also take in a visit to other historic London sites: Parliament Buildings, Whitehall, Buckingham Palace, St. Paul's Cathedral, etc.

• *Windsor Castle.* The sense of history comes alive here where present day monarchs still reside. Watch the Changing of the Guard, always exciting and much less crowded than its Buckingham Palace counterpart.

OUTDOOR ACTIVITIES

Backcountry Camping. This is possible in a number of national parks at approved campsites. Areas that specialize in backcountry camping include The Pennine Way (a 400 km hike through northern England), Northumberland National Park (along the Scottish border), Lake District National Park, and Peak National Park (including camping in "barns", converted stone farm buildings with basic amenities).

Hiking. England is definitely one of the hiking meccas of the world, with over 200,000 km of public footpaths alone. A country where walking is a national pastime, public footpaths seem to pop out around every corner. Some are long, ambitious treks, others gentle rambles linking one village to another. Local tourist bureaus can always supply you with leaflets on walks in the area.

• *Public footpaths.* Representing ancient right-of-ways, these are indicated by small public footpath signs. All pass through private property, so act accordingly (no litter, leaving farm gates open, etc.).

• *National Trails.* England has 13 of these long distance trails (or "ways"), formed by linking together a series of public footpaths in a given area. All pass through areas of lovely scenic beauty and can be walked as day trips or in their entirety. The British Tourist Authority publishes a helpful leaflet on all the Ways.

• *National Parks.* All feature extensive hiking, the ideal way to explore these varied areas of natural beauty. Some, like Yorkshire Dales and Cumbria National Parks, offer challenging climbs as well as easy walks. Park headquarters can provide leaflets on trails, including recommended circular hikes.

• *Southwest Coast Path.* One of the national trails, this encircles the southwest peninsula of England, passing through Somerset, Dorset, Devon, and Cornwall, and offering spectacular, pastoral hiking. The path can be joined at any seaside village. Easy, yet exciting, hiking.

• *The Cotswolds.* A lovely, rural area filled with gentle footpaths linking villages of unsurpassed beauty. Easy walking, even for little children, with plenty to look at. Includes the longer Cotswold Way.

• *The Yorkshire Wolds.* Excellent family walking through gentle hills and quiet villages in northwest England. Includes the national trail, Wolds Way.

Bicycling. Bicycling can be the ideal mode of transportation here, as you delve into the countryside under your own steam. The cost of bicycle travel is low, the level of enjoyment high for the whole family, and the country is filled with appropriate places to explore. Quiet country roads are plentiful, while traffic is light to non-existent in many areas. Children will love bicycling through a countryside filled with farms and animals, lovely rivers and streams, miniature villages and a country pace of life. Try day outings or longer tours, biking from village to village. Provisions are plentiful, B&Bs and Youth Hostels prolific for nightly stops, and camping spots easy to find (both in campgrounds or in farm fields - ask first, though). Bicycles can be carried on trains for covering long distances. The British Tourist Authority publishes a helpful pamphlet on cycling in England, including suggested tour routes.

• *Southwest England.* A two or three week tour could easily be planned here. Take a train into the countryside and start biking. Stick to backroads and explore some of the prettiest, most easily accessible counties in England. Terrain is gentle. Appropriate for families with small children.

• *The Broads.* Wonderful, level bicycling through England's eastern coastal region. Ideal for young children or a family pulling an infant in a trailer. A popular bicycling area.

• *The Yorkshire Wolds.* Lovely, scenic countryside, perfect for day rides or a mini-tour. Gentle, hilly terrain.

• *Cumbria and North Yorkshire.* More challenging bicycling through hilly, sparsely populated countryside. Best for experienced children.

• *Isle of Wight.* Easy touring around this lovely, rural island off the south coast.

The best season for bicycle touring is September, after the tourist crush, but while weather is still nice. This is really a wonderful country for touring, one where the culture, landscape, and lifestyle all help make the experience fun yet exciting, relaxing yet challenging.

Canal Boat. An unusual, adventurous way to explore the countryside, canal boats are available for charter along the many lovely, inland waterways. As anyone who has traveled this way knows, the exposure to an area by water is totally different, the experience a magical one. The gentle pace, ease of travel, sense of self-sufficiency, and scenic viewpoint it affords all make canal travel a wonderful way for families to adventure. Areas to cruise include the Norfolk Broads and over 4,000 km of rivers, tributaries and canals through the heart of England. Weekly charter rates are very reasonable, especially during the off-season months in spring and fall. The British Tourist Authority has information on charter operations throughout the country.

Sailing. In a country made famous by its naval prowess, it's not surprising that sailing is one of England's most popular sports. The South Coast offers the best cruising, with many small coves and harbors nestled along the shore, plus the Isle of Wight and Scilly Isles. Sailing here is for the knowledgable, due to the currents, tidal changes, boat traffic, and changeable weather. A fee is always charged for anchoring in town harbors during the summer season. Chartering is available in a number of locations in southern England. Although this type of sailing is only for those with experience, newcomers, or families with very small children, might like to try their hand at sailing in the Norfolk Broads, a lovely area with natural surroundings and completely protected sailing. Charter boats are available at reasonable cost.

Swimming. It could be said that you have to be English, or at least from a northern climate, to want to go swimming in England. There are some lovely beaches, and weather can get temptingly warm at times during the summer, particularly in the southwest. Personally, we've never been tempted enough to take the plunge, but it's best to come prepared with at least a bathing suit if you plan to visit in summer. It's practically impossible to acquire a tan in England, which tells you something about how often you might want to swim. On the other hand, time spent along the south coast with children will invariably involve some hours at the beach, even if it's just to build sandcastles and jump in the waves.

Nature Studies. Guided nature walks are possible at a number of England's national parks.

Exmoor National Park

Occupying a large portion of Somerset County in southwest England, Exmoor National Park is made for families that seek wild, adventurous places. Despite the stark picture the word "moor" conjures up, in actuality it is a place of untamed, rugged beauty, of contrasts and a people who live close to the elements of nature. Vastly different from the gentle lanes and cozy villages that typify much of the country, here the landscape seems bigger than life, with high, wind-swept moors plunging down into wooded valleys cut by rock and streams. The whole area is magical, most appreciated by those who love a sense of aloneness, of nature's supreme powers. Here, man and nature live side by side in harmony. Domestic sheep graze the hills where wild ponies roam. Scattered villages shelter in hidden valleys, their presence only guessed at from a distance. Despite its inhospitable guise, man has occupied this region since prehistoric times. It is a special place, untouched by modern trends, protected from man's destructive forces, ruled by a natural harmony. Filled with places for families to explore and enjoy, it makes a complete destination in its own right.

The best way to appreciate the area is to camp. We discovered a wonderful campground about 5 km outside Exford, located on a 500 acre working sheep farm. Like all England's national parks, land is in private hands and park boundaries are a nebulous affair. Lying deep within the park, the campground offers the ideal base, not only for its convenient location, but for its fascination for children as well. Camping is in lush, green grass beside a river, just beyond the rambling series of farm buildings. The setting is exquisite, with hills rising all around, the intense green color of the English countryside, and the sense of isolation instilled in Exmoor. Children will love the working farm atmosphere, with all the usual activities going on around you by day. Evenings are livened by the sight of sheep dogs herding home the animals with the precision of machines. Sheep shearing can be watched in certain seasons, or perhaps a litter of sheep dog puppies discovered in one of the many outbuildings. With four hikes of their own, the owners encourage guests to explore the property. An abundance of tame ducks greet campers along the stream's edge (they'll make themselves quite at home during mealtime). Swimming is possible in the deep pond beside the campground. To enjoy the place in relative quiet, visit off-season, either before or after the summer school holidays (July-August).

Exmoor is a hiking paradise, especially for families. Varying from short rambles to all day outings, there are about 600 miles of footpaths and bridleways throughout the park. The hikes are wonderful, appropriate for children of all ages. Even five and six-year-olds can easily handle any of the walks, while babies can comfortably be carried in backpacks. There's plenty of visual stimulation for children: grazing animals, wild ponies, open meadows, mysterious, moss-filled woods, rushing streams crossed by narrow footbridges, isolated cottages, and everywhere a sense of history. Set in Lorna Doone country, one of the hikes treads the area made famous by this novel. Familiarize your children with a brief version of the story (we used one of those miniature children's classics editions).

One of the joys of hiking here are the many possible circle routes, always more interesting than out and back hikes. The guidebook *Walks for Motorists in Exmoor* outlines 30 circular walks throughout the park. All are equally lovely and most within easy reach of the campground. With public transportation all but non-existent in the park, you'll need either a car or bicycles to reach the trailheads. Leaving bicycles or a parked car for the day is perfectly safe. Weather is usually cool, ideal for walking. Take rain gear (just in case) and plenty of picnic food for hungry children. As trails cross private property and are frequently nothing more than devised routes, expect to spend the occasional moment sorting out where you are. Hiking directions in the guide book are very clear. Animals frequently graze in fields you walk across, so be sure to close gates, something children love to take responsibility for. This is a magical corner of England, one that's easy to reach even on a short visit.

RESOURCE SECTION

TOURIST BUREAUS
British Tourist Authority, Thames Tower, Blacks Rd., London, England W6 9EL   Tel: (081) 846-9000.
British Tourist Authority, 40 W. 57th St., Ste. 320, New York, NY 10019-4001   Tel: (212) 581-4708.

CONSULATES
British Consulate General, 845 3rd. Ave., New York, NY 10022   Tel: (212) 745-0202.
British Consulates are also located in Boston, Chicago, Dallas, Los Angeles, San Francisco, and other major North American cities.

NATIONAL AIRLINE
British Airways, 75-20 Astoria Rd., Jackson Heights, NY 11370   Tel: (800) AIRWAYS.

SUGGESTED READING
Affordable Great Britain by A. Hoffman. Fodor Travel Publications, New York.
Off The Beaten Track: Great Britain by T. Roby. Harper Perennial, New York.
Let's Go: London by S. Blyth & M. Fischhoff. Harvard Student Agencies, St. Martin's Press.
Great Britain Walker's Guide 2, Ordinance Survey Books, England.

SUGGESTED MAPS
Great Britain & Ireland Pocket Atlas, Reise und Verkhersverlag, Scale: varies.
Great Britain Motoring Atlas, Ordinance Survey, Scale: 187,000:1
Great Briain & Ireland, Michelin Travel Publications, Scale: N/A.
The tourist board also sends a servicable travel map with their tourist package.

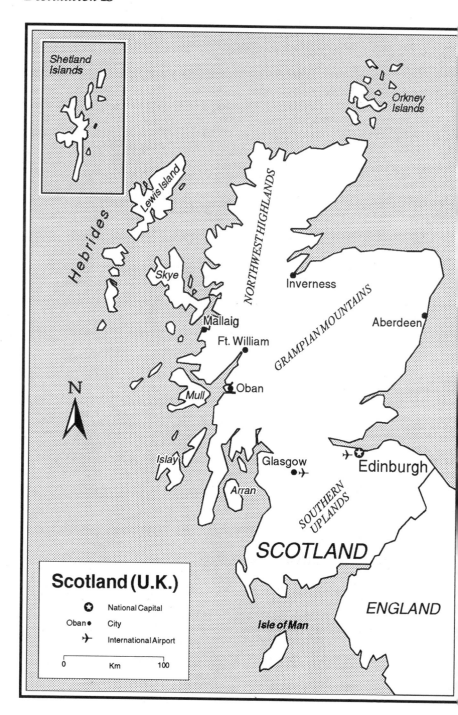

Shetland
Islands

Orkney
Islands

Lewis Island

Hebrides

NORTHWEST HIGHLANDS

Skye

Inverness

GRAMPIAN MOUNTAINS

Aberdeen

Mallaig

Ft. William

N

Mull

Oban

Islay

Glasgow

Edinburgh

Arran

SOUTHERN
UPLANDS

SCOTLAND

ENGLAND

Scotland (U.K.)

National Capital

Oban ● City

✈ International Airport

0   Km   100

Isle of Man

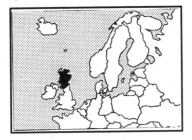

Scotland

Adjacent to England and akin to Ireland, Scotland is a world of its own, a land of rock and heather, of craggy mountains and scattered islands, of hardship and endurance. Like all remote, northern places, it exudes a sense of awe, of the force of nature and man's will to survive. The people are warm and welcoming, as isolated people always are, their soft, lilting speech offsetting the rugged, raw land. From the elegant streets of Edinburgh to the far reaches of the Highlands, this is a land where an ancient history and the harsh dictates of nature have forged a distinct culture, one that can't help but enchant you.

GENERAL DESCRIPTION

Location. Thrusting out into the North Sea with a rawboned defiance, Scotland forms the northern portion of the British Isles. To the south lies its one shared border, dividing it from the powerful presence of England. Everywhere else the country is bounded by water, its scoured, well-carved shores bearing testimony to the continual onslaught of northern waters. Despite a relatively mild climate, Scotland lies at the same latitude as the north coast of Labrador.

Terrain. Beginning in the gentle lowlands of southern Scotland, the land rises to the north, culminating in the Grampian Mountains, which boast the highest peak in Great Britain. The Highlands dominate the country, a barren, remote land possessed of its own haunting beauty. With 800 islands and a coastline that extends 6,300 miles, there are coves and inlets, rocky shores and dramatic headlands. The west coast is undoubtedly Scotland's most impressive area, a meeting place of sea and mountain, wind and waves. Throughout the country, the land is hilly and open, imparting an immense feeling of space.

Climate. There's no denying the fact that Scotland's weather is its one drawback. Weather here is extremely changable, with the west coast experiencing the most rain. The good news is that sun can also be a surprising presence, with more sunny days than many areas to the south. Given Scotland's extreme latitudinal setting, temperatures are mild, warmed by the passing Gulf Stream and the ocean waters. The climate is harsher than England, with weather usually staying cool even in summer. Winters can be cold and raw.

Culture & Lifestyle. Of Celtic origin, Scotland has experienced a near lifetime under English dominion. Despite centuries of hardship, deprivation, and cultural oppression, a strong sense of heritage has survived. Scottish people are intensely aware of their origins and differences from the rest of Great Britain. A sense of culture is most keenly felt in the Highlands and Hebredian Islands, where an Old World lifestyle prevails and Gaelic is still frequently heard. Village life predominates throughout the country, with homes clustered together in small, intimate communities surrounded by expanses of nature. Despite an overall prosperity, the pace of life remains slow, the lifestyle traditional. Even Edinburgh, the country's capitol, seems more like an overgrown town, with none of the fast pace that personifies city life. On the islands, time stands still, continuing a hard-won way of life that has survived countless generations.

PRACTICAL CONCERNS

Political Background & Safety. Once a land of ruling monarchs and powerful clans, Scotland endured a tumultuous history, including a series of bloody clan rivalries and the infamous Land Clearances. After years of English suppression, Scotland formally became part of Great Britain in the early 18th century. Today, it is a peaceful place, comfortable to travel through and little troubled by crime. Families can feel very safe visiting here.

Travel Documents. Passports are all that's required for citizens of the United States, Canada, and Commonwealth countries. EC members need only an identification card. All others will need a visa. Passports are stamped for visits up to 6 months.

Money. Currency is the British pound, comprised of 100 pence. Travelers checks and most credit cards are widely accepted. Banks are easy to find and open Monday-Friday.

Travel Costs. Scotland is a medium range budget destination for families. Like the rest of Great Britain, travel costs here are less than throughout most of northern Europe. Much of what you see and do is free. Camping offers the least expensive accommodations, followed by B&Bs and youth hostels (open to all ages). Public transportation costs are reasonable (there's no need for a rental car). Food prices are equivalent to Canada, or about half again as much as in the United States.

Language. English is the official national language. Despite decades of English rule prohibiting the use of Gaelic, Scotland's native language, it is still spoken in the western Highlands and outer islands.

Health. There are no health concerns. Do not drink out of streams passing through grazing land unless you use a water filter effective against bacteria and virus. Health clinics with excellent facilities are situated in most major towns. Medical supplies are also widespread.

Food. Scotland has very good, basic food, the kind even fussy children don't seem to object to eating. Food shopping is a pleasant, sociable affair, mostly out of small, specialized shops. There's the sweet shop, the bakery, the meat shop and grocer. Perhaps best of all is the one small village shop in very small or remote places, seemingly crammed with every imaginable food. Traditional fare includes an assortment of dried and fresh fish, meat and sausage pies, and frequent use of oats, barley, and potatoes. Scottish baked goods are particularly wholesome and filling. Try oatcakes (sold fresh in bakeries) in place of crackers. Cool weather vegetables like cabbage, carrots, potatoes and onions are easy to find, as are cheese, eggs, dairy products, baked goods, hot and cold cereals, fish and meat. Teahouses and pubs are widespread (a visit to either is an inexpensive cultural experience), as are food shops, even in small villages.

Clothes. Weather is usually mildly cool, even in summer, so bring warm clothing as well as the usual assortment of lightweight summer clothes. Include two sets of warm clothing per child (long pants, long-sleeved shirt). Also a rain jacket, some kind of windbreaker, and good walking shoes. Scotland is well known for its lovely wool clothing, both woven and handknit, so you might want to leave room in your bags for adding a few items. Our children went wild over the Scottish caps, made in traditional plaids. Regular, everyday clothing can also be easily bought at very affordable prices.

Laundry & Bathing. Laundromats are available in all good sized towns as well as at many campgrounds. Bring enough clothing to last you a week between washings. Hot water bathing is possible at hotels, B&B's, campgrounds and hostels. Like all of Great Britain, Scotland often relies on instantaneous heaters for hot water, only turned on when needed. These can frequently be seen mounted on the wall.

Baby Needs. Aside from the risk of finding yourself camping in the rain with a baby, there's not much to worry about. Baby food, both jarred and dried, is available, as are disposable diapers. Cloth diapers can easily be laundered. Bring a good baby backpack, the kind that includes room for carrying additional baby paraphernalia. This way you can comfortably explore the outer islands by ferry for overnights or longer without any need for a car (a number of islands are only serviced by passenger ferry). Include a warm hat for those cool hikes when the baby is being carried in a backpack. Babies and toddlers will find plenty of foods they like to eat. Both fresh and longlife milk are available.

Bugs. Come prepared to encounter a few no-see-um invasions, particularly if camping in the Highlands or on the islands. These are tiny stinging sand flies that appear out of nowhere, usually on still, muggy days. Wind is the best deterrent, so choose a windy campsite or picnic spot. Avon "Skin So Soft" works well against the little devils, a non-toxic bath oil that even babyies can use safely. Apply full strength.

TRANSPORTATION

Getting There. Scotland has two international airports, at Edinburgh and Glasgow, with connections all over the world. International flights are often less expensive to London, in which case you can either fly to Scotland or travel overnight by train. Daily trains from London to Scotland leave from Euston Station (to Glasgow) and King's Cross Station (to Edinburgh). It's possible to reach Scotland from England by car via three main highways, one from Carlisle, the other two from Newcastle.

Regional Travel. Scotland has an excellent public transportation system, incorporating trains, buses, and ferries. Train routes originate in Glasgow and Edinburgh, radiating out across the country right up to the far north. Small villages can be reached by bus. Traveling by public transportation in a predominantly rural country like this is always an adventure, one made easier by the fact that you can speak the language and communicate with local people. A number of ferries service the inhabited islands, including the Shetlands, Orkneys, and Hebrides, with car ferries to the larger ones and passenger ferries to all others. Service to smaller islands is less frequent, but staying a night or two on an island is always more exciting. An entire trip could be planned just around island hopping on the variety of ferries. Children will love this mode of transportation best of all (bring good backpacks or bicycles with panniers for easy travel). To reduce costs, use any one of a number of good fare reduction plans offered by the transportation system. These include passes for rail, bus, post bus and ferry travel, or a combination of all four.

Roads. Aside from a handful of highways (called trunk roads) in southern Scotland, roads are rural and two-lane affairs (or smaller). Roads through the Highlands are spectacular, imbued with a sense of nature's grandeur. Along the coast, the western shore is most impressive. Driving can be slow in bad weather, with little visibility. Traffic is sparse outside the two cities. Cars can be rented from a number of urban locations. As throughout Europe, rentals are high and gasoline (called petrol) expensive. Remember, driving is on the left.

ACCOMMODATIONS

Campgrounds. Designated campgrounds are all over Scotland, particularly in the south and coastal regions. The British Tourist Authority publishes a book on campgrounds in Scotland. Although usually located in scenic surroundings, campgrounds can be a bit of a shock to North American camping enthusiasts. During peak season, space can be at a premium in popular spots, with RVs and tents sharing close quarters. Think of it as a cultural experience as you find yourself chatting with the neighbors. Campgrounds in Scotland are regarded more as cheap holiday homes than as an opportunity to commune with nature. Cost is reasonable. This is by far the least expensive way for a family to travel. Facilities usually include hot showers, a small canteen, and bathrooms. Another option is to free camp, best when traveling by car or bicycle. Be sure to ask permission first.

Rooms. Bed & Breakfast places and country inns are the most affordable alternatives to camping. B&Bs are located in private homes, usually in simple, yet comfortable surroundings. People who run them are generally interested in guests and eager to talk. This is a good opportunity to experience a bit of the local color firsthand. Inns offer a measure of privacy and anonymity lacking in B&Bs, something you may or may not want. Bathing facilities vary from cavernous porcelain tubs to temperamental showers, adventures in themselves.

Rentals. With Scotland's capricious weather, renting can be one of the best ways to enjoy a visit to this lovely country. Pick a rural corner, perhaps a coastal Highland village or island community, and stay a while, experiencing what it's really like to live there. Contact the nearest tourist bureau, a local real estate office, or just go there and look around once you have arrived. Even short term rentals are usually available.

POINTS OF INTEREST

Natural. Scotland is filled with the
magnificent presence of nature: spectacular seascapes, cloud-studded skies,
dramatic weather, vast expanses of
wilderness land, craggy mountains,
and haunting glens. Its beauty is
unsurpassed on the British Isles, a
beauty that speaks eloquently of
nature's rugged extremes. It is almost
impossible to recommend where to
go, for all is worth seeing.

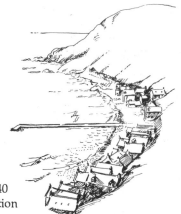

• *National Scenic Areas.* Scotland has 40
of these areas, set aside for the preservation
of the environment.

• *The Highlands.* Cutting across central Scotland from coast to coast, the
Highlands are every bit as dramatic as their reputation claims. A land of
untamed wilderness and few people, they encompass mountains and
moors, glens and lochs. A visit here is a must.

• *Hebrides.* An entire trip to Scotland could be confined to visiting a few
of these inhabited islands off the west coast. With free access permitted to
all island land, walking is an excellent way to explore. This is a true
adventure as you arrive by ferry, hike the countryside, and experience a
taste of the traditional island culture. Consider renting for a week or two.

• *West Coast.* This is one of Scotland's most spectacular areas. Off-shore
islands loom in the distance. Long finger lochs reach up into the land, a
magnificent combination of mountain and sea. Follow the train route
north, past the popular seaside towns of Oban, Fort William, and Mallaig.

Cultural. With its strong sense of culture and distinctive heritage,
Scotland has a great deal to offer, from a visit to a local teahouse to
attending a local festival.

• *Outer Hebrides.* Visit these islands to experience Scotland's greatest
traditional stronghold. Gaelic remains the principal language in this area
where the simple crofter's lifestyle still prevails.

• *Shetland & Orkney Islands.* Discover a vastly different culture on these
northern islands, isolated from the rest of Scotland and influenced by years
of Nordic invasion and settlement.

• *Festivals.* These are wonderful, authentic affairs, designed for the
pleasure of local inhabitant and tourist alike. Events range from sheep dog

trials to musical events. Located all over the country throughout the year (contact the tourist bureau for specifics), attending any one of these is worthwhile and fun. One of the most thrilling (although crowded) is the Edinburgh Tatoo, a truly amazing gathering of bagpipers and drummers performing at Edinburgh Castle.

Historic. It's hard to know where to begin in a country so steeped in history. Most towns have at least one interesting museum, if not a local castle or ruin as well. Scotland is littered with historic antiquity: castles and crumbling abbeys, royal palaces and prehistoric standing stones.

• *Edinburgh.* By all means spend a day in this small, charming city. Historic sites include Edinburgh Castle, Palace of Holyrood House, plus various historic houses and one Gothic church, all located on the city's famous Royal Mile (easy to visit on foot).

• *Castles.* This is the best of historic Scotland, something that conjures up the intense drama of its past and that never fails to excite children of all ages. Like historic pebbles cast across the land, castles are everywhere, from the strategic border castles of the south to the isolated homes of Scottish Highland lords. Once an integral part of the country's line of defense, many remain today, open to the public for a nominal fee. Conditions range from crumbling ruins to presentday residences.

• *Standing Stones.* Remnants of a prehistoric era, shrouded in mystery, these are always an impressive sight, a reminder of man's past achievements and mysterious beliefs. Among the most impressive in Great Britain are those on Lewis Island in the Outer Hebrides.

• *Skara Brae.* Remains of a Stone Age village in the Orkney Islands.

OUTDOOR ACTIVITIES

Hiking. Hiking is probably the best way to explore Scotland: along trails, down country lanes, across islands, through rural villages. There are places to walk everywhere, some along designated trails, others freelance wherever the mood strikes. The islands offer some of the best hiking for families, places that can easily be explored on foot from a central base. All island property is open to the public provided you maintain a courteous

distance from private homes. If you see a tempting footpath, feel free to take it. Weather can be unpredictable, particularly on the west coast, so hike prepared (always with rain gear - even if the sun is shining brilliantly!). Hiking in the Highlands and mountains should be done with care. Extensive wilderness hiking on your own should always be done with a good ordinance survey map and compass. Although Scotland has some of the toughest hiking in Great Britain, don't let that deter you. Hikes here are a way to explore, even if it's nothing more than a relaxed ramble across the countryside.

• *National Trails.* Scotland has four of these long distance trails, or "ways", which can be hiked as easy day outings or in their entirety. These are Southern Upland Way (runs coast to coast through southern Scotland), West Highland Way (through the western highlands), Speyside Way (through rural countryside in the north), and Fife Coastal Walk (east coast footpath).

• *National Scenic Areas.* These offer wonderful hiking in a variety of scenic settings throughout the country. Some are very remote, others easily accessible.

Bicycling. Bicycling here can be surprisingly good for families, given the hilly terrain. Country roads tend to follow valleys and lowlands, making it easier to bicycle in many cases than places like England where roads go up and down every hill along the way. The easiest bicycling is in the south Lowlands, where touring is a good possibility. Terrain is gently rolling and villages, with food and accommodations, frequent. Island hopping with bicycles is another excellent choice, one that combines perhaps the best of Scotland with an exciting mode of travel. Bicycles can be taken on ferries, then each destination can be explored extensively, covering far more territory than you could on foot. Children love to bicycle, usually preferring it to the slower activity of hiking. Island roads are rural and almost entirely free of traffic, ideal conditions for day outings. Wind and weather can be a factor, so keep the daily itinerary modest. If traveling with bicycles throughout Scotland, consider using trains for covering major distances, or escaping a bout of bad weather. Campgrounds, B&Bs, and youth hostels are all conveniently located for inexpensive, overnight stops.

Sailing. Scotland's west coast is Great Britain's finest cruising ground, one best suited to experienced sailors. Beautiful, uncrowded and remote, this is a place for sailors who like getting away from it all. Helensburgh serves as the country's main yachting center. Anchorages are prolific, the sailing protected (albeit filled with navigational challenges), and villages well supplied with provisions. Even if bad weather keeps you to a modest itinerary,the experience of sailing a magnificent corner of the coastal world like this will be unforgettable. Chartering is possible at reasonable prices. Inquire with the Scottish Tourist Authority.

Swimming. Although Scotland has some lovely, deserted beaches, swimming isn't something you'll find yourself wanting to do very much in this cool climate unless you hit a real warm spell. When visiting in summer, however, it's always worth bringing along bathing suits just in case.

Nature Studies. Excellent birdwatching is possible in both the Shetland and Orkney Islands, home to over a million seabirds. The Shetlands also offer opportunities to see otters and seals, as well as the small ponies named for the islands.

The Isle of Skye

Only a short ferry ride off the west coast lies almost another world, one that in many ways encapsulates the essence of Scotland. Wild and wind-swept, assaulted by the powerful forces of nature, dramatic in its stark beauty, the Isle of Skye provides a glimpse into the deeply-rooted culture of the Scottish Hebrides.

Volcanic in origin, the island rises from the cold Atlantic, its treeless, jagged mountains startling against a cloud-studded sky. Isolated and sparsely populated, it beckons those with a true love of nature and a spirit of adventure. Only 50 km long, its small size is deceptive. Rugged mountains, wide open, empty spaces, and expanses of treacherous bog dominate the interior, while the coast is a tortuous contest between rock and water. Travel is slow, forcing the visitor to adapt to the unhurried pace of island living. A trip here is special, particularly off-season (October-April), when island life prevails and the dictates of nature are keenly felt. Mid-winter storms can temporarily shut down the ferry service, offering you intimate exposure to the isolation of an island. Blessed with a relatively mild climate, Skye is as enjoyable in February as in July, with snow dusting the hill and mountain tops, and the scenery breathtakingly beautiful. Weather can be damp at any time of year, for Skye lies along Scotland's wettest coast, one frequently shrouded in mists. A far cry from the torrential, icy downpours than can ruin any trip, mists here are more often gentle rains, oddly appealing and rarely a disturbance to outdoor activities. Nightly refuge can always be sought in one of the many B&Bs that dot the island.

Skye's two main coasts are widely different: the eastern shore protected and comparatively cozy, the west one jagged and craggy. Arriving at Dunvegan by ferry from the mainland town of Tarbert, the first approach to Skye is a gentle one. Portree, nestled along the east coast, is the island's main tourist town, an excellent place to stock up on food and essentials. To experience a more authentic and spectacular facet of the island, continue on to the northeast and west coasts. Crossing the island can be done either via the winding coastal road, or across the interior, a barren moonscape like the far reaches of Tibet. The sense of space is enormous, far greater than its size suggests. Dominating the island is the impression of water: brooks and streams, rivers and waterfalls, ocean waves, and softly falling mists. The sound of water is everywhere, tumbling down the hillsides and across meadows, spilling across the land in its race to the sea.

Like its landscape, Skye's culture is almost mystical. Deeply religious, traditionally entrenched, hardworking, and provincially loyal, the people of Skye evince a powerful cultural integrity. Gaelic is still  frequently heard, particularly among the old people. Culturally different from the English, who's rule they have endured for centuries, the islanders combine a Scottish highland heritage with a strong island identity. Try to attend a village "ceidlh", an unforgettable music fest of local talent. The sense of history is strong and eloquently expressed, harking back to the turbulent days of clan rivalries and struggles for survival, of wresting a living from an unforgiving land. Like the music that rises from a distant past, the island and its people represent a stronghold of culture and beauty, one we can all appreciate and learn from and strive to emulate.

To fully enjoy the beauty and pace of the island, explore on foot or by bicycle. Walking can be done anywhere, for Scotland has no trespassing laws. Locals can always point you in an interesting direction: up into the hills, across sheep-dotted fields, to a black sand or pebble beach, up to a spectacular waterfall, or poking among some burned-out ruins of an ancient church. Every ruin seems to have its lurid past, stories local inhabitants are only too happy to tell you. Most commonly seen are the scattered remains of empty crofts, sad reminders of the Land Clearances that once devastated the Highlands. If heading inland to hike in the mountains, be well-prepared for a swift change in the weather, as Skye's mists are quick to descend, and losing your way can be easy.

Bicycles offer the ideal means of transport, allowing you to explore all over the island along mostly level roads. Main roads are roughly paved, adequate for bicycling with regular touring bikes. Communities lie scattered along the shore, some little more than a handful of fishermen's homes and a village school. The sense of isolation is intense in some areas, but the rewards when touring are immense. Cars are almost non-existent (particularly off-season) and accommodations plentiful, with a number of campgrounds open in summer and B&Bs in most villages. Even in winter, when places look closed up for the season, a mere knock on the door will usually produce a warm welcome. Rooms are simple and comfortable, the breakfast the usual generous fare of cold toast and fry-up. Tea is, of course, the preferred drink, served with a ceremonial flair that reduces the American teabag to the status of sacrilege. Bathing facilities are the habitual four inches of hot water in an otherwise icy tub. Hearty to the core, islanders seem to assume their guests to be as well. If not, it's best to book into one of Portree's finer establishments.

For a more intimate experience of island life, consider renting a village croft for a few weeks or longer. Finding a place is rarely difficult, with no need to book in advance. Homes are white-washed, made of stone, and attractive in their stark beauty. Scandinavian influences, remnants of long-ago Viking days, are reflected in the architecture and local names, and in the prevalence of blonde hair and blue eyes. The people live modestly and resourcefully, enjoying a cross between modern comforts and the sparse lifestyle of the Third World. Food is typically Scottish, plainly cooked and with a strong emphasis on fresh fish, soups, scones, oatcakes, puddings, bread, and an assortment of cold climate vegetables like cabbage and potatoes. Small villages often have their modest food shop in a local home. For maximum selection, try Portree.

A visit to Skye is a wonderful experience for children, offering them the freedom of the outdoors to roam and an ancient, still vital culture to explore. Like a miniature version of Scotland, Skye offers an intimate insight into the culture and people of this lovely country.

RESOURCE SECTION

TOURIST BUREAUS
Scottish Tourist Board, 23 Ravelston Terrace, Edinburgh, Scotland EH4 3EU Tel: (031) 332 2433.
British Tourist Authority, 40 W. 57th St., New York, NY 10019 Tel: (212) 581-4700.

CONSULATES
British consulates are listed under England.

NATIONAL AIRLINE
British Airways, 75-20 Astoria Rd., Jackson Heights, NY 11370 Tel: (800) AIRWAYS.

SUGGESTED READING
Cadogan Guide to Scotland by R. Miers. Globe Pequot Press, Chester, CT.
Exploring Rural Scotland by G. Summers. Passport Books, Lincolnwood, IL.
Scotland - Camping & Caravan Parks. Scottish Tourist Board, Edinburgh.

SUGGESTED MAPS
Scotland, Michelin's Great Britain Series, Michelin Maps, Scale: 400,000:1.
Scotland & N. England, Reise und Verkhersverlag, Scale: N/A.
Great Britain & Ireland Pocket Atlas, Reise und Verkhersverlag, Scale: varies.
Great Britain Motoring Atlas, Ordnance Survey, Scale: 187,000:1.

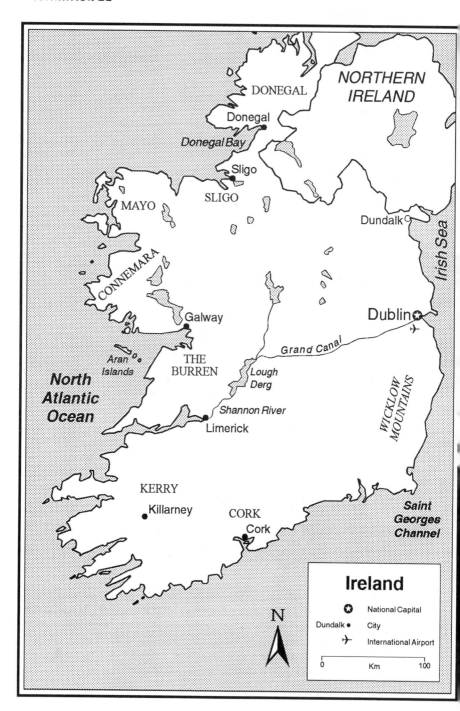

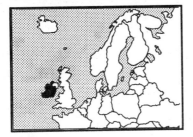

Ireland

Ireland is a country from another era, a piece of the past merged with the present. Set off in its island kingdom, deeply entrenched in a rich culture, the country exudes a mystical, elusive quality, like a jewel cast adrift on the sea. Despite a reputation for rain, Ireland is an easy place for family adventuring, by bicycle or canal boat, camping or renting a traditional cottage. Like the music that permeates their lives, the Irish are exuberant and enticing, welcoming you to their softly beautiful land.

GENERAL DESCRIPTION

Location. Ireland is situated off the west coast of Great Britain in the Atlantic Ocean. To the east is the Irish Sea, to the north its border with Northern Ireland, the only Irish territory still part of the United Kingdom.

Terrain. The terrain is breathtaking, filled with variety and a sense of nature's grandeur. Mountains and sea dominate, surrounding the central plain that lies in the island's interior. White sand beaches, rocky headlands, scattered islands, and barren mountains line the tortuous coast, an area of poignant beauty and isolation. Inland is equally unspoiled and diverse, a landscape of lakes and rivers, valleys covered with patchwork quilt fields, and always the distant mountains.

Climate. Ireland's climate is like its landscape, both gentle and rugged. Reputed for its rain, spectacular cloud effects, and lack of sunshine, the climate is nevertheless easy to cope with, due to its mildness. Rains are light, temperatures comfortable, the air warmed by the presence of the Gulf Stream. The best time to travel is spring or fall, with fewer tourists and warm weather. The one exception is southwest Ireland, where even winter makes a lovely time to visit, with mild temperatures and no tourists.

Culture & Lifestyle. Populated as long as 8,000 years ago, Ireland has experienced a number of invasions, each which left its mark on the island's culture. Two prevailing forces proved the most significant, the Celts and Catholicism. Today, Ireland is a place of music and poetry, of a convivial, exuberant people and an almost subsistence lifestyle, of modern awareness and timeless tradition. Despite centuries of habitation, the country remains a rural place, with the lowest population density in Europe due to continual emigration. Agriculture, conducted at a local level, predominates, with sheep dotting the hillsides and white-washed stone houses scattered across the land. Almost a Third World country in European guise, Ireland treads its own path, linking two worlds.

PRACTICAL CONCERNS

Political Background & Safety. Following years of turmoil and exploitation, Ireland achieved independence in 1949. Since then, the country's peace has only been marred by the ongoing dispute over the northern province of Ulster, still recognized as part of the United Kingdom. Ireland itself is a very safe, friendly place to visit.

Travel Documents. Citizens of the U.S., Canada, Australia, and most EC countries need only a passport. A few EC nationals, including the British, require only some form of identification.

Money. Currency is the Irish punt, equal to 100 pence. Money is best carried in travelers checks. Standard credit cards are also widely accepted. Banks are located in all main towns and open Monday-Friday, with a one hour midday closing. One day a week is usually reserved for a later evening closing, but this varies from place to place.

Travel Costs. Ireland is a real bargain, the ideal destination for a low-budget trip. Compared to England, for instance, prices are considerably lower. Everything about it is inexpensive: the food, accommodations (both campgrounds and B&B's), public transportation, and outdoor activities. This is one country where you'll rarely have to think about how much money you are spending, even traveling as a family.

Language. English is the official language, although Gaelic (or Irish), the traditional language, is still spoken widely in the west. Signs are frequently written in both English and Gaelic. Although most people can speak English, their preferred use of Gaelic should be treated with respect. Ireland is currently undergoing a renewed interest in the survival of their native language, with increased use in schools and everyday life.

Health. There are no significant health concerns. Water, food, and hygiene standards are all excellent, as is public health care. Both medical facilities and supplies are widespread throughout the country. Even small villages carry basic first aid supplies.

Food. Food is inexpensive, wholesome, and delicious, the kind of plain fare that children love. Lamb, fish, dairy products, potatoes, root vegetables, baked goods, and the ubiquitous brussel sprouts are all good local buys, either in food shops or restaurants. For dining out (something even budget-minded families can afford to do), there are plenty of wonderful little restaurants, with tasty, simple meals and ample servings. Try the meat pies, destined to please even fussy children. Shopping is done from small, specialized shops along the main street of each town or village. Allow plenty of time; shopkeepers will all want to talk with you.

Clothes. Bring a good cross-section of clothes, from lightweight T-shirts and shorts to something warm for brisk days. Good raingear is a definite must. Include appropriate shoes for hiking, something you're bound to do in this rural, alluring countryside. If visiting during summer, bring a bathing suit, although you can leave the sunhat at home. For fall travel, include a warm hat and gloves, especially if bicycling or boating. Even late fall, however, can be warm enough for a T-shirt and shorts when exercising. Babies in backpacks or bicycle trailers should always have warm clothing available and sufficient rain protection. Ireland produces some lovely clothing, particularly handknit items like their famous Aran sweaters. Leave room in your bags should you succumb to temptation.

Laundry & Bathing. Laundry is easy to do in laundromats, located in any sizeable town. Campgrounds often include laundry facilities as well. If staying at B&B's, getting your laundry done can be arranged with the owner. Hot water for bathing is the norm. Expect showers in campgrounds, bathtubs elsewhere. Unlimited hot water is something most families don't enjoy, so be sensitive to the fact. Water is usually heated just before bathing, sometimes at a particular time of day. Avoid using it lavishly.

Baby Needs. Children are greeted with delight is this country that loves its young, so bringing a baby will make you universally popular. Baby foods, diapers, and assorted paraphernalia are plentiful, and the local diet very appropriate for little children. Fresh milk is easy to find. Taking your baby anywhere is quite acceptable, other than the local pub, a cultural institution that remains sacrosanct from the presence of children. Bring a good child carrier for hikes or strolls around town, preferably one with an optional rain cover, such as Tough Traveler's *Stallion* or *Kid Carrier*.

TRANSPORTATION

Getting There. As an island, Ireland can only be reached by airplane or boat (other than through Northern Ireland). Ireland's international Shannon Airport is a popular first stop on transcontinental flights, with excellent fares from the United States. APEX usually offers the best fare reduction plans, so be sure to check into these. Flights to Ireland are also frequent from various European countries and Great Britain. Ferries make the crossing to Ireland from England, Wales, and France, linking with train routes at both ends.

Regional Transport. Public transportation is excellent, on trains, buses and ferries. Train service has been curtailed in recent years, but still links all major towns to Dublin. Buses reach even the furthest, most remote communities, while passenger ferries provide transport to a handful of inhabited islands off the west and south coasts. Various fare reduction plans are offered to foreigners, including the Rambler, Overlander, and Eurail Passes. Remember, though, these types of passes do encourage you to move around a lot, not necessarily the best way to travel with children. A complete, updated bus schedule is available from the Irish Tourist Board. Children under the age of 16 pay half fare. Rental cars are also widely available and fuel is expensive, as in all of Europe.

Roads. Ireland has lovely roads; lovely to look at, drive on, bicycle, or stroll along. Most wind timelessly through the countryside, providing a gateway to country rambles, to remote landscapes, to isolated communities. Irish roads, like the country itself, should not be taken in a hurry. Narrow, roughly paved, and lined with stone walls or hedge rows, most are two-lane affairs (or narrower), including main roads. With little traffic away from cities, they beckon you to explore. Driving is on the left, something that can take a bit of time to get used to (especially when it comes to shifting with that left hand).

ACCOMMODATIONS

Campgrounds. Weather aside, Ireland is really a lovely country to camp in, with over 100 official campsites and plentiful opportunities for free camping, all in scenic surroundings. This is definitely camping for the outdoor enthusiast, or hearty souls who don't mind a bit of inclement weather. Make sure you bring sufficient rain protection. A tent annex, for instance, works well, providing room to store wet clothes and gear or prepare a meal when bad weather moves in. The two biggest advantages to camping are its rock bottom price, hard to beat with a family, and the independence and outdoor focus it affords you. Campground rates are charged per tent. The Tourist Board's "Caravan and Camping Parks" carries a complete listing of approved campgrounds. You might want to combine camping with Bed & Breakfast stays, depending on the weather. Free camping is permissible provided you ask first, an ideal way to really enjoy some gorgeous, isolated nights out. Bring a water filter to ensure a safe water supply when free camping (finding a water source won't be a problem).

Bed & Breakfast. These ubiquitous, low-cost accommodations in private homes offer a nice alternative to camping. Facilities are always comfortable and the breakfast lavish. Always a meal of prime importance in Ireland, breakfast at a B&B is delicious and filling, guaranteed to get your children through a good portion of the day.

Farm Vacations. Farm vacation accommodations can range from large farmhouses to humble dwellings, all fascinating in the opportunity they afford to share the rural lifestyle. Ideally suited for children, farm vacations offer endless scope for outdoor activities, from helping with farm chores to exploring the surrounding countryside. All approved farms are listed in the Tourist Board's "Farm Holidays in Ireland".

Cottages & Rentals. A number of tourist cottages are available for rent at various locations around the country. All are modest, attractively situated, and grouped together in small clusters on the edge of a village. Although often traditional in appearance, amenities are modern. Ideal for families in this potentially damp climate, they allow independence and the ability to cook your own meals (a great money saver). Contact the Tourist Board to book early if traveling during peak summer season. Other informal rental cottages can often be found just by asking around in a community that appeals to you.

POINTS OF INTEREST

Natural. A country possessed of a wild, haunting beauty, Ireland abounds in natural points of interest. One of the last great stongholds of nature in

Europe, each region of Ireland seems as lovely as the last, luring you on to turn one more corner, to travel one more kilometer, to explore one more area. Most beautiful and dramatic are undoubtedly the western regions, although the east, south coast, and interior Lakelands all possess their own gentler appeal. With four national parks, 68 nature reserves, and 12 forest parks, Ireland has committed itself to preserving its natural treasures.

• *Dublin.* Although Ireland's largest city and capital, Dublin is an excellent example of how natural points of interest can be incorporated into urban areas, something Europeans specialize in. Within the city limits are numerous spacious parks, including the huge Phoenix Park, Zoological Gardens, Botanic Gardens, and St. Stephen's Green.

• *Killarney National Park.* A large area of forests and mountains in the heart of the Killarney lake district, with dense, luxuriant forest growth. Once a private estate, the park has been greatly expanded, with no cars permitted within the park limits. Visitors must explore on foot, by bicycle, on horseback, or in the traditional two-wheeled horse cart.

• *Glenveagh National Park.* A lovely park in the northern reaches of Ireland, with forests, moors, lakes, and mountains, including the two highest peaks in Donegal. Wildlife features the country's largest herd of red deer. Excellent hiking, guided nature walks, and visitor center with natural history display.

• *Wicklow Mountains National Park.* A fascinating area of heath and bog, located in the eastern portion of the country, with a wide variety of moorland birdlife. Excellent hiking and bird-watching.

• *The Burren Nature Reserve.* An unusual area of limestone rock formations, caves, and underground streams and lakes. Appearing barren at first glance, the reserve is filled with abundant wild flowers and plant life, fascinating for botanists.

• *Galway.* A spectacular region of western Ireland, isolated, rugged, wild, and dominated by mountains and sea. Man has had little impact on the natural beauty of this area. Off-shore lie scattered islands, among them the three inhabited Aran Islands. A hiker's paradise, all three feature abundant bird and plant life.

• *Connemara National Park.* Located in the western portion of County Galway, the park occupies much of Connemara, a region renowned for its dramatic physical beauty. Combines mountains, ocean, and lakes. Wonderful hiking.

Cultural. Ireland's traditions and culture are both tenuous and deeply entrenched, threatened and secure. Steeped in poverty, the country seeks to better itself while retaining its independence, its sense of heritage and cultural ties. While the usage of English dominates in the east, Gaelic prevails in the more isolated west, enjoying a recent resurgence of interest. Despite a number of cities and industrial areas, it is rural Ireland that seems to personify the country, exhibiting the powerful bonds of family and village that dominate daily life.

Tradition and Irish culture are most prevalent in the west, the regions that make up what's known as the Gaeltacht, or Irish-speaking area. Here, the culture is not something seen in a museum, but a matter of every day life. When visiting, try to have as little impact as possible, to treat their cultural and language differences with the respect you would any foreign country. Despite the infiltration of English influences, the traditional Irish are trying hard to survive. Take advantage of the tremendous friendliness of these people to learn about the country you are traveling through.

• *Dingle.* A Gaelic-speaking region with strong links to the past. Traditional crafts and music still play a strong part in everyday life. A *seisian*, or informal musical get together, is a common occurrence at local pubs.

• *Connemara.* The western portion of County Galway, this coastal region is proud of its commitment to the traditional culture and language.

• *Aran Islands.* Traditional and isolated, the people of the Aran Islands continue a way of life entrenched in their past. There's perhaps no better place in Ireland to experience the depth of Irish culture, particularly on the island of Inishnaan.

• *Donegal.* Ireland's northernmost county, the region is still very isolated and unchanged, based on a hardworking agricultural economy, with the people steeped in tradition and Gaelic speaking. Includes the island communities of Tory and Aranmore.

• *Folk Museums.* A number of regions have a local folk museum, depicting aspects of traditional life in the area. Children usually love these, learning much about a region and its people, as well as acquiring a respect for art, music, and crafts. Visit the Kerry Folklife Center in Killarney National Park, with its live exhibits of traditional crafts.

Historic. Historic sites abound in this island occupied for thousands of years: abbeys and churches, manor houses and castles, museums and megalithic tombs, ancient forts and standing stones. Try a bit of each to gain a real feel for Ireland's fascinating, tumultuous, diverse past.

• *Dublin.* Explore this historic town (founded by the Vikings) with the aid of the "Tourist Trails", signposted routes through the city. An accompanying map and guidebook are available through the Tourist Board. Historic points of interest include Dublin Castle and a host of museums.

• *Castles.* Castles are everywhere; irresistible, exciting, and fascinating for children and adults alike. Among the best areas for castles are Counties Clare and Limerick, with nearly 900 castles alone. Literally hundreds are in the barren area known as The Burren. A variety of well-preserved castles, manor houses, and gardens are maintained by the Irish Heritage Properties and open to the public.

• *Megalithic Tombs.* Remnants of early inhabitants who built extraordinary stone structures, these lie scattered throughout much of the country. A number are found in County Mayo, principally just outside the village of Cong, including the Giant's Grave. One of the largest groups of tombs in Europe lies outside Sligo Town in northwest Ireland, including Creevykeel, probably the best in the country.

• *Rock of Cashel.* Once the ruling seat of kings and an important religious site, this is probably the country's most impressive ruin, with buildings dating from the 11th, 12th, and 13th centuries. Situated atop the highest hill in the area, with imposing views and historic structures.

• *Grianan of Aileach.* Well-preserved remains of an ancient circular stone fort from early Christian times, built impressively on a mountain top.

• *Dun Aengus.* Remnants of a prehistoric stone fort, dramatically situated on a 200 foot cliff on the Aran island of Inishmore.

• *Lough Gur.* Reconstructed, 5,000-year-old stone age dwellings and excavated remains at one of the country's most important archaeological sites.

OUTDOOR ACTIVITIES

Hiking. As with most rural countries, Ireland offers wonderful hiking, either freelance or on designated trails. There's no better way to explore the lovely countryside than getting out and walking: along well-trodden footpaths and white sand beaches, up mountaintops with magnificent views, and along the edge of cliffs, overlooking the water. Although just about anywhere can be enjoyed on foot, the following are some of the best places to hike. Be sure to include raingear on any hike, no matter how short or how fine the weather looks, as mist is a common occurrence. A good ordnance map should also always be carried when venturing out on your own across the countryside.

• *National Parks.* All four national parks can be explored throughout on foot, offering a wide range of lovely areas, from the heath and bogland of Wicklow to the remote wilderness of Glenveagh. Hiking here ranges from freelance to self-guided nature trails.

• *Forest Parks.* A type of nature preserve, these offer scenic hiking in a variety of different settings. Many are set in what were once private estates.

• *Islands.* These make wonderful bases for day hikes, or even overnight camping expeditions. All inhabited islands can be reached by boat. The islands themselves have few, if any, cars, narrow country roads, and footpaths, all ideal for hiking. Try Cape Clear and Sherkin Island, the Aran Islands, Achill Island, and Tory and Aranmore. The Arran Island Ways combine to make a lovely, fascinating walking route across the three islands, while the Cape Walking Trail offers similar hiking on Cape Clear Island.

• *Public Ways.* Ireland has a series of long distance footpaths, called ways, offering unsurpassed hiking through a variety of landscapes. With 12 already complete, an equal number are in the works for the future. Ways can be hiked in part or as an ambitious trek through the countryside, with conveniently located villages and accommodations along the route. Freelance camping is also possible provided you seek permission from the landowner first. Easiest among the routes are those that follow canal towpaths, guaranteed to offer level walking most of the route. Kerry Way and Sli Chorcha Dhuibhne (Dingle) follow the contours of the lovely peninsulas they are based on, while others like Slieve Bloom Way and Wicklow Way climb to the top of various mountain groups.

• *Mountains.* Experienced hiking families with older children can hike any of the many mountains ranges. For an easy climb even little children can do, try Croagh Patrick, the holy mountain overlooking Westport, Clew Bay, and the west coast. Mt. Knocknarea, another easy climb, offers the reward at the summit of one of Ireland's most impressive megalithic cairns, 2,000 years old and 80 feet tall. There's a trail up Mount Brandon, the second highest peak in Ireland, as well as numerous places to hike in Macgillicuddy's Reeks and the Purple Mountains of Kerry.

Bicycling. Bicycling is a natural way to travel through Ireland, one of the best ways to experience real adventure. Children old enough to ride a ten-speed won't have any trouble, nor will parents pulling young ones in a trailer. For the most part, terrain is more moderate in the east, hillier in the west. Bicycling is most spectacular along the west coast, with narrow roads that twist and turn along the dramatic shore. Exciting day outings include circumnavigating any of the peninsulas that reach out into the sea. Try Beara, Dingle, or any other that strikes your fancy. Local tourist bureaus can always help outline good areas for you to bicycle, a popular outdoor activity throughout the country. Other wonderful touring areas include the more remote counties of Mayo and Donegal in the north, or interior regions less frequented by tourists. Here the biking is not only easy and spectacular, but the timeless quality of life seductive as you find yourselves experiencing the friendliness and generosity of rural Ireland.

If you don't want to bring your own, bicycles can easily be rented at a variety of locations, perhaps most practical for families who only want to do day outings. When touring, villages, campgrounds, and B&Bs are conveniently located for nightly stops, even in more remote corners of the country. If pulling a baby or toddler in a trailer, choose one with a rain cover. Ireland's roads are ideal for bicycling: narrow, scenic, free of traffic, and exciting. For more information on this ideal mode of travel through Ireland's rural countryside, see the sidebar for this destination.

Sailing. Ireland offers some of the best sailing in Europe. Uncrowded, surrounded by breathtaking scenery, with numerous lovely anchorages, coves, bays, and islands to discover, this is sailing for true outdoor enthusiasts, families that like the feeling of wildness. The prime cruising ground is the southwest coast, including counties Cork and Kerry, where both weather and water are warm and kindly to sailors. Cork serves as the main yachting center of the country, with marina and yacht club facilities. Heading west, things become wilder and grander, culminating in the dramatic coastline around the Dingle Peninsula. Other exciting cruising areas along the west coast include Connemara and Donegal, with the same abundant choice of places to explore and delve into.

Weather is usually warm, but come prepared for the inevitable showers and mists that frequent the west coast. Sailing is also possible on Ireland's largest freshwater lake, Lough Derg, a gorgeous inland sea surrounded by mountains with plenty of places to explore. Chartering is available in a number of coastal locations, including Cork County, Limerick, Connemara, and Dromineer, on Lough Derg.

Canal Boats. Unusual and Old World, timeless and peaceful, canal travel is an ideal way to explore the interior of this lovely, rural nation. Once used as a means of commercial transport, canal routes are now quiet navigable waterways, drifting through the pastoral countryside past tiny villages and flower-filled meadows, grazing animals and ancient abbeys. A wonderful way to travel with children of all ages, canal boats supply a home away from home as you explore. Three routes are open to boat travel: the Shannon River, River Barrow, and Grand Canal. All are linked to each other, although larger boats are used on the Shannon than the other two waterways. Weekly rental costs are surprisingly low, particularly off-season, and boats available at a number of locations along each route. Excellent times to cruise include May, June, and September.

Swimming. Contrary to popular belief, Ireland does have swimming and some lovely beaches, particularly on the southeast coast where the weather is sunniest during the summer. A number of beach resorts in Counties Wexford and Waterford cater to those who like abundant facilities, while other areas bask in lonely splendor, ideal for families who like to get away from it all. Some of the most beautiful, unspoiled beaches of all are found on the islands. Try Sherkin and the Aran Islands. Numerous inland lakes also offer opportunities for swimming.

Nature Studies. As one of wildest, most unspoiled environments remaining in Europe, Ireland has its share of opportunities for nature studies.

• *Bird-watching.* Bird-watching is excellent along west coastal areas, particularly on the islands, where thousands of seabirds nest seasonally. Ireland is also a principal wintering place for many species of northern birds.

• *Seals.* Children will love the opportunity to see abundant seals swimming along the shallows and sunning on rocks.

• *Parks.* With its strong emphasis on environmental preservation, Ireland provides plenty of opportunities to learn more about nature in its many parks and preserves. Guided walks, self-guided trails, exhibits, and nature literature are all available.

Cycling Where the Grass *is* Greener

By bicycle, Ireland is such an enchanting place to visit that no one comes home from riding there without being a firm believer in the fairies. The country seems made for it, with even the roads seemingly provided just for the benefit of bicyclers. Three hours of pedaling along a narrow lane trafficked only by sheep will leave you wondering if they even drive cars in Ireland.

Yes, there are cars, but right outside of Shannon International Airport you can find a maze of country roads that will soon have you pleasantly lost and away from motor traffic. Pick up the Cycling Ireland Map from the Tourist Board right at the airport, then choose the region you'd like to visit. There are rugged cliffs and green fields dropping into the ocean on Ireland's Atlantic coast, mystical mountains and cathedral skies in Connemara, salmon-filled lakes and streams and gentle hills in the central lake lands. Ancient monuments and ornate gardens grace the east near Dublin, while the lilt of Gaelic and traditional music and dancing prevail along the gulf stream coast. The Cycling Map outlines 23 scenic routes around the island, all easily covered within a week. The accompa-

nying description of each area will be helpful in choosing which regions to tour. Once you've selected an area, pick up the corresponding Ordinance Survey Maps, available at both the 1:25,000 "Holiday Map" scale, and the very detailed "Half-inch" scale. The latter is recommended for planning a trip along minor, rural roads.

Forget about towns you must see or reservations you must make, distances that have to be covered or schedules to keep. Ireland is a place where life moves slowly, a natural environment for bicycle travel. Pick a daily route that covers about 50 km, a relaxing pace for children as well as adults. Whether you're all riding your own bicycles or pulling children in a trailer or two, this will allow plenty of time to mingle with the locals during your inevitable morning and afternoon tea breaks, to slow down and listen to the song sung by the woman hanging her laundry, to linger to watch collies herd sheep across the patchwork fields rising up around you, or even occasionally to get lost.

Traveling the narrow, timeless roads, the country will woo you with its magic, inviting you to stop and enjoy each bend in the lane. Everywhere there are stone walls to climb, green fields to run through, ruins to explore, flowers to gather, hills to climb and people to visit. Follow signs marked "Strand", "Tra", or "Fishing", all of which lead to water, where you can picnic, linger, admire the view, or explore. The many state-owned forests also have scenic picnic places, many with signposted footpaths ready to be explored as a change from all that bicycling. Forests and points of interest are all marked on the Holiday Maps, or you can just follow your whim and discover them on your own at unexpected moments along the route.

Campgrounds and isolated fields abound where you can set up tents for nightly stops. Camping in a campground, you'll find yourselves with neighbors from all over the world; camping in a field, you'll keep company with flocks of shy, woolly sheep. If camping doesn't appeal, or you fancy something with a bit more cultural exposure, consider the Irish Tourist Board's Farmstay program, an excellent way to combine nightly accommodations with an insight into the people that inhabit the land you are bicycling through. Costs are very economical, well within the means of most budget-minded families. Besides your room and giant Irish breakfast (cereal, brown bread, marmalade, eggs, bacon, sausage, tea, coffee, juice, and sometimes scones, smoked salmon or crepes), you'll enjoy a chance to share tea with the family and explore their farm. Arrive early, leave late, or stay a couple of days and you'll experience a taste of rural farm life, from seeing how the peat that heated your water and cooked your breakfast was cut and dried, to learning how to make Rhubarb Crunch. You might have a chance to walk to school with the family's children, or attempt some notes on a penny whistle.

While camping is always a nice way to bicycle tour, the opportunity to avoid carrying all that gear and meet a new family each night along your way makes a farmstay bicycle trip a wonderful option. Instead of setting up tent and cooking dinner, you might find your children out milking the cows while you enjoy a sociable cup of tea. Irish farms are rarely full, so finding a place at whatever village you happen to be in at the end of the day is easy. Those offering bed and breakfast are always signposted. The Tourist Board also has a complete listing of farmstays, available at any tourist office. If all else fails and you find darkness falling with no place to stay, inquire at the local pub.

So what about rain, you might be thinking. Yes, it does rain in Ireland and sometimes it even rains hard, but more often the rain simply adds to the fun and excitement. When the sky lowers and you find yourselves riding in and out of the mist, with only the gentle sound of sheep on the hillsides around you, you'll wonder why you ever were enchanted with sunshine.

Pack up the children, load up your bicycles, and take a tour around Ireland. Some mountains may be tall, but since no one will be in a hurry you won't mind if you have to walk a little. On the downhill side the view will be so incredible you'll find yourselves slowing down anyway to savor the view. There will probably even be a rainbow, nature's tribute to this magical, mystical land.

RESOURCE SECTION

TOURIST BUREAUS
Tourist Information Offices, Bord Failte Eireann, Baggot St. Bridge, Dublin, Ireland Tel: (01) 765871.
Irish Tourist Board, 757 3rd. Ave., New York, NY 10017   Tel: (212) 418-0800.
Irish Tourist Board, 160 Bloor St., Ste. 934, Toronto, ON M4W 1B9, Canada   Tel: (416) 929-2777.

CONSULATES
Irish Consulate, New York, NY   Tel: (212) 319-2555.
Other consulates in Boston, Chicago, and San Francisco.

NATIONAL AIRLINE
Aer Lingus, 122 E. 42nd. St., New York, NY 10168   Tel: (212) 557-1110.

SUGGESTED READING
Real Guide: Ireland by Doran, Greenwood, & Hawkins. Prentice Hall Travel, New York.
Bicycle Tours of Great Britain & Ireland by G & K. Hendricks. Plume Book, Penguin Books, New York.
Round Ireland in Low Gear by E. Newby. Penguin group, Viking Penguin, New York.

SUGGESTED MAPS
Great Britain & Ireland Pocket Atlas, Reise & Verkhersverlag, Scale: varies.
Michelin Ireland, Michelin Maps, Scale: N/A.
Ireland East, North, South, & West (four maps), Ordnance Survey of Ireland, Scale: 1:250,000.

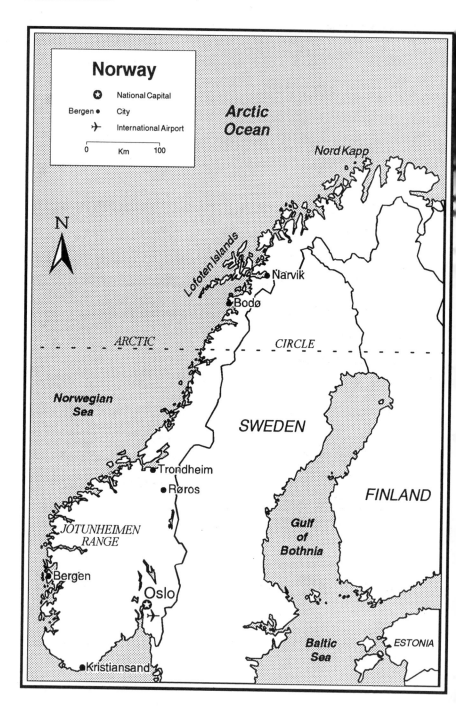

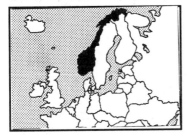

Norway

A country of unsurpassed northern beauty, populated by a people deeply committed to their heritage and passionate in their love of the land, Norway is a natural for family adventuring. The best way to explore is on foot, by sailboat, or by bicycle and ferry, delving into a rural countryside perched on the edge of spectacular

wilderness. More than almost any other country in the world, Norwegians live in harmony with their environment, seizing every opportunity to enjoy the outdoors. It is a place the rest of us can learn from, a country where adventuring is almost a way of life.

GENERAL DESCRIPTION

Location. Together with Sweden, Finland, Denmark and Iceland, Norway makes up the region called Scandinavia, situated in the extreme north of Europe. The proverbial land of the midnight sun, much of the country's northern portion is located above the Arctic Circle. To the east, Norway shares borders with Finland, Russia and predominantly Sweden. Water forms the remaining boundaries, with the Arctic Ocean to the north, the North Sea in the west, and the Skagerrak separating it from Denmark to the south.

Terrain. Norway is a country of mountains and sea, a place where the forces of nature seem to have surpassed themselves. Like a long-handled ladle dipping down from the Arctic, the country hugs the European continent, a buffer between land and sea. With 2,735 kilometers of coastline, water is a constant presence, assailing its shore, delving inland in a series of fjords, like fingers clawing at the land. Most of the country is mountainous and wooded, with little arable land, while offshore, islands lie scattered like protective armor.

Climate. Climate varies throughout the country, influenced by latitude, ocean and season. Southern coastal areas enjoy a moderate climate year round, due to the warming effects of the passing Gulf Stream. Inland and north of the Arctic Circle, winters are cold and snowy, summers hot. Rain is most common on the west coast, particularly around Bergen. North of the Arctic Circle, daylight is continuous during the summer.

Culture & Lifestyle. Once the land of the Vikings, Norway developed a culture that far outreached its modest size. Driven by dauntless seamen, Viking ships were the first to cross the Atlantic, planting the seeds of their culture along the way. Today, Norway remains deeply committed to its heritage, a fact that evidences itself in daily life. There is a sense of continuity and tradition that influences even the present-day modern lifestyle. Traditional food is served, Old World aesthetics valued , a way of life preserved. More than anything, it is a culture and lifestyle that embraces a love of the outdoors.

PRACTICAL CONCERNS

Political Background & Safety. Once the land of marauding Vikings and internal turmoil, politically allied for centuries with Sweden and Denmark, Norway finally gained independence in 1905. Having established its own king, the country is now ruled by a constitutional monarchy, with free elections. Today Norway is probably one of the safest countries in the world, politically sound and virtually crime free.

Travel Documents. Most nationals, including those from the U.S., Canada, and Australia, need only a passport for visits up to three months in all Scandinavian countries combined. EC citizens need only a national identity card. A handful of countries do require visas. Check at the nearest consulate.

Money. Local currency is the krone, equalling 100 ore. Travelers checks are widely accepted, as are standard credit cards. Banks are in all main towns and open five days a week.

Travel Costs. This is one country where you're going to have to stretch the budget a bit. There's no getting around it; cost is definitely Norway's one drawback. Fortunately, ingenuity and a sense of adventure should help you avoid some of the high cost of a visit to this exquisite country. Camping is the best way to go unless you mean to stay in one place. "Rorbu" holidays offer another unusual option for comparatively inexpensive accommodations. Food is expensive, so eat the local fare and cook your own. Public transportation can be costly, although a number of fare reduction plans are offered. Don't try to see the whole country. Everything is equally breathtaking and rewarding, so save some money by cutting down on travel time. One of the best ways to cut travel costs is to ferry hop up a part of the west coast with bicycles, relying on them for local explorations at each stop.

Language. Norway has two official versions of Norwegian, Nynorsk and Bokmal. Similar to Danish and Swedish in origin, a knowledge of any will get you by in all the countries. Use of English is widespread, particularly with the younger generations who are introduced to it very early in school. Try to pick up some Norwegian, a very easy, phonetical language. Children won't have any trouble with it.

Food. Food here is what you might expect of a northern country: filling, hearty and wholesome. The emphasis is on locally produced goods in this country where farming and fishing are heavily protected by the government. Staples include fish, meat, cheese, potatoes, baked goods, root vegetables, and whole grains. Stick to the basics and you should be able to feed the family somewhat economically. Avoid imported foods with their high prices. Seafood is one of the best buys (both dried and fresh), with Norway the leading producer of cultivated salmon. One inexpensive snack or lunch food is flatbread (a kind of cracker) with local cheese. Norwegians eat this for breakfast.

The very popular goat's cheese is the one that looks like a brown cake of soap, with an acquired taste that can take some getting used to. Norwegian school children thrive on it. For fresh fruit, keep your eye out for wild berries on hikes, walks, or bicycle rides. Children love berry picking, devouring fruit at a rate that will have you wondering why they don't do the same thing at the dinner table. Most towns have at least one food shop, usually well-stocked with all the basics. Prepackaged foods like cold cereals, cookies and crackers are plentiful, but always expensive. Figure on doubling your food bill while in Norway.

Clothes. Come prepared for every range of weather, from summer through fall. One minute you might be swimming, the next huddled around a fire. Include two lightweight and two warm outfits per person. Raingear is essential, also good walking shoes (with hiking treads). To reduce the amount of clothing you carry, choose items that can be layered: a vest for a sweater, leggings under shorts, etc. Bring a wool hat and mittens if visiting in September. Nights can be cool. Norway produces some gorgeous clothing, particularly in the color we call "Norwegian blue". Handknit sweaters and children's jackets are particularly tempting, but again, prices are usually prohibitive. If you have the extra money, they're well worth it. Basic clothing is widely available in main towns. It's best to bring what you need, however, to avoid the higher cost.

Laundry & Bathing. Laundry facilities are usually easy to find at most accommodations, including campgrounds. Laundromats are also available in large towns and cities. Bathing facilities are equally plentiful, with hot water in all types of accommodations.

Baby Needs. Norway is a clean, safe place, ideal for babies and toddlers. Baby food is easy to find, though it's more economical to manufacture your own by mashing up regular food. All the basic children foods are available: bread, crackers, eggs, cheese, oatmeal, rice, meat, fish, and yogurt. There's nothing exotic about the local cuisine, so babies should like it. Cloth diapers can easily be laundered. Disposable ones are also available. Leave the stroller at home and bring a good child backpack for ferry hopping, train rides, hiking, or whatever. If bicycling, a baby could be pulled in a trailer (get the collapsible kind for easy transit on public transportation) or ride in a baby seat. Stick to southern coastal roads or island explorations if bicycling with a baby. Include a warm hat and ample raingear.

TRANSPORTATION

Getting There. Scandinavian Airline (SAS) is the main airline servicing Norway, with daily flights to Oslo from around the world. Another popular route is by ferry from either Jutland, Denmark to Christiansand, or from Newcastle, England to Stavanger and Bergen. Norway can also be reached by train or car via Sweden, or by car ferry from Denmark.

Regional Travel. Public transportation is very well-developed, albeit expensive, on trains, buses, and ferries. Trains offer the best interior and long distance transport, while ferries service all coastal communities and cross numerous inland fjords. A number of fare reduction plans are offered,

so be sure to contact the tourist
office for particulars.
Children under the age of
four travel for free on all
public transportation
(provided they don't
take up a seat), and
for half price between
the ages of four and
fifteen. For a family,
ferry travel is probably
the most exciting and
affordable, exploring the
breathtaking coast in a series of
leisurely hops. Slower ferries cost less than high
speed hydrofoils. The Hurtigute (mail and passenger boat) continually plies
the coast between Bergen and Kirkenes, near the Russian border. Fares are
considerably lower off-season (spring and fall). The Norwegian Tourist
Board publishes a helpful pamphlet on train, bus, and ferry schedules
throughout the country.

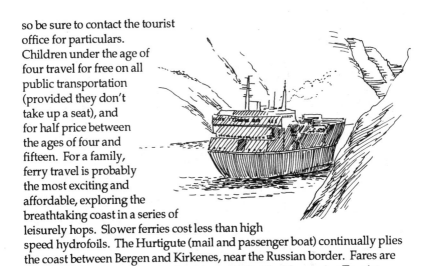

Roads. Norway's roads tend to be engineering feats through mountainous
terrain. Driving is spectacular, time-consuming, and occasionally hair-
raising. It's also expensive. The main advantage to driving is that you can
camp anywhere you like (as long as it's away from private residences). Both
car rentals and gasoline prices are high. Roads are excellent for bicycling on
short outings: few cars, endlessly scenic, and exciting. Most are narrow and
subject to the continual assault of Norway's winter weather.

ACCOMMODATIONS

Campgrounds. Camping in Norway is wonderful, a good way to
combine enjoyment of the country's lovely natural areas with beating the
high cost of accommodations. About 1400 official sites are located throughout the country, with a grading system based on the level of amenities. The
fancier the facilities, the higher the cost, although all are well within the
means of families on a budget. Amenities range from rustic to well-serviced.
Most are scenically located. To enjoy them with maximum privacy, visit
during June or September, before or after the school holiday. Fortunately,
even during peak season, people who camp in Norway are outdoor-oriented
and good neighbors, even in the close quarters you can find in crowded
campgrounds. Free camping for one night is permitted throughout the
country, away from private homes. Ask first if camping on farmland. No
open fires are allowed between April and mid-September, and campsites

must be left as found. A complete list of official campgrounds is available through the tourist bureau.

Farm Holidays. These are accommodations located on working farms, a wonderful way to enjoy a taste of rural life in Norway. Children will especially love the opportunity to participate in daily farmlife, something they're welcome to do as much as they like. Accommodations are simple, comfortable, and affordable. For information, contact Den Norske Hyttefermidling, A/S Box 3207, N-Olso 4.

Norwegian Youth and Family Hostels. Part of the International Youth Hostel Organization, the hostels in Norway have taken on a definite family focus, offering inexpensive accommodations in family-size bunk rooms. Many include prepared meals, saunas, and private baths. Cooking facilities are always available, a definite money saver for families with perpetually-hungry children. If traveling extensively, inquire about the hostel holiday passport for a reduction in costs.

Rentals. Two types of rentals are available: holiday cabins in rural settings (very popular with urban Norwegians) and rustic "rorbu", a type of fisherman's cottage on the Lofoten Islands. For a real taste of adventure try a week or two in a rorbu, an experience the whole family will never forget. Contact the tourist board for their Norsk Hytteferie brochure, listing available rentals (for more information on rorbus, see the accompanying sidebar).

POINTS OF INTEREST

Natural. All of Norway is a natural point of interest. Where you go matters little in this country where everything you see is beautiful and inspiring, unspoiled and environmentally-focused. A sense of wilderness and nature's grandeur predominates in this land of mountains and sea, deep gorges and immense waterfalls, steep-sided fjords and magical valleys. Norwegians have handled the natural gifts of their country well, fashioning man's needs to the needs of the environment. There is no hidden ugliness here, no areas to be avoided in this land where nature rules and man adapts.

• *Fjord Country.* Fjords are Norway's most famous characteristic. They pierce the west coast from Stavanger to the Arctic, a splendid melding of mountain, sea and forest. This is an area of the country that should not be missed.

• *Jotunheimen Mountains.* Norway's principal mountain range, the Jotunheimen offer the best alpine-style hiking in the country, with a system of huts extending throughout the region.

- *Lofoten Islands.* High and rocky, with tall peaks and cliffs rising from the sea, the Lofoten Islands are really pieces of a massif surrounded by water. Sparsely populated and unspoiled, they offer the ultimate escape, a stepping back in time to a world where nature dictates and man follows (see sidebar).

- *National Parks.* Norway has three types of protected park areas: national parks, protected landscapes, and nature reserves. All are lovely areas of natural beauty filled with protected wildlife, from virgin forest and wilderness peaks, to coastal fjords and tundra plateau. Here you can not only hike to your hearts content (the best way to explore any of the parks), but catch sight of herds of wild reindeer, musk-oxen, and abundant species of birds. Parks like Dovrefjell are typified by some of richest mountain flora in Europe. To discover what parks are in the area you plan to visit, contact the local tourist bureau. Some of the most accessible are Jotunheimen, Hardangervidda, Dovrefjell, Rondane, Rago, and Saltfjellet-Svartisen.

Cultural. Perhaps nothing typifies Norway's culture more than the people's love of the outdoors, something that's evidenced everywhere you look. In winter, children cross-country ski to bus stops, leaving their skis parked beside the road for the day. Summer homes lie hidden along the shores of the Oslo fjord and village life prevails on numerous small islands. Farmers continue to till the fields of tiny hill farms and urban dwellers flock to the great outdoors in their free time. Most telling of this national passion for the outdoors is the city of Oslo, where huge tracts of unspoiled land have been incorporated into the city limits themselves. Nothing seems more distinctly Norwegian than this embracing of the outdoors into everyday life. Norwegians are immensely proud of their country, not only its physical beauty but its traditional culture, its sanity in a world wracked with crime, its sense of identity. People in Norway do things the Norwegian way, gaining a sense of strength and identity from ways carried over through generations.

- *Festivals.* Norway celebrates festivals throughout the year, many of them traditions that have carried over for centuries. Summer is the principal festival time, with celebrations honoring everything from historic events to traditional music and dance. One of the most traditional is Midsummer Night, celebrated throughout the country in local fashion, with night-time bonfires.

Historic. It's not surprising that there are numerous interesting historic sites and museums in Norway, many of them dating from the early Viking period. Among the most interesting are the following five museums, all located a short ferry ride from downtown Oslo .

- *Norsk Folkemuseum (Folk Museum).* Contains many historic buildings depicting early life in Norway-period dress, craft exhibits, farmhouses, stave church, etc.

• *Vikingskiphuset (Viking Ship Museum).*
This includes a 9th century ship
excavated from the bottom of a fjord,
plus ornate jewelry and treasures
from Viking days.

• *Maritime Museum.* Covers the
nautical history of Norway from
early Viking days to the present
fishing industry.

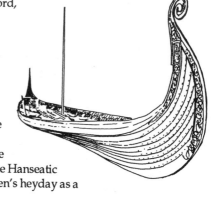

• *Bergen.* This city contains some
of the best preserved buildings
dating from Medieval times. Once
Norway's most important port, the Hanseatic
Museum portrays aspects of Bergen's heyday as a
medieval center of trade.

• *Roros.* Potentially a future World Heritage Site, this architecturally
beautiful village is one of the best preserved in the world, with a history that
extends back 350 years.

• *Norland County Museum, Trondheim.* Exhibits concerning life of the
Lapps and the Norlanders, or north country people.

OUTDOOR ACTIVITIES

Hiking. Hiking is definitely one of the best way to explore the outdoors,
with good family hikes practically everywhere. Norwegians love to hike
and have trails all over the countryside, good for day outings or longer.
Contact the nearest tourist bureau in any given area to discover what's
available. Guided hiking tours are widely available throughout the country
for families who prefer this option. Contact the Norwegian Tourist Board
for a list of tours. The following are a few of the many areas to hike, all of
which are appropriate for children.

• *Jotunheimen.* Norway's highest mountain range, these offer a system of
huts, with day hikes between each well within the capabilities of experienced hiking families. Similar to hiking in the Alps, trails are well maintained and huts staffed, thus negating the need to carry food and gear.
Membership in the Norwegian Touring Club is a must if you plan any
serious hut-to-hut hiking, to help reduce costs. Contact Den Norske
Turisforening at Stortingsgate 28, Oslo. They also carry hiking maps and a
list of mountain huts.

• *Islands.* Explore any of the many inhabited islands off the west coast on
foot, an excellent way to discover the island pace of life and physical beauty.

- *National Parks & Reserves.* Hiking is always wonderful in these areas of scenic beauty. Children should have no problem here, although some mountain areas can be quite strenuous, so keep the itinerary modest. National Parks with designated hiking trails include Hardangervidda (high plateau), Jotunheimen (highest mountain range, lakes), Dovrefjell (rugged mountains), Saltfjellet-Svartisen (mountains, valleys, glacier), Rondane (barren mountains, gorges, deep valleys), Femundsmarka (lakes, rivers, forest), and Ovre Dividal (forest, mountains, lakes, bogs). Most provide huts for overnight or longer hikes.

Bicycling. Bicycling here tends to be rigorous, due to the mountainous terrain. A tour through some areas would be enough to exhaust all but the most energetic cyclists. There are some places, however, where bicycling can be fun and not too energetic, an exciting way to explore the countryside. Easy day trips and touring are possible in southern Norway, especially along the coast and around the Oslo area. One excellent choice is to ferry hop up the west coast with bicycles, using them for day explorations and for carrying camping gear. Getting around the area would be easy this way, far easier than carrying everything in backpacks. Many islands have dirt roads, so be sure your bike tires are appropriate. Bicycles can easily (and inexpensively) be carried on ferries and provisions bought at each destination. Bicycles can also be rented in a number of tourist area and used for local explorations.

Canoeing. With so much sheltered water, Norway offers a wonderful variety of places to canoe: fjords and lakes, rivers and protected coastal waters. There's something for everyone, from novices or families with little children to experienced paddlers. Canoes can be rented at many resorts scattered around the country, as well as from a wide variety of canoe outfitters, most of which offer canoe rentals and guided trips. Some good areas to canoe include the Telemark Canal, the Lagen River, the Nordmarka lake district outside Oslo, the Tana River (some parts of which have never been canoed), and almost any of the thousands of lakes that dot the landscape.

Sailing. There are few places in the world more beautiful to sail than Norway's west coast. When the weather is good, this is heaven on earth for outdoor enthusiasts, with fjords to sail up, quiet anchorages to discover, tiny villages to explore,and interesting people to meet. The long summer hours just add to your pleasure. The wide Olso Fjord, filled with islands, makes a pleasant, sheltered cruising ground, popular with Norwegians. Despite the prevalence of sailboats, conditions are never crowded. Boats can be chartered from a variety of places along the south coast.

Swimming. Swimming in Norway is for the intrepid. Beaches are in short supply and the waters cold enough to make most people think twice.

It's still worth bringing bathing suits for summer travel. There's no shortage of places to take a dip; in lakes, rivers, fjords, and the ocean. The best beaches are along the south coast.

Nature Studies. With its abundance of wildlife, birds, and protected areas, Norway offers a number of opportunities for nature studies. Bird-watching is best in the Lofoton Islands, the site of Europe's largest bird sanctuary. Whale-watching tours operate out of northern Norway in the Arctic, offering glimpses of the sperm whale, among the world's largest. National parks and preserves offer some of best opportunities to study and learn about all aspects of Norway's natural world.

Adventure on the Lofotwall

Rising from the sea like cathedral spires fashioned from rock, the dramatic Lofoten Islands march southwest, paralleling the Norwegian coast. Lying north of the Arctic Circle, their inspiring landscape is matched by their remote environment. Isolated and harsh, rugged and inhospitable, they nevertheless support a large, stable population, a people who have successfully combined the advantages of modern times with the constancy of traditional ways. A place of jagged peaks and sheltered hamlets, abundant bird life and migrating whales, of timeless farms and a vast fishing industry, the Lofotens invite visitors to come and stay awhile, savouring the adventure of life in these remote parts.

Once the outer edge of the ice cap that covered Scandinavia, the Lofoten Islands were carved by glaciers over 10,000 years ago. With the receding of ice and water, they remained behind, testimony to the powerful natural forces that created them. Today, they rise almost like a solid wedge of rock. Frequently called the "Lofotwall", they appear like a fortress wall, guarding the mainland across the Vestfjord. Everywhere you look the land is imposing: vertical expanses of rock plunging to the sea, narrow fjords chiseled from the shore, pinnacle peaks, deceptive in their air of fragility, and lakes that are among the deepest in the world. The mountains themselves are treeless displays of rock and moss. Pockets of fertile lowlands hug the shore, once part of the seabed during the ice age, now the site of the islands' many communities.

Despite their seeming inaccessibility, the Lofotens have been inhabited for thousands of years. Once the site of Europe's most northern settlement, they achieved early prosperity during Viking times, principally due to a unique marine condition. Each winter, the

Vestfjord and surrounding waters, warmed by the presence of the Gulf Stream, become a major breeding ground for cod. The consequent fishing industry is the largest in Norway, with boats arriving from all over the country to partake in the seasonal catch. Coupled with the successful development of fish farming, this remains the economic mainstay of the islands.

One interesting side-effect of this seasonal fishing was the appearance of the ubiquitous "rorbu," a Lofoten trademark. Simple wooden structures, they were built to provide accommodation for visiting fishermen. Traditionally idle during the quiet summer months, they've now been made available to tourists at a modest cost. A stay in one is the next best thing to being an islander yourselves, allowing you to easily inhabit one of the many fishing hamlets and share in daily life. Facilities are simple but comfortable, with all the basic modern amenities. Other accommodations on the islands include various campgrounds (a total of 10), guesthouses, and an upgraded version of the rorbu, or seahouses. Larger and somewhat more modern, these usually occupy the upper story of fish houses along the wharfs.

Getting to Lofoten is surprisingly simple, given its distant setting. Coastal steamers stop daily at Stamsund and Svolvaer, arriving from Bodø on the mainland. Flying from Bodø is also possible, with airports located on the islands of Vaerøy, Røst, Verstvagøy, and Austvagøy. Inter-island ferries and public buses make local travel an easy affair, with no need for a car. Instead, consider taking bicycles, a wonderful way to explore the islands along narrow, paved roads. Cars are few and far between, the scenery breathtaking, the roads well suited to family bicycling. Most follow the low coastal land, thus avoiding any strenuous climbs through the mountains. A bicycle tour around various islands, stopping nightly at any number of small guesthouses, would be an exciting way to travel. Provisions can be bought at the many fishing hamlets along the coastal routes. Vestvagøy, with its rich farming region, offers a lovely, relaxing area to explore by bike, with easy terrain set against an impressive backdrop.

Hiking is also possible, whether along coastal roads, across fields, or up into the mountains. Work is presently underfoot to provide marked trails for hikers, helping establish safe, easy routes through some of the more difficult terrain. With no trespassing laws, Norway's countryside is always open to the public for walking. Other possible outdoor activities include sea kayaking, horseback riding and fishing. Be sure to take along simple fishing tackle for enthusiastic children so they can try their hand off the many wharfs. A small rental boat can usually be arranged while staying in a rorbu, always fun for children to explore in or fish out of.

In addition to its other natural attributes, Lofoten has a rich bird and marine life. Vaerøy and Røst, the two outermost islands to the south, both contain large bird colonies, with practically every kind of seabird sighted at one time or another. Whale-watching in the Vestfjord is also plentiful during the summer months. The Lofoten Aquarium and Museum at Kabelvåg are well worth a visit, depicting the marine environment of Loften, modern fish farming practices, and the region's historic background. Other points of interest include the museum at Å, the Vestvagøy museum with its collection of historic buildings showing island life and industry through the ages, and the hamlet of Nusfjord with its well preserved, traditional rorbus.

Despite an active, lively winter season, the islands are best visited in summer or early fall, when weather is warmest and the outdoors waiting to be enjoyed. Come prepared for a broad range in temperature, rather like a visit to any northern coastal area of Europe or the United States and Canada. Due to Lofoten's extreme latitude, days are very long in summer, with little darkness, something that's bound to have repercussions when it comes to trying to put the children to bed. The best thing is to ignore the time and revel in the extra daylight like the natives do. This is simply one of the many charms of a visit here, more hours to enjoy it in.

Even if you linger in only one village, or explore just one island, the experience will a fascinating, rewarding, exciting one, something the whole family can enjoy equally. Lying north of the Arctic Circle, yet warmed by the Gulf Stream, a breathtaking meeting of mountain and sea, inhabited by a people who value their unique island environment, the Lofotwall cannot fail to touch you with its grandeur. It represents the very essence of Norway.

RESOURCE SECTION

TOURIST BUREAUS
Norwegian Tourist Board, Havnelageret, Langkaia 1, Oslo 1, Norway.
Norwegian Tourist Board, 655 3rd. Ave., New York, NY 10017   Tel: (212) 949-2333.

CONSULATES
Royal Norwegian Consulate General, 825 3rd. Ave., 38th Fl., New York, NY 10022   Tel: (212) 421-7333.
Other Norwegian consulates are located in Houston, Los Angeles, Minneapolis, and San Francisco.

NATIONAL AIRLINE
Scandinavian Airlines System (SK), 9 Polito Ave., Lyndhurst, NJ 07071   Tel: (800) 345-9684.

SUGGESTED READING
Real Guide: Scandinavia by J. Brown & M. Sinclair. Prentice Hall Travel, New York.
Visitor's Guide to Norway by D. Philpott. MPC/Hunter, Englewood, NJ.
Insight Norway by T. Wilkie. Prentice-Hall, Englewood Cliffs, NJ.

SUGGESTED MAPS
Norway, Terrac, Scale: 1: 1,000,000.
Norway Regional Series (7 maps total), Terrac, Scale: 1:300,000 & 1:400,000.
Norway, Hallwag, Scale: 1:1,000,000.

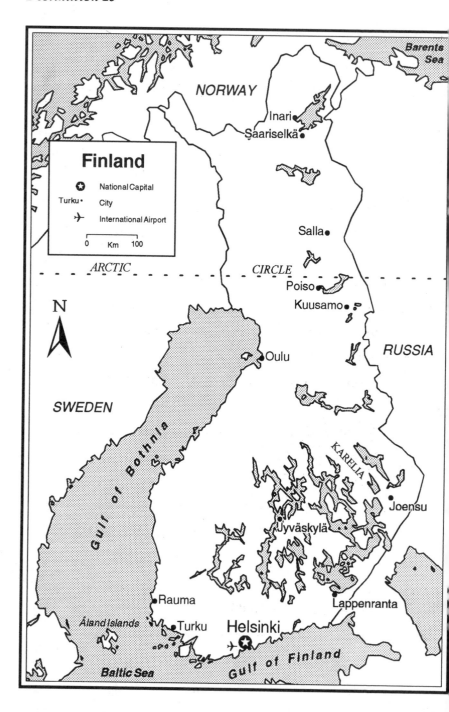

Scandinavia

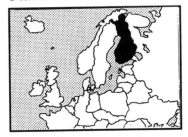

Finland

Isolated and inspiring, Finland forms a natural link between the settled fabric of Europe and the vast wilderness tracts of northern Asia. A cultured, modern country, it nevertheless seems poised on the brink of unbridled nature. As with all Scandinavians, the Finns are an outdoor loving people. Enjoying and protecting their natural environment is as integral to their culture as their language or customs. A destination for true outdoor enthusiasts, the country can be experienced a

number of adventurous ways: bicycling island and country roads, hiking wilderness trails, canoeing the vast inland waterways, sailing the intricate Baltic archipelago, or indulging in a taste of rural living.

GENERAL DESCRIPTION

Location. Finland is situated in northern Europe, comprising one of the five countries that makes up the region called Scandinavia. A quarter of the country lies north of the Arctic Circle. Its nearest neighbors are Sweden in the west, across the Gulf of Bothnia, Norway in the north, and Russia to the east. The south borders the narrow Gulf of Finland, an inlet of the Baltic Sea. In far northern Lapland lies the Three Countries Frontier, the spot where Finland, Sweden and Norway all meet.

Terrain. A land of water and forests, islands and tundra, Finland is a country of northern splendor. With an inland lake region of over 50,000 lakes, water seems to infiltrate the forested land. The coastline stretches over 4,6000 km, while to the north, the vast woods of central Finland march relentlessly towards the Arctic tundra. Off the south and west coasts, an island archipelago lies scattered across the sea, a region of rock and water, conifer forests and peaceful isolation. North of the Arctic Circle, Lapland stretches away to the horizon, its tundra and dramatic fells both fragile and compelling.

Climate. Finland experiences a temperate climate, with warm summers and very cold winters. Due to the broad longitudinal range, temperatures can vary widely between the north and south, particularly in winter. The absence or presence of sun helps determine the weather, with long hours of daylight in the summer and little or no sunlight in winter. The best time to visit is May-September.

Culture & Lifestyle. Culturally unique, the Finnish people have always seemed set apart from the rest of Scandinavia. Tall and spare, independent and loyal, they speak a complex language that few others master. Most of the country is populated by descendents of a nomadic people who once migrated across northern Europe. The Finns themselves call their land Suomi, a name that probably originated from some ancient tribal territory. A small segment of the population is Swedish in origin, principally along southern coastal regions, while the northern reaches support a sparse, intrepid group of Lapps, or Sami, as they prefer to be called. Bound to a beautiful, but harsh land and climate, the Finns have developed a culture closely allied with nature. Combining a profitable modern European economy with an appreciation for their environment, the people today seem to have struck a balance between affluence and moderation. Like all their fellow Scandinavians, the Finns have integrated a sense of physical beauty and love of the outdoors into their culture. The people themselves are warm and welcoming to visitors.

PRACTICAL CONCERNS

Political Background & Safety. Historically a pawn between Swedish and Russian expansionist forces, Finland changed hands a number of times, only emerging as an independent nation in 1917. The post-WW II years saw a policy of fence straddling, as Finland sought to politically appease it powerful communist neighbor while maintaining democratic independence. With the dissolution of the Soviet Union, the country has finally gained complete freedom in an international sense, something that's sure to manifest itself in the future. Peaceful and virtually crime-free, Finland is one of the safest countries in the world to visit.

Travel Documents. Citizens of the United States, Canada and Australia need only a passport for visits up to three months. All Scandinavian, British, and a number of EC nationals need only some form of identification.

Money. Currency is the markka, equalling 100 pennia. Both travelers checks and credit cards are widely accepted. Money can easily be exchanged at banks (open Monday - Friday), airports, railroad stations and seaports.

Travel Costs. Although hardly a bargain destination (nowhere in Scandinavia is), Finland is one of the easiest European countries for cutting costs. Both trains and buses supply widespread, inexpensive public transportation to all corners of the country. With plenty of campgrounds, hostels, B&Bs and rentals, the price of accommodations can be kept low, as can food, provided you cook your own. The outdoor and nature focus of a visit here means much of what you'll be doing will cost little or nothing. Camping, hiking, or bicycling, and cooking your own meals is the cheapest way to travel, a real budget experience with plenty of adventure and family fun.

Language. Both Finnish and Swedish are official languages, with Finnish the most widely used. Lapp is also used regionally by the Sami people of Lapland. English is taught early in the schools, so communicating, particularly with the young, will not be a problem. Many signs are also written in English to aid tourists.

Health. Finland has no health concerns. Food, water and hygiene are all excellent, as are health care services. Bring a water filter if you plan any backcountry camping or extensive hiking. This allows you to use the extensive fresh water supply as you need it.

Food. Food is what you would expect of a country in the far north: hearty and filling, with a nice ethnic twist. Children will love it. Fish, meat, potatoes, bread (dark and rye), and dairy products (cheese, yogurt, milk) form the basis of the diet, destined to keep the whole family filled at reasonable cost. For an inexpensive meal out, try meat pies, potatoes served with a meat sauce, or bread stuffed with fish or meat, all Finnish specialties. One summertime delight is berry picking, sure to excite children and play havoc with your hiking plans. More than one woodland hike will probably deteriorate into an orgy of blueberry or lingonberry picking. Carry some small containers in your daypacks so you can stock up for future occasions.

Cloudberries, an Arctic special, have an elusive quality, as distinctive as their habitat. Picking them, however, is only permitted by local inhabitants. Food is available in numerous well-stocked grocery stores and wonderful open air markets. To keep prices down, frequent the markets, an excellent source of inexpensive, locally-produced food. Despite only a fraction of arable land, the country is extraordinarily self-sufficient in food production. All the basics are readily available in any sizeable town. Fresh food in rural areas can often be bought from local farms.

Clothes. With a cool, temperate climate, Finland requires a broad range of clothing, from bathing suits to heavy sweaters. Bring a smattering of everything if traveling during summer. An early spring or fall visit will warrant the addition of a wool hat, gloves, and some kind of parka or windbreaker. On the other hand, days can also be hot, even in the Arctic, especially when exercising, so don't leave behind the shorts and T-shirts. Raingear is always imperative, as Finland is subject to frequent, short showers. If sailing, remember it's always cooler out on the water. Include a good pair of hiking shoes, something with appropriate treads (real hiking boots aren't necessary unless you plan some extensive backpacking).

Laundry & Bathing. Hot water bathing facilities come with all accommodations. How often and how much hot water you see depends on the place, where bathing can range from copious showers to frugal baths. Finland's real bonus is the ubiquitous sauna, as culturally entrenched as England's tea. Although hardly bathing in the conventional sense, it provides a similar cleansing effect when combined, in traditional Finnish style, with a dip in an adjacent lake. Saunas are usually included with accommodations, often at minimal extra cost or on a twice-a-week basis. Expect young children to find them initially hot, as they are much more sensitive to heat.

Baby Needs. Everything you might need for a baby is easy to find: food, diapers, clothing, and other paraphernalia. Definitely bring a good child carrier for endless walks, hikes, village rambles, and so on. Include one very warm outfit (hat, mittens, jacket, heavy socks) for cool weather when the baby is sitting still while everyone else is exercising. No bug protection is needed unless going to Lapland in summer, in which case you might want a pack with an optional cover, something you can drape mosquito netting over. Babies travel free on all public transportation and are welcome at all types of family-oriented accommodations.

TRANSPORTATION

Getting There. Finland has one international airport at Helsinki, with numerous direct flights from all over the world. Coming from North

America, use APEX to reduce fare costs if possible. Coming from Europe, Finland can be easily reached via car ferry from Sweden, Germany and Poland, with Sweden providing the shortest, least expensive route. Ferries from Sweden dock at both Turku and Helsinki. Trains from Stockholm, Copenhagen and Hamburg also link with ferry connections. On land, Finland can be reached by car or train via Sweden or Russia.

Regional Transport. As with all European countries, Finland has a wonderful public transportation system, serviced by trains, buses, lake steamers and ferries. Cost is reasonable, especially with one of the many fare reduction plans. Try to avoid those that encourage maximum travel in minimum time, the kind of schedule that can turn a family holiday into a traveler's nightmare. Either trains or buses reach even the most remote communities, while lake steamers serve as a major source of transport on inland waters. Ferries service all the inhabited Åland Islands off the west coast. On trains, children under the age of six travel free, and half fare from six to seventeen. Buses offer a 20% discount to families traveling long distances. To really keep costs down, consider bicycles, a popular mode of travel and well suited to the scenic, rural, often low-lying countryside. Car rentals are widely available, although fuel is very expensive.

Roads. Roads range from good paved to rural dirt, with the emphasis on good along all major routes. Don't expect dual highways, hardly a necessity in this sparsely populated country. Cars are infrequent outside urban areas and drivers considerate. Using your headlights outside of cities is required. The biggest road hazard is wildlife, something you definitely have to watch out for. Roads are excellent for bicycling.

ACCOMMODATIONS

Campgrounds. The country has numerous campgrounds, always located in lovely natural surroundings. Facilities are good, with covered cooking areas (in case the weather turns bad), bathrooms, showers, and often a small food store with the basic necessities. Saunas are also often available at a small extra cost. Many include cottages that can be rented for little more than the cost of camping, ideal for families who don't like tents or want to escape inclement weather. The Finnish Tourist Board publishes

"Finland, Camping and Youth Hostels", with a listing of all approved sites. This is a very nice, inexpensive way to travel, whether by public transport, bicycle, or in your own car. Most campgrounds close at the end of August.

Youth Hostels. Finland's youth hostels are open to all ages, often with special family rooms available. Friendly, congenial places, they offer inexpensive, comfortable accommodations, complete with cooking facilities. Surroundings are always attractive.

Cottages. These range from government-owned holiday villages to privately run cottages. Facilities can vary from the elegant and well-equipped to the sparse and simple. Most economical are the privately owned ones, with some very simple indeed. All tend to be located on or near water, often with swimming, rowing or sailing nearby. Some of the least expensive and most adventurous are those on the coast or islands in the archipelago, wonderful for families seeking the great escape into nature. Children invariably love this kind of holiday, with an emphasis on making a base rather than distance covered.

Farm Vacations. These combine outdoor adventure, rural settings, and a certain degree of independence with the added attraction of comfort and cultural interaction. How much you participate in farm activities is up to you (count on your children wanting to do everything). Arrangements can be made for just about anything: bed and breakfast, full board, or self-catering. Surroundings are lovely and rural, with water in the vicinity. The sauna experience is guaranteed, usually twice a week.

Bed & Breakfast. A recent type of accommodation to come to Finland, these are similar to B&Bs throughout other parts of Europe, with pleasant facilities in private homes. Breakfast is always abundant and the brief chance to meet local people in their homes welcoming.

POINTS OF INTEREST

Natural. With over 4000 km of coastline and an archipelago of 30,000 islands, acres of forest and the largest inland water system in Europe, Finland has more than its share of natural wonders. Choosing where to go is the biggest problem in this country graced with abundant beauty.

• *Åland Islands.* These lovely islands off the west coast are numerous and varied, enjoying some of the best weather in the country. Each island has its own flavor, from hills and fjords to cultivated fields and flat, rocky terrain. Best explored by bicycle or sailboat (or a combination of both), they offer endless beauty in a manageable size. Inter-island ferry travel is frequent, and camping facilities provided.

• *Finnish Archipelago.* A magical region of abundant islands in the Baltic Sea, with no end of places to explore. Best experienced by sailboat, discovering numerous quiet anchorages, poking among the rocky and wooded islands, enjoying unspoiled, deserted places. Weather is usually sunny and warm in summer.

• *Lake District.* An immense inland water system, with thousands of islands dotting the lakes and rivers. Hills and headlands, forest and farms, and the ever present water typify this area. Linked by rivers and canals, straits and inlets, the whole lake system becomes a wonderful area to explore by bicycle, boat, or on foot. Local tourist boards can offer information on bicycle routes, boating, hiking trails, and scenic points of interest.

• *National Parks.* Finland has 27 of these, a number that reflects the environmental commitment of this relatively small country. Scattered throughout the country, the largest parks are located in the north where the population is sparse and the land still an area of often undisturbed wilderness. Wildlife abounds, particularly in the forest region, including bears, lynx and wolves. Some national parks, like Lemmenjoki, Urho Kekkonen, Pallas-Ounas, and Pyhatunturi feature the fragile beauty of the arctic fells and forest, bogs and rivers. Bothnian Bay, the newest park to be established, offers a dramatic contrast with its island archipelago along the northwest coast, while inland Hildenportti is a true wilderness area of forest and gorge. Most of the national parks offer services in the form of an informative park headquarters, numerous marked hiking trails, and camping facilities.

• *Lapland.* The indisputable mystique of the Arctic and its intrepid people makes this an alluring place. If you have the time, go there. Its immensity and loneliness, its inhospitable guise and physical grandeur will awe you. To avoid rampant mosquitoes, visit in late August or September.

Cultural. Despite a small population, Finland has its share of cultural diversity, evident through the many regional dialects, architectures, cultural habits and celebrations.

• *Åland.* Like stepping stones across the Baltic, the Åland Islands link Finland to Sweden. Culturally and geographically set apart from the rest of the country, they form an enclave of Swedish culture in a predominantly Finnish land. A visit here is like a glimpse into another country, coupled with the unique regional qualities always inherent in island cultures.

• *Karelia.* For a long time a part of Russia, Karelia is uniquely itself. The center of the Finnish Greek Orthodox population, it possesses its own characteristic food, architecture, customs, and religion.

• *Ostrobothnis.* A fascinating, Old World coastal region, with inhabited off-shore islands, sandy beaches, fertile farmland, and picturesque fishing villages. The culture is traditional and deeply entrenched, with many inhabitants of Swedish origin.

• *Lapps (Sami)*. Perhaps Finland's most intriguing cultural group, the Laplanders' very elusiveness and rugged environment adds to their appeal. To see them, head to the far north, where a handful of tiny villages dot the immense landscape, base for what was once a nomadic people. Visit the Sami Museum in Inari to learn more about the traditional lifestyle.

• *Festivals*. With its strong music heritage, Finland has many of these, offering an enjoyable window into the traditional culture of a region or people. Festivals in summer vary from traditional village celebrations to lumberjack competitions and prestigious music events. Local tourist boards can always let you know what is happening in the area during your visit. One of the best known is the Kaustinen Folk Festival, a week-long event during July featuring traditional music and dancing.

• *Architecture*. Much of Finnish art is expressed through its distinctive architecture, both past and present. Ranging from the historic grandeur of Rauma's lovely wooden buildings, now a World Heritage Site, to the striking works of such modern architects as Alvar Aalto, Finnish architecture strives to impart a sense of the natural beauty of its surroundings.

Historic. The country is filled with historic points of interest, particularly in the south where castles, museums, preserved buildings and ancient towns proclaim Finland's long history.

• *Rauma*. A wonderful historic coastal town with a distinctive culture of its own. Renowned for its ancient seafaring and lacemaking industry, the town remains very much as it was a hundred years ago. Visit the Rauma Museum to learn more about the history of the town's two enterprises. A visit during Lace Week in July will offer opportunities to see this traditional art practiced.

• *Åland*. One of the oldest areas of habitation, Åland first reached prominence as a seafaring base during the Viking era. With remnants of Stone Age settlements, an historic museum, Old World towns, and a fascinating four-masted ship to visit, there's much of historic interest on these islands.

• *Museums*. Finland has plenty of these, depicting the histories of various towns, demonstrating traditional crafts, displaying works of famous artisans and musicians. Children, with their innate curiosity, are usually receptive to museums and historical sites if prepared properly. Discover what interests them. Traditional crafts? Try a visit to Turku's Handicraft

Museum. Sami culture? Visit the Inari Sami Museum.
Old-fashioned lifestyles? There's the Kuopio Museum,
with exhibits of turn-of-the-century local life, or
the Riuttala Farmhouse Museum in Karttula,
with its many historic buildings, animals,
and live demonstrations.

• *Castles.* These are scattered across
southern Finland, a reminder of early
defense needs, and always a hit with
children. Visit the Olavinlinna Castle of
Savonlinna, Kastelholm Castle in the
Åland Islands, or the impressive Turku
Castle in Turku.

OUTDOOR ACTIVITIES

Backcountry Camping. There are wonderful opportunities for this in
some of the parks or on long-distance hiking trails. Facilities have often
been provided in the form of simple huts, cabins, or tenting areas. Carrying a tent during peak season or on a popular hiking trail such as the
Karhunkierros is always a good idea anyway. For a real wilderness
backcountry camping experience, try backpacking in one or more of the
national parks in northern Lapland or along the UKK Trail (see sidebar).

Hiking. Finnish people love to take to the outdoors and hike, as evidenced by the abundant trails all over the country. Just about anywhere
has at least one or two good designated trails, some short and easy, others
excellent long-distance routes through undisturbed natural surroundings.
Although terrain is usually manageable and any type of walking shoe
sufficient, bring hiking boots if you plan extensive outings or backcountry
camping. Local tourist boards can point you in the direction of good hikes
in any area. Hikes along areas with water (plentiful in Finland) are always
popular with children. If hiking in Lapland, remember that tundra
vegetation is extremely fragile. Stay on designated trails to avoid unneces-
sary damage.

• *National Hiking Areas.* There are six of these around the country,
protected areas with extensive hiking potential. Information centers,
marked trails, camping and wilderness huts are all available. Surroundings include waterways, sand beaches, bog, forest, and fell. The largest
area is in central Finland, with Hossa and Kylmäluoma Hiking Areas
adjacent to each other, linked by a 30 km trail.

• *National Parks.* As always, national parks offer some of the best hiking
in the country, with extensive trail systems, backcountry camping facilities
and wilderness huts.

• *Jyväskylä.* A good base from which to hike the forests of central Finland. Hiking trails are extensive, with huts and farmhouse accommodations conveniently located on all long-distance trails. Contact the local tourist office for maps and information on designated trails.

• *Kuusamo.* A popular hiking region of forest, rivers and canyons, with many marked trails. Most popular is the 80 km Karhunkierros , passing through spectacular scenery in Oulanka National Park. The trail can be done as a whole or in part.

• *The UKK Trail.* See the accompanying sidebar to learn about this most ambitious of trails, extending the length of the country.

Bicycling. Finland is a terrific country to bicycle. Ever popular in this outdoor-oriented nation, bicycling can be done with your own bikes or utilizing one of the many bicycle rental places. Touring a region of Finland is as exciting and adventurous a way to travel as you could hope for. Roads are generally narrow, rural, and almost empty of traffic, other than around urban centers. Campgrounds, hostels, farms, B&Bs, inns and cottages are plentiful in the countryside, as are villages with provisions. With its predominantly gentle terrain, this is an excellent country for bicycling with young children, either biking on their own, or carried in a trailer or bike seat. Good places to explore include the Åland Islands, the Lake District, southern farming regions, and coastal areas. Both the Åland and Lake regions offer planned bicycle routes along untrafficked, country roads. Contact local tourist offices for more information.

Sailing. With its archipelago of lovely islands and immense inland waterway system, Finland offers plenty of scope for sailing, always an adventurous way to travel. Facilities are plentiful in this country with a seafaring heritage that extends back hundreds of years. Although the intricate navigation among the numerous rocky islands of the archipelago warrants a good knowledge of sailing, the rewards are plentiful: secluded anchorages, scenic islands of every size and shape, deserted beaches, pleasant sails, and an overwhelming sense of nature's beauty and your own self-sufficiency. The Åland Islands, once a mecca for sailing ships during the era of square riggers, now offers an appealing cruising ground for yachts. Inland, Savonlinna serves as the boating center for this vast, protected, uncrowded cruising area, ideal for families. Access between the inland lake district and Gulf of Finland is possible via the Saimaa Canal. Both coastal and lakeside communities usually offer facilities for sailboats. Chartering is possible out of Savonlinna, Nauvo, Lappeenranta, and Mariehamn, giving access to both coastal and inland waters.

Canoeing. With so much water, it's not surprising that canoeing has become a popular outdoor activity in Finland, with many areas appropriate for families, novices, and young children. The main canoeing regions are the rivers, lakes and canals of the Lake District and the more remote wilderness areas of the north country. With 1,8000 lakes, all connected by a waterway system, opportunities for lengthy outings or day trips are plentiful. Both group trips and independent travel are possible, with local tourist offices supplying information on planned routes for those who want to venture out on their own. Canoes can easily be rented locally at a reasonable price. Accommodations along the route are possible in farm-houses, wilderness huts, cabins or camping. This is a wonderful country to try your skills at family canoeing in these scenic, protected waters, paddling out on some overnights and enjoying the unique vantage point of this peaceful, gentle mode of travel.

Swimming. Despite its extreme northern latitude, Finland has some delightful swimming. Swimming is most pleasant on inland lakes where the relatively shallow water warms quickly in the summer heat. Along the coast, the southwest area enjoys the most sun and mildest temperatures, as well as a number of lovely sand beaches. The most impressive beaches are those around Ostrobothnia, complete with sand dunes. Swimming is always popular, with many accommodations located on lakes and water areas.

Nature Studies. With so much uninhabited land, Finland has a number of areas with potential for nature studies. National Park visitors centers are always a wealth of information. Note the fascinating variance in flora and fauna between the different regions, with some of the richest and most varied found in Urho Kekkonen, a national park in northern Lapland. Seabirds abound in the Eastern Gulf of Finland National Park, only accessible by boat, but well worth the trip. One of the best areas for large mammals and birds of prey is Patvinsuo National Park, predominantly an area of peat and bogs.

Hiking the UKK Trail

In a part of the world known for its hiking potential, the UKK Trail of Finland offers some of the best. Running the length of the country from the arctic border town of Nuorgam to the narrow Gulf of Finland, the trail passes through a variety of landscapes. Arctic fells, river gorges, inland lakes, deep forests, expanses of bog, and Ice Age-carved ridges all comprise portions of the route. The overwhelming feeling along most parts of the trail is one of isolation and peace, of undisturbed nature and pastoral countryside, of wilderness tracts and physical grandeur. Passed along the way are waterfalls and ancient churches, hilltop views and fascinating historic towns. Although more than 1,500 km in its entirety, a distance that takes about two months to cover exclusively on foot, the trail can easily be sampled in small segments, much of it appropriate even for even children. Unlike many long distance hikes, numerous sections of the UKK can be walked without carrying camping gear, a definite bonus with children. No matter what your level of hiking expertise, exploring a portion of this impressive national trail is well worth incorporating into any visit to Finland.

The UKK was first conceived by Urho Kalera Kekkonen, a former president of Finland for whom the trail is named. Having skied part of the route, he devised the idea of creating a single trail running the length of the country and tying together numerous scenic, historic and cultural points of interest. Although still short of completion, nearly the entire route can now be hiked along marked trails, particularly south of Salla.

Beginning in the south, the first portion travels through the densely populated southeast corner of the country, from the Gulf of Finland to Karelia. Although the route south of Lappeenranta is still incomplete, heading north a marked trail follows the shore of Lake Saimaa. Hiking is an excellent way to enjoy this popular summer tourist destination, experiencing the beauty and tranquility of the inland lake system in uncrowded, natural surroundings.

The Karelia district offers a variety of changing landscapes and easy hiking for families. One of the most spectacular portions is the 90 kilometers (about a four day hike) from Joensuu to Koli, passing through the Kolvananuuro ravine, forested hills, and fertile valleys. Kerimäki, a nearby town in North Karelia, features the world's biggest wooden church, the site of various concerts during the famous Savonlinna Opera Festival each summer. Given the time, leave the UKK to venture up some of the surrounding hills around Koli, considered some of the most spectacular hiking in Finland. All reward you with wonderful vistas across the untouched lakes and forests that comprise much of the southeast interior.

North of Koli, the route follows that skied by former president Kekkonen, covering 210 kilometers to Vuokatti. Another popular hiking district, there are numerous facilities catering to outdoors enthusiasts and many alternative trails one can explore while in the area. Hiking from Koli to Vuokatti takes about a week, although as always, covering smaller portions is equally feasible, with convenient bus connections to various entry and exit points. One of the most popular parts of the UKK, the section here includes spectacular hilltop views.

Continuing north, the trail arrives at Hyrnsalmi and the beginning of the Kainuu wilderness area. A seemingly isolated expanse of ancient land, the walk here is fascinating and intriguing, incorporating two waterfalls, one of them the largest in Finland. Arriving at Puolanka, the trail has reached the midway point and the beginning of its more rigorous half. The short distance from Puolanka to Syöte is strenuous and isolated, passing along a number of ridges and crossing various rivers. Syöte marks the beginning of the arctic fells, rolling expanses of treeless hills that represent the remnants of ancient mountains. Looping to the right, the UKK passes Posio, a well serviced winter recreation town, before entering the Riisitunturi National Park. Joining with the famous 80 kilometer Karhunkierros Trail, the route continues on to Oulanka National Park, covering some of the country's most magnificent territory. Once again, various alternative trails in the park offer a tempting diversion, among the best being the overnight trip through a magical forest to the cabin at Aihkipetsi.

From Salla north, the route is for those with real backcountry experience. Accommodations and facilities are scattered and the terrain rougher for hiking. Nor is the trail always marked. Carrying full gear becomes necessary north of Tulppio, although well-supplied cabins and huts have been provided along much of the route. While covering these northern distances exclusively on the UKK is demanding, don't overlook the wonderful hiking potential of this remote region. Various areas can easily be explored from towns along the way, including Saariselkä with its numerous trails appropriate for families. The far north is a world of its own, dominated by a tremendous sense of isolation. Passing Kultala, once the site of Finland's gold rush, the trail travels along frequently unmarked territory of fell and lake to Inari. Beyond lie expanses of heath and fell, vast peatlands and scattered lakes.

One of the nicest things about the UKK is its accessibility to facilities and accommodations along most of the route. South of Salla, there's little need to carry camping gear. Trailside huts, cabins and camping spots have been provided, while abundant nearby villages offer hotel, farm, B&B, and youth hostel accommodations. A very pleasant five to seven day outing could easily be planned along the southern portion of the route, with nightly stops at nearby farms, an exciting experience for children and the perfect antidote to a day of hiking. For those on a tighter budget, simple cabins along the trail supply nightly shelter, with water, cooking facilities, firewood, and bathrooms. In the far north where towns are few and far between, each provides a welcome measure of comfort at the end of a week or so of backcountry hiking.

Although well marked along much of its distance, the UKK should not be attempted without a good trail map. Both the 1:50,000 recreation map and the 1:30,000 ramblers map are available from the National Board of Survey. Contact the Karttakeskus Pasila, Opastinsilta 12, P.O. Box 85, 00521 Helsinki. The hiking season extends from mid-March through October in the south and June-September in Lapland. To avoid rampant mosquitoes in Lapland (and to experience the beauty of fall colors), visit the north in late August or September. Families with little hiking experience or small children should confine themselves to areas south of Salla or Syöte. Others will find all portions of the route exciting and rewarding, nor too demanding. Bring good hiking boots for the whole family, plus frame packs if taking gear for overnight camping. If not camping, young children can probably limit their load to lighter daypacks.

RESOURCE SECTION

TOURIST BUREAUS
Finnish Tourist Board, Töölönkatu 11, PB 625, SF-00101, Helsinki, Finland.
Finnish Tourist Board, 655 3rd. Ave., New York, NY 10017   Tel: (212) 370-5540.
Finnish Tourist Board, 1200 Bay St., Ste. 604, Toronto, ON M5R 2A5, Canada   Tel: (416) 964-9159.
A Finnish tourist office is also located in Los Angeles.

CONSULATES
Consulate General of Finland, 380 Madison Ave., New York, NY 10017   Tel: (212) 573-6007.
Consulate General of Finland, 1200 Bay St., Ste. 604, Toronto, ON M5R 2A5   Tel: (416) 964-0066.

NATIONAL AIRLINE
Scandinavian Airlines, 9 Polito Ave., Lyndhurst, NJ 07071   Tel: (800) 345-9684.

SUGGESTED READING
Real Guide: Scandinavia by J. Brown & M. Sinclair. Prentice Hall Travel, New York.

SUGGESTED MAPS
Finland, Hallwag, Scale: 1:1,000.000.
Finland, Terrac, Scale: 1:1,000,000.
Finland, Terra Regional Series (6 maps total), Scale: 1:300,000.

UNITED
KINGDOM

GERMANY

BELGIUM

*English
Channel*

LUX

LORRAINE

Le Havre
Rouen

Strasbourg

Paris

Versailles

ALSACE

Chartres

BRITTANY

Orléans

BURGUNDY

SWITZERLAND

Nantes

Loire River

POITOU

Lyon

*Mont Blanc
4807M*

Grenoble

ITALY

*Bay of
Biscay*

Bordeaux

Rhône River

ALPS

MASSIF
CENTRAL

Nice

AQUITAINE

GASCONY

Marseille

Gulf of Lions

SPAIN

Corsica

France

Grenoble •   National Capital

City

International Airport

0   Km   200

N

Continental Europe

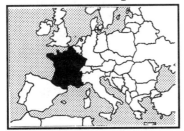

France

A country of immense diversity and natural beauty within a workable size, France is a natural destination for adventuring families. No matter what your inclination or level of experience, there's something for everyone. Perhaps a bicycle tour through the châteaux-filled Loire Valley, or coastal exploration along the isolated Brittany coast. There's hiking in the Alps along a well-groomed network of trails and travel by water along the ancient system of canals. Renting a cottage offers a firsthand opportunity to experience life in rural France, challenging without being overwhelming. For newcomers to adventure travel, France provides a comfortable introduction to a foreign culture, one filled with scenic beauty and outdoor opportunities, with a wealth of historic areas and a distinctive heritage. Experienced families will find it a welcome respite from more rigorous destinations, although still adventurous in its own right.

GENERAL DESCRIPTION

Location. One of the largest countries in Western Europe, France is bordered by water on three sides: the Atlantic, the English Channel, and the Mediterranean. To the east, France shares borders with Belgium, Luxembourg, Germany, Switzerland and Italy, while to the southwest lie Spain and Andorra.

Terrain. Despite a relatively compact size, the country has a wide range of terrain, each with its own scenic appeal. Much of France is countryside, some of it flat and spacious, some deeply carved with valleys and gorges. Mountains rise along the eastern and southwestern borders, the massive Alps and the craggy, pinnacles of the Pyrenees, while in the center looms the Massif Central. Rivers ramble through the countryside and towns, carving patterns in the landscape. With nearly 3000 km of coastline, a sense of the sea is often felt, from the popular white sand beaches of the Mediterranean to the rocky, hazardous shores of Brittany.

Climate. Most of France experiences a temperate climate, although weather varies widely between the south and north during winter. Eastern mountain areas have cold winters with plenty of snow, while just to the south, the Mediterranean coast stays considerably milder except when the notorious mistral blows, bringing stormy weather. Brittany enjoys some of the country's mildest weather due to its close proximity to the Gulf Stream. Summers are hot throughout the country. The best time to travel is spring and fall, both of which are lovely and mild, with few tourists and no summer crowds.

Culture & Lifestyle. France is intensely French. This may sound strange, but there's no better way to describe it. Since time immemorial, the French have been fiercely proud of their culture, resulting in a cultural heritage that is very much a part of everyday life. So many things typify the French culture and lifestyle: their language and social code, their fantastic cuisine and distinctive national temperament, the flowers spilling out of every nook and cranny, and people passing the time of day in sunny, congenial cafes.

Traditionally viewed as inflexible and possessed of a cultural snobbism that was off-putting to foreigners, recent years and a new generation have seen the emergence of a deeper friendliness to outsiders. In the end, however, it is this total disregard for compromise that reflects their deep sense of cultural commitment. When traveling to France, it's best to do things the French way. Learn some phrases if you can't already speak the language. Brush up on the accepted code of behavior: how to shake hands the French way (one shake - no more), when to kiss (which cheek and how many times), how to address strangers (always Monsieur, Madame, etc., even in shops). Simple things like this not only make a visit go more smoothly, but also offer an added insight into the French way of life.

PRACTICAL CONCERNS

Political Update & Safety. Once the home of Europe's most wealthy, decadent monarchy and aristocracy, France has been a republic on and off since the Napoleonic era in the early 1800s. Always active in world politics, the country has traditionally shown the same disregard for international opinion that it does in everyday life. Despite some tempestuous moments in its past, France is a very safe country to visit, with little crime and no political violence.

Travel Documents. Canadian, U.S., and Australian citizens all need a passport to visit France, issued a three-month visitors visa upon entry. Most EC nationals need only a valid identification card, including all countries neighboring France. Visas are required for most nations outside Europe and North America.

Money. Currency is the French Franc, worth 100 centimes. Travelers checks are widely accepted, although rates vary between different banks and when changing money at hotels. Ask the rate first before committing yourself. Standard credit cards can also be widely used. Banks are in all major towns and open five days a week (some close on Saturday, others on Monday). Closing at lunchtime for an hour or two is also common.

Travel Costs. Travel here is typical of Europe: expensive, but not too expensive. Budget travelers will have to be somewhat money conscious, reducing costs by camping, riding public transportation, doing their own cooking, etc. Food prices in shops and markets are reasonable, as are campgrounds and pensions (sometimes with meals) in country farmhouses. Public transportation offers a huge variety of cost cutting options on trains. Both Paris and the south coast are extremely expensive compared to other areas of the country. For a low-cost trip, try bicycling or renting a cottage. Canal boats aren't inexpensive, but the additional cost is well worth it for this wonderful experience.

Language. French is the national language, spoken with a variety of regional variations. If you don't know any, start learning. Some English is spoken in tourist areas, but the French definitely prefer to use their own language and are noticeably receptive to those who make the effort to speak it. Both Breton and Basque are spoken regionally, in Brittany and Gascony.

Health. There are no health hazards or need for immunizations. Food and water are both good, although some newcomers to travel can experience minor gastronomic complaints at first. Health services are widespread and excellent, although expensive for non-residents.

Food. France is famous for its food and considered the culinary capitol of the world. Not only is the food wonderfully varied and creative, but the French take eating very seriously. Shops and businesses frequently close during the traditional two-hour lunch break as owners retire to enjoy their midday meal, an occasion no one would dream of rushing. An American family can order, eat an entire dinner, pay and depart in the time it takes a French couple to enjoy their after-dinner coffee.

Food shopping is a pleasant, sociable experience, with housewives taking their time and no one in a hurry. Typically, different food groups are sold in different shops: the bakery, pastry shop, the cheese shop, the butcher, etc. Although most shops are small, a growing chain of Supermarches has infiltrated some urban areas. Built somewhat like American-style malls and located on the edge of town, they comprise an entire range of food shops, all under one roof like a mini-village. Local foods include delicious, freshly baked bread, a wide variety of fruits and vegetables, excellent cheese, wine (watered when served to children), meat, and seafood.

Finding foods to keep your children happy is easy and affordable. Produce is locally grown and of excellent quality, usually sold at open-air markets. Feel free to carefully examine produce before purchasing. French house-wives do this liberally and expressively. Restaurants and cafes abound, both irresistible and well worth the occasional splurge. Prices are usually posted outside. Cafe sitting is a national pastime, one parents can happily enjoy as children play nearby.

Clothes. Take whatever clothing you would be wearing at home for any particular season, bearing in mind that spring comes earlier and summer lingers longer in France than North America or northern Europe. If hiking in the Alps, bring some warmer clothing just in case. Raingear is a must, as are bathing suits. Locally-made clothes are easy to find, in case you forget or lose something.

Laundry & Bathing. Neither of these is a major concern. Pensions, hotels, and campgrounds all have bathing facilities and often some way to get clothes clean (a wash basin, set tubs, or local laundry service). Hot showers are the norm, sometimes at extra cost.

Baby Needs. By all means go to France with a toddler or baby, a lovely, relaxed place to introduce your infant to foreign travel. The presence of a baby will open doors to you, particularly in the south and out in the countryside. Bring a good child backpack, but don't worry about much else. France sells everything needed for babies: food, diapers, clothing (very nice and stylish), extras. Babies ride for free on all public transportation. Diapers are easy to launder, even at campgrounds (by hand). This is an easy place to travel with a baby on public transportation, by backpack, bicycle, or boat.

TRANSPORTATION

Getting There. France has two major international airports, Orly and Charles de Gaulle, both located just outside Paris. Frequent overseas flights from all over the world use one or the other. Ferries make the crossing from England to a number of ports along the north coast, the quickest passage being Dover to Calais. Getting to France by train or car from neighboring European countries is easy, with frequent rail service (to and from Paris), and excellent roads. Train service is also possible from England, linking with an appropriate ferry until future completion of the channel tunnel.

Regional Travel. France has probably the most sophisticated public transportation system in the world. To the foreign-speaking outsider, the whole thing can seem incredibly confusing at first, leaving you dashing for a rental car. Don't; with its reasonable prices, extensive service, and precision performance, public transportation in France is well worth the effort of sorting out. Train service is extensive and includes the TVG, the fastest train in the world. All kinds of fare-reduction plans are offered, some only sold outside the country to benefit tourists. Within France, there are special fare reductions for families, young people, or travel on certain days of the week. Other plans include discounts on things like car and bicycle rentals and travel on the Paris metro. Contact the tourist bureau or inquire at ticket offices. Where trains don't go, buses service regularly.

Roads. France has all types of roads, from highways (autoroutes) to country lanes. Long-distance travel on highways is fast except during peak season (July-August) when traffic in the south coastal region can be formidable. Avoid this at all costs. Lovely country roads permeate the countryside, ideal for relaxed exploration by car, or better yet, bicycle. Traffic is light away from the south coast and urban areas, villages frequent, and the landscape scenic.

ACCOMMODATIONS

Campgrounds. There are thousands of campgrounds throughout the country, making this an easy and affordable means of accommodation for families. Like all European campgrounds, facilities are usually well developed and privacy minimal. Expect plenty of company during peak summer months. Off-season, in spring and fall, campgrounds can be almost empty, a lovely time to enjoy them. All provide potable water and bathing facilities. Don't expect picnic tables, a luxury that North Americans take for granted. Bring beach mats for the ground (one per person) or a folding table and chairs if traveling by car. One unusual camping option is offered by France's Guest Farm Organization, whereby you camp (with facilities) on a local working farm. A natural setting for children, this combines the freedom, outdoor orientation, and low-cost of camping with the pleasures of a farm vacation stay.

Pensions & Chambre D'Hôte. Pensions or rooms in a private home are very easy to find. Few villages are without accommodations of any type. Some come with various meals included, an entertaining occasion in private homes that can involve sharing the meal with the whole French family. While pensions are run like small hotels, chambre d'hôte are the equivalent to a Bed & Breakfast. Both offer an affordable option for families.

Gîtes D'Étape. Simple, affordable, and run similar to hostels, gîtes d'étape offer basic accommodations in private rooms or dormitories, with cooking facilities included. Particular emphasis is on providing nightly stops for hikers, bicyclers, and horseback riders, making this a fun, interesting way to meet fellow outdoor enthusiasts.

Rentals. With young children, renting a place in the countryside is a wonderful way to enjoy a visit to France without the normal rigors of travel. Prices are highest during peak tourist season, and prohibitive in the extreme south. Instead, try the north or west coast, or just some lovely corner of the country that strikes your fancy. The pace of life is slow here, ideal for families with children . Contact the Tourist Office to find out about the Gîte de France, cottages and apartments in country settings, available for tourists to rent seasonally. Another option is to just pick a spot and go there. Something always seems to turn up when asking around for a rental.

POINTS OF INTEREST

Natural. Almost everywhere in France seems to possess the same element of natural beauty, making it hard to choose where to go. The following are a handful of the many areas of interest.

• *Brittany.* The coast forms much of the character of this region in the northwest corner of the country. Bordered by water on three sides, typified by a rocky, rugged shore, the area also offers a surprising number of lovely beaches. One of France's least populated regions, the prevalent feeling here is still one of wildness, of a raw and untamed environment. The tides are extreme (up to 50 feet), the currents treacherous, the land rugged, the climate unpredictable. Inland lie low hills, remnants of the Earth's oldest mountain range.

• *Alsace.* A lovely area of eastern France along the border with Germany, Alsace is filled with river valleys and fruit orchards, pine forested hills and inland waterways. An excellent region to explore by bicycle, canal boat, or on foot along numerous trails.

• *Provence.* Southern France's most popular region, this area is a delight to visit, particularly in fall or spring. A region of hills and cozy valleys, a hint of the Mediterranean Sea and the Alps rising behind. Nature here is at its most comfortable, with blue skies (except when the notorious mistral blows) and pastoral landscapes. To enjoy Provence at its wildest, visit the Massif des Ecrins National Park, a mecca for hikers and those who like remote areas.

• *National & Regional Parks.* With seven national parks, 27 regional ones, and 100 sanctuaries, France has done much to preserve and protect its natural wonders. Visiting any is a fascinating, educational experience for families, as well as an opportunity to enjoy an unexploited environment. While national parks protect wilderness areas, regional natural parks demonstrate an environmentally-sound balance between man's presence and the equally valid needs of nature. Sanctuaries are specifically selected to preserve the natural habitats of animal, bird, and plant life.

Cultural. Just about everywhere you look is something of cultural interest. The language and lifestyle, the local cuisine and architecture, the sense of history and social norms. Get away from the tour groups and tourist spots, the rental car and crowded beaches to experience the real France.

• *Brittany.* Of Celtic origin, ties with the past are strong here, a cultural identity that sets this region apart from the rest of France. The Breton language, traditional dress, unusual architecture, and social customs all are markedly different, with closer ties to Cornwall in southern England than elsewhere.

• *Alsace & Lorraine.* Bordering Germany, this region has frequently changed nationality between the two countries in the past, a fact that has affected its cultural development. Architecturally reminiscent of Germany, a visit here is like straddling two cultures.

• *Food.* There's no question that food is, in essence, a cultural experience. In a country that has elevated eating and cooking to a fine art, the cultural importance of food in France should not be overlooked. Where else could you drive numerous, rigorous backroads out into a remote corner of the countryside, arrive at an ancient, rustic farmhouse, and find yourselves at a five star restaurant, with all the tables previously booked? The French cook and dine as they do everything - with immense and lingering pleasure.

Historic. France is rich in historic points of interest. Castles and walled cities, ancient aquaducts and ornate châteaux, prehistoric cave drawings and cer- emonial standing stones, Roman ruins and majes- tic churches; all bear testimony to a rich and diverse heritage. The following are a handful of what's available to see on a trip through France.

• *Paris.* Paris is almost a walking museum, from the famous, art-filled Louvre to the impressive Arc de Triomphe. Just outside the city lies Versailles, unquestionably Europe's most elaborate royal residence, built during the height of French aristocratic power.

• *Loire Châteaux Country.* This area offers a trip back in time that can't fail to delight children and adults alike. Fairy-tale châteaux dot the banks of this lovely river valley, once the homes and country retreats of France's aristocracy. Many are open to the public, some mere remnants of their former grandeur, others restored and magnificent. An evening Son et Lumiére performance is always a thrill for all ages.

• *Burgundy.* Burgundy is filled with 15th century buildings, dating from its era as a powerful, independent kingdom: fortified castles and Romanesque churches, monasteries and abbeys, many of them religious holdings from a time when the church owned much of the region's wealth.

• *Dordogne.* A region of castles and walled towns dating from Medieval times, the Dordogne is also the site of a number of cave dwellings, evidence of early Cro-Magnon man. The most renowned drawings are at Lascaux, although only reproductions can be seen now at a nearby site. Also included are a museum and zoo of prehistoric animals and artifacts.

• *Perigueux (Poitou-Charentes).* Exciting castles from Medieval days abound, situated along the many rivers of this region, once a strategic defense point against invaders.

• *Colmar (Alsace).* A lovely, preserved Medieval city, with the narrow cobblestone streets and half-timbered houses typical of this period.

OUTDOOR ACTIVITIES

Hiking. France is an easy place to hike with children, whether on simple country rambles or more ambitious mountain treks. Visual stimuli are plentiful, from vineyards and farms to rivers and lakes. Hiking here is a far cry from uphill slogs along densely wooded trails to some elusive view which children could care less about. Instead, there's plenty of scope for the imagination, an everchanging view, and a village or mountain hut just when you always seem to need one.

• *Towpaths.* Some of the best and easiest hiking is along the many towpaths, quiet trails that ramble through the pastoral countryside beside canals. Children invariably love this kind of hiking: level and unhurried, always with the alluring presence of water.

• *Designated Footpaths.* France has a multitude of these, totalling about 120,000 km of trails. Grand Randonnee paths, marked with red and white trail signs, offer excellent long-distance hikes, with inexpensive accommodations always available for nightly stops. The equally prolific Petite Randonnée paths supply shorter hikes throughout the countryside, ideal for children of all ages. For a topographical guide to all designated trails, contact the Federation Francaise de la Randonnée Pedestre (64 rue de Gergorie - 75041 Paris). Hiking guides to specific areas can also be bought locally.

• *French Alps.* For challenging hiking on groomed trails, try the French Alps. Here you'll find the most developed trail system in the country, with a string of mountain "huts" similar to those found throughout the Alpine Mountain range. Huts are located for convenient overnight stops along each trail, with meals and simple sleeping accommodations provided, thus eliminating the need to carry most gear. This is a wonderful opportunity for introducing younger children to ambitious hikes.

Membership in the French (or any other) Alpine Club gives you a significant discount at huts. One of the most exciting hikes is a week-long tour around Mont Blanc, Europe's highest mountain, passing through three separate countries.

• **National Parks and Preserves.** Like most preservation land, these offer excellent opportunities for hiking in a variety of settings, from the forests and lakes of Aquitaine's Parc Naturel Régional des Landes de Gascogne to the high, remote mountain regions of Parc National du Mercantour.

• **Franche-Comté.** Situated in the country's northeast corner, this area is particularly well-suited for families with young children, with easy hiking along 7,000 km of designated trails. A scenic region of lakes, streams, waterfalls and forests, the walking here is lovely, destined to keep children interested.

Bicycling. France is a lovely country to bicycle around, certainly one of the best in the world. The French have long had a love affair with bicycles, making them a popular mode of travel and always eliciting a favorable response from local people. Motorists are considerate, rural roads abundant, the countryside lovely and fascinating, villages frequent, and terrain manageable in most areas. Just about anywhere is appropriate for a day outing, heading out into the countryside to explore. Transport on local trains is often free for bicycles, making this an easy, economical way to cover distances between desirable areas for touring. Some places are more appropriate for touring than others, particularly for first time families or ones with small children.

• **The Coast of Brittany, the Loire Valley (best off-season), and the Poitou-Charentes Region** all provide easy, interesting touring.

• **Alsace** is a beautiful, culturally interesting area with orchard-filled valleys and wooded hills, best for families with older children.

• **The Parc Naturel Regional des Landes de Gascogne** in southwestern France has a 200-mile bicycle path, an exciting opportunity for a lovely tour.

• **Canal Boat.** Carrying bicycles for use on the towpaths while boating is a wonderful, unusual way for families to explore a region of the country. For more details, see the sidebar.

Sailing. The principal sailing region is the Mediterranean, along the country's south coast. Popular with sailors from all over the world, the sailing can get crowded here during peak summer season. Better yet, cruise during spring or early fall, exploring the lovely coastal villages, docking Mediterranean-style (stern first) in cozy harbors. Provisions and yachting facilities are readily available and distances short between nightly stops. For a taste of something different, sail to the island of Corsica, an exciting, rugged, wild place to explore. Winds in the Med are notoriously temperamental, typified by dead calms or sudden gales. Boats can be chartered from a number of locations along the southern coast. A wonderful alternative to sea sailing is a cruise through any of the many canals. Sailboats need only lower their masts to make the trip. Currents run north to south, making this the better direction to travel in. The one exception is the Canal du Midi, France's most popular canal, that can be accessed from the south.

Swimming. Wonderful beaches for swimming are numerous. Most popular are those along the south coast, where peak season can bring record crowds. For those who like something more isolated, try the beaches of Brittany, beautifully situated along the predominantly rocky shore. Swimming is appropriate for children of all ages, except along the Atlantic coast where surf can be strong . Fresh water swimming is also available at a variety of lakes and rivers throughout the country, including those in national parks .

Nature Studies. France's parks and preserves offer the best opportunities for nature studies, with guided nature walks and exhibits.

Cruising the French Canals

Permeating France is an ancient system of inland waterways, canals that have long served the country as an important means of transport. Today, in addition to their commercial purpose, they offer an unusual type of vacation, one that combines the independence and excitement of boat travel with the beauty and tranquility of France's pastoral countryside. While sailors have long recognized the special exposure to an area that boat travel affords, others with little or no nautical experience are denied the opportunity.

The charm of France's canal travel is that anyone can do it, including families with children of any age. Free from the potential stresses and navigational hazards of coastal cruising, travel by canal offers only the best of boating: a slow, relaxed pace; intimate exposure to a region; easy interaction with local inhabitants; comradery among fellow boaters; the independence and convenience of a home that moves with you; an ever-changing scenery; peaceful surroundings and a sense of timelessness.

Children will take to it like the proverbial ducks to water, for canal boat cruising has just the outdoor, active focus they thrive on. Put a child on, near, or beside water and he'll remain perennially content. Even little ones can play happily and safely on boats designed to incorporate children of all ages. As with all boat travel, canal cruising means your home goes with you, a definite asset for families. There's no need to hurry or pack up, disturb their play or marshall them into a car. Gone is the backseat boredom, the plaintive cries for release, the demands to know if they're almost there. Whether moving or moored, canal boats provide an ideal play place, with towpaths along the shore doubling as backyards. Older children will enjoy helping to steer, handling boat lines, and assisting the lockkeeper when locking through.

Navigable canals are located all over the country, from the Vosges Mountains of Lorraine and the rocky shores of Brittany to the wine growing region of Burgundy and Mediterranean flavor of the Carmargue. All are equally enticing, filled with lovely landscapes, historic sites, rural villages, and a peaceful sense of life along the water. Choosing where to go is almost arbitrary. Some people might fancy the rugged appeal of Brittany, others the forested hills and Germanic feel of Alsace. In early spring or late fall the sun and warmth of the Carmague or Midi might prove irresistible, or the Sarthe River region lure you with its unspoiled nature and wildlife. Trips can be planned to last from a few days to two weeks.

Consider renting bicycles for the duration of your cruise, easily arranged through charter operations. Towpaths offer ideal bike routes as you explore the immediate area, go shopping, or encourage the children to burn off steam. Provisioning can be done at villages and towns along the canal, or bought directly from lockkeepers, many of whom sell fresh produce from their gardens.

The boats themselves are easy to handle, well-equipped, and comfortable. There's no need to bring anything other than a small selection of clothes and whatever recreational things you want (books, camera, toys, etc.). Boats range from small compact models to spacious abodes, with even the smallest capable of accommodating a family of four. It's possible to charter any time of year, with peak season lasting from July - August. Off season rates can be reduced as much as 50%. As most boats include a heating system, even winter travel can be fun and comfortable, as well as guaranteeing you uncrowded waters.

Other than peak season, canal travel offers a very affordable vacation for families. With your accommodations and transportation already taken care of (other than the cost of fuel), there's little additional expense except indulging in France's gastronomic pleasures. Free overnight mooring is permitted almost anywhere along the canals. Just tie up when the mood strikes, making sure you're not obstructing the canal. Be sure to assist the lockkeeper at manually-operated locks, all part of canal etiquette. Transit through the locks is free and usually takes about 15 minutes, but be forewarned that like all the French, lockkeepers take a generous time off for lunch at midday.

Chartering is possible in all major canal regions, principally Brittany, Burgundy, Franche-Comté, the Loire Valley, Alsace-Lorraine, Midi, Camargue, Sarthe, Champagne, and Quercy. In addition to bicycle rentals, charter companies offer a variety of other services, including provisioning, cleaning, extra furnishings, fishing equipment, and baby service (high chair, baby bath and folding cot). A good contact for arranging a canal boat charter in France, Britain, or Ireland is Le Boat Inc., P.O. Box E, Maywood, N.J. 07607 USA, (800) 922-0291.

RESOURCE SECTION

TOURIST BUREAUS
Tourist Information Office, Maison de la France, 8 Ave. de l'Opéra, 75001 Paris, France Tel: (1) 42 60 3738.
French Gov't Tourist Office, 610 5th Ave., New York, NY Tel: (212) 757-1125.
Other tourist offices in many major North American cities.

CONSULATES
French Consulate General, 934 5th Ave., New York, NY 10021 Tel: (212) 606-3688.
Other consulates in many major North American cities.

NATIONAL AIRLINE
Air France, 888 Seventh Ave., New York, NY 10106 Tel: (800) AF-PARIS.

SUGGESTED READING
Real Guide: France by K Baillie & T. Salmon. Prentice Hall Travel, New York, NY.
Green Guide: France. Michelin Tyer Public Limited Company.

SUGGESTED MAPS
France, Map Art, Scale: 1:1,000,000.
France, Institute Graphic National, Scale: 1:1,000,000.
France, Michelin, Scale: 1:1,000,000.
France Topographic Series (recommended for local hiking and bicycling), Institute Graphic National, Scale: 1:100,000.

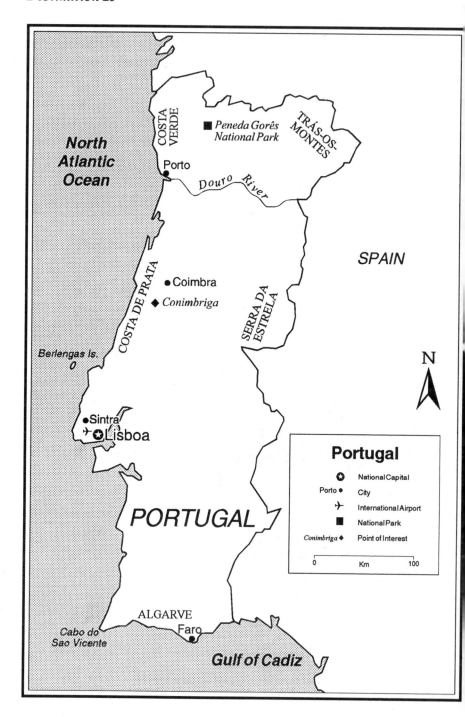

Portugal

Portugal is an excellent destination for traveling families. Scenic and friendly, quiet and self-contained, its culture is different and unusual without being intimidating or daunting. Graced with a beauty that extends from the mountains in the

north to the coastal spendors of the southern Algarve, the country offers pastoral surroundings and unspoiled areas to explore. Whether for the experienced or novice adventuring family, Portugal is a welcoming, enticing country.

GENERAL DESCRIPTION

Location. Located in the extreme southwest corner of Europe, Portugal forms a long, thin buffer between the ocean and the rest of the Iberian Peninsula. Bordered by water on two sides, it faces the Atlantic to the west and south, with its larger neighbor, Spain, to the east and north.

Terrain. Portugal is a mix of mountains, plains and sea. To the south lie the pristine beaches of the Algarve, to the west the surf-swept shore of the Atlantic. Mountains and gentle hills, rivers and broad plains dominate the interior. Villages nestle in wide valleys and seaside coves, while small farms dot the countryside.

Climate. The climate is essentially that of the western Mediterranean countries, with a slight cooling effect from proximity to the Atlantic. Winters are cold and wet, summers hot and dry. The best time to travel is spring or fall, when weather is good and the summer tourist season not in full swing. Temperatures are noticeably cooler in the north than south. Visiting in May, for instance, you can have beach weather in the Algarve and still be uncomfortably cold in the northern mountains.

Culture & Lifestyle. Despite a long history of Spanish influence and occasional dominance, Portugal's culture is distinctly different from its neighbor's. Originally occupied by Moors, the country's ethnic origins can still be felt today, in the appearance of the people themselves, the language and architecture, the temperament. Portugal enjoys a comfortable, yet modest lifestyle. Despite recent efforts to modernize and bridge the economic gap that separates it from a number of other EC countries, people still retain many of their old ways and the lifestyle remains simple in the countryside. Homes are small, open-air markets the norm, cars few away from cities and tourist meccas. The pace of life is slow, the people noticeably family oriented. Children are free to roam, their boisterous behavior in marked contrast to the more sedate character of their parents. Unlike other Latin countries, the Portuguese are quiet and self-contained, with little of the proverbial Latin temperament.

PRACTICAL CONCERNS

Political Background & Safety. Like many European countries, Portugal underwent the transition from a monarchy supported by vast colonial holdings to democracy. Today it is a completely safe place to travel, with little crime and no political discord. Children are looked on with affection and tolerance and can freely explore villages, towns and country-side safely on their own. This is a relaxing, family-oriented culture where whole families traditionally turn out for Sunday evening promenades. Theft is rare.

Travel Documents. In most cases, only a passport is required, including citizens of the United States, Canada, and most EC and Commonwealth countries. A two-month visa is issued upon arrival.

Money. Currency is the escudo. Travelers checks can easily be cashed throughout the country. Banks are found in all large towns and open Monday-Friday.

Travel Costs. By European standards, Portugal has the justified reputation for being a budget destination. Compared to neighboring France and Spain, it's decidedly affordable. By shopping at local markets, riding public transportation, and camping, it's possible to travel on a tight budget and still enjoy yourselves. Gasoline prices and car rentals are high, but bringing your own car or traveling by bicycle are two good, low-cost alternatives. Prices are highest in cities and tourist areas like the Algarve coast.

Language. Portuguese is the official language. With some knowledge of Spanish you can easily get by. English is usually spoken in tourist areas, cities, and large towns. Otherwise, you'll have to rely on your ingenuity when it comes to communicating. Take along a basic phrase book to learn the rudimentary words and phrases.

Health. There are no health concerns when visiting Portugal. Water is safe to drink, fresh produce clean. Food preparation at restaurants is hygienic, so there's no cause for concern when dining out, even in small, local places. Medical supplies and services are readily available.

Food. The food selection is excellent. Buy fresh produce at open-air markets. Cities have them on a daily basis (just ask for directions to the "mercado"), towns usually once or twice a week. Saturday is the main market day and attracts the biggest turnout and selection. Choice is wide and varies with the season. Shops range from small supermarkets to tiny stalls. Bread is sold in bakeries, meat at meat markets, fish at fishmongers, etc.. Both powdered and fresh milk are available, also a variety of cheeses, yogurt, grains, eggs, pastas, cereals, and canned goods. For unsweetened fruit juice, look for liter-size jars of orange concentrate. Eating out can be very affordable, even for families. Order half portions for children.

Clothes. Given the temperate climate, it's best to take a range of clothing when visiting off-season, lightweight clothing for summer. To be on the safe side, include one warm outfit. Portugal has lovely, hand-made clothes for sale at reasonable prices, so you might want to leave room in your bags for adding to your selection. For a different cultural experience, buy from Gypsies selling alongside the road. Bring or buy a sunhat if traveling during the summer heat or in the south. Bathing gear is imperative (little children, including girls, only need bottoms to their bathing suits).

Laundry & Bathing. Hotels and pensions can always provide laundry service, although the cost is usually fairly high for this sort of thing. Consider doing your own in the sink, tub, or bidet (wonderful for soaking dirty laundry). Campgrounds have the best facilities, excellent wash basins with a built-in washboard effect on the front edge. Be sure to carry a piece of clothesline and handful of clothespins for hanging clothes to dry. Rented apartments often come with a small washing machine, a real luxury. If traveling by car, carry a bucket for doing your own laundry. Bathing is rarely a problem, with hot showers provided at most pensions and campgrounds. An extra fee is often charged for hot showers in a pension (check to see how hot it is first!).

Baby Needs. Everything for babies can be easily found: cereal, jarred food, milk, fruit, diapers, laundry services. Bring a good child carrier and possibly a stroller if traveling by car. Include plenty of sun protection (sun hat, cotton clothing, sunscreen) for hot days. Expect your baby to figuratively open doors for you and attract plenty of attention in this southern European country, an area that traditionally dotes on its young. Babies can always be taken to restaurants. Local children never seem to go to bed.

TRANSPORTATION

Getting There. Portugal can be reached by air, land or sea. If flying, try TAP (Air Portugal), the country's excellent national airlines. Good fares are offered from North America and Europe. For reduced costs on longer stays, book APEX (advanced purchase). By car, Portugal can be entered in a number of locations from Spain. It's also possible to bring a car on the ferry from Plymouth, England. Passenger train links Lisbon with Paris and London.

Regional Transport. Portugal's rail service is excellent, linking most major towns. Family tickets help cut costs, with one adult paying full fare, the other half fare, and one quarter fare for all children over the age of four. Under four rides free (if not occupying a seat). The tourist bureau publishes a very comprehensive, helpful train schedule. Comfortable, well-run bus service covers areas not reached by train.

Roads. Most roads are well paved and easy to drive or ride by bicycle. Traffic is light on backcountry roads, heavy near cities, tourist areas, or on weekends. Avoid traveling on Sunday afternoons, a time when carloads of local families like to go for an outing .

ACCOMMODATIONS

Campgrounds. Portugal has a wide network of campgrounds, mostly located along the coast. Facilities are usually clean and simple, although the occasional glamorous campground will have a pool, restaurant, and assorted other resort-style amenities. Grounds are well kept, with flowers, grass, shade trees, and quiet surroundings. Many are located near beaches. In those with no designated sites, conditions can be crowded in summer. Off-season, they're a delight - nearly empty, wonderful to stay in, and frequently 30-50% off peak season prices. Children will have plenty of room to exercise and burn off steam. Few offer any provisions, but shops are generally nearby. The tourist bureau publishes the very comprehensive guide "Camping Portugal", including a list of campgrounds, their facilities, outdoor activities, distance from the nearest bus or train station, and locater map. Free camping is permitted anywhere other than urban areas, or less than one km from an official campground or beach. Ask before camping near someone's home, and never use an open fire.

Pensions & Rooms. Pensions are numerous and located all over the country, with comfortable rooms and clean, modest facilities. Another equally affordable option is a room in a private home. Look for signs or ask at the local tourist bureau. For an interesting cultural experience, try staying in at least one farmhouse, many of which offer accommodation. Children will love it (and they will love your children). Prices are best off-season or if you stay a week or longer. For a taste of luxury with a cultural twist, try a night in one of the country's many lovely pousadas, government-run hotels located in ancient, historic buildings, from castles to convents. Equally luxurious, but even more intriguing is the opportunity to spend a night or two in some of Portugal's most elegant, private homes. Similar to staying on a farm, the experience is shared with a resident family, a wonderful way to gain some insight into the local culture and lifestyle. Young children, of course, will prefer the farm experience to the manor house, with less to worry about in terms of their behavior. Off-season prices (November-March) are by far the best.

Rentals. This is an excellent country to base yourself in for a while and enjoy living in a foreign community. Off-season is best, when summer cottages and apartments are vacant and prices down. Check with local tourist bureaus or ask around when you find a town or village that appeals. Try out the amenities before paying, but expect some surprises.

POINTS OF INTEREST

Natural. Portugal has its share of lovely areas of scenic beauty and natural points of interest, from the remote, mountainous regions of the Trás-os-Montes province to the gentle, wildflower-covered hills and sand beaches of the Algarve. Most of Portugal remains pastoral and unspoiled, with nature intermingling easily with areas of cultivation and habitation. The following are only a few of Portugal's many areas of interest.

• *Peneda Gerês National Park.* Located on the Costa Verde, this encompasses 170,000 acres of mountainous countryside, forests, and inland waters, with abundant wildlife. Exploration is best done by hiking or horseback riding.

- *Cape São Vincente.* Southwestern most point of Europe; a spectacular meeting place of cliffs and sea. Where Nelson defeated the French navy in 1797.

- *Northeastern Portugal.* A remote region of fertile river valleys, high mountains, wind-swept plateaus, and health-giving mineral waters.

- *Serra da Estrela.* The country's highest mountain range, located in south central Portugal.

- *Berlengas Islands.* A group of small islands off the west coast, completely unspoiled and ideal for walking or camping.

- *Buçaco Forest (Costa de Prata).* A lovely, small national park with good hiking.

- *Caves.* Visit the caves at Alvados, including Mira de Aire, the deepest cave in Europe.

Cultural. In many ways, Portugal's culture is an amalgamation of other cultures, gleaned from the years when Portuguese sailors and navigators roamed the seas. Coupled with this are the years of conquest, when Celtic, Roman, and Moorish cultural influences were felt. Today, the most interesting pockets of culture can be found inland, with each region revealing its individual characteristics.

- *Architecture.* This can be fascinating, even for children, providing insights into the evolution of Portuguese culture: the distinctive Moorish influences in southern Portugal (white-washed houses with ornate chimney pots); the Manueline design, unique to Portugal; and the Roman architecture found in northern regions.

- *Festivals.* These take place annually all over the country and are an expression of ancient culture, with traditional costumes, dances, and music. Attending one is always

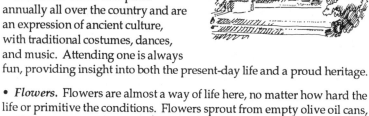

fun, providing insight into both the present-day life and a proud heritage.

- *Flowers.* Flowers are almost a way of life here, no matter how hard the life or primitive the conditions. Flowers sprout from empty olive oil cans, spill down steps, crowd walkways, and grace windows. More than anything, they express the Portuguese love of beauty and nature.

- *Handicrafts.* Portuguese handicrafts are a reflection of a rich heritage. Among the best are hand-painted pottery, ceramic tiles, colorful clothing, and wicker weaving.

Historic. Portugal seems to have an historic point of interest at every turn in the road. Churches and castles, Medieval walled towns and fortresses, Roman aqueducts and ancient bridges, convents and monuments, historic houses and palaces, all interweave the country's rich past with its charming present. It's almost impossible to suggest anywhere in particular, as all are equally interesting. Instead, choose historic aspects that interest your children. Castles are always popular, as are palaces and ancient ruins. If architecture has been studied, visit some churches so they can have the fun of identifying styles. Many towns have at least one museum, while Lisbon is filled with every type, focusing on everything from military and musical instruments to archeology and ancient art.

- *Sintra.* Children will delight in a visit to this magical town. Once the summer retreat of Portuguese royalty, this mountain town outside Lisbon retains an elegant, fairy-land appeal, with castles and fortress walls, turreted mansions and narrow, cobblestone streets (refer to the accompanying sidebar).

- *Conimbriga.* Impressive Roman ruins of what was once a summer resort, with temples, houses, waterways, a forum, and mosaics.

OUTDOOR ACTIVITIES

Hiking. Hiking is a wonderful way to experience the countryside, following footpaths, animal tracks, dirt roads and designated trails. Bring good hiking shoes or boots (ones with appropriate treds) for the whole family if you plan any mountain rambles. While walking can be done freelance all over the country (follow any path that looks enticing), various national parks and preserves offer hiking on designated  trails. Good places to hike include Peneda Gerês National Park, Buçaco Forest, and the Berlengas Islands.

Bicycling. Many parts of Portugal are excellent for bicycling, from easy day outings to ambitious tours. Backroads and scenic countryside are everywhere, offering an abundance of attractive, easy routes. On a tour, campgrounds are conveniently located along the coast for nightly stops. In the interior you'd have to rely more on pensions or free camping for accommodations. The south coastal route makes a wonderful, easy tour. Stick to the backroads to avoid coastal traffic. Cars are few, the terrain gentle, and the riding safe. Backroads here are appropriate for babies in bicycle trailers and older children riding themselves. If traveling by car, consider bringing bicycles for enjoyable day explorations into the country-side, always more fun and exciting for children than being cooped up in a car all the time.

Sailing. Portugal has some lovely sailing, with coves, fishing ports, and marinas to duck into at day's end. Boating facilities are numerous along both coasts, and chartering available. Although this is perhaps not the best way to visit the country, boating enthusiasts will discover a wonderful side to coastal regions, one that's only accessible to those traveling by water.

Swimming. Swimming is excellent at the many sand beaches along both coasts. The south coast is the most crowded, with numerous resorts throughout the Algarve. On the other hand, the east has some lovely, unspoiled areas, particularly far away from Lisbon (the surrounding metro area can get very crowded on weekends). To enjoy Portuguese beaches at their best, visit in May or September, before or after the summer rush. The south coast has the best swimming for young children, with no surf.

Sintra - Village of Palaces

We first heard about Sintra when our bicycle trip to Portugal was still in its formative stage. A friend, knowing what our children liked, insisted we go there, assuring us the boys would love it. They did, of course, and thereafter, when asked what they liked best about the trip, invariably answered "Sintra".

Although we arrived by bicycle, an exciting approach through the dense forest that shields the town, Sintra is easy to reach by car or train from nearby Lisbon. Like a child's fairy tale come to life, turrets and peaked roofs appear above the trees, offering a first glimpse of what's to come. Sintra seems of another world, one where all men are princes and all homes

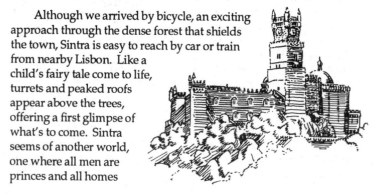

palaces. Once the summer retreat of Portuguese kings, the area served as an enclave of nobility and wealth for about 500 years.

Today, the town casts a spell like magic, enchanting you with its mystery and intrigue, its elegance and splendor. Palaces and quintas peek out from among the wooded hills, ancient castle walls crest the hilltop, and ornate gates offer glimpses of unimagined , elaborate gardens. Everything seems reduced in size, like a miniature fairy land constructed from a child's set of blocks.

Built around the small central square, the town tumbles down the hillside along narrow streets, overshadowed by the tall, conical chimneys of the National Palace in the center of town. Village architecture is elaborate and fanciful, with each building as enchanting as the one before it.

Walking is the best way to explore, along the main street, with its wooded park and waterfall, past teahouses and tempting shops, up steep cobblestone lanes lined with private mansions. Beyond stretches the lush expanse of forest, enveloping Sintra like a green protective cloak.

Most exciting for children will be visiting Pena Palace and the Moorish Castle, both situated high above the town. Romantic and fascinating to all ages, children will find them the perfect spark for their imaginative play as they walk the castle ramparts or explore rooms once inhabited by royalty. The walk from town, about an hour hike up a steep yet scenic hill, reaches the Moorish Castle first. Only the wall and ramparts remain, following the contours of the hillside and offering spectacular views as you tramp the battlements. At night the walls are lit up, a magical, tantalizing sight from the village below. Another easy half hour of walking through palace grounds brings you to Pena Palace. By all means explore the parkland and gardens, even if you arrive by car. Lush and lovely, they conjure up images of bygone wealth and elegance. Children will particularly enjoy the duckhouse, appearing out of the lush surroundings on its miniature pond like a diminutive Sleeping Beauty's castle. Swans swim along the water's edge, another unfailing source of entertainment.

Summer home of Portugal's last royal family, Pena Palace retains an inhabited feel, with each room appearing as though someone had just stepped out of it. Built in the Bavarian style, its romantic architecture and small size seem made for children.

Other historic places in the area include the National Palace in the center of town (less interesting, but still worth a visit) and the Convento dos Capuchos, a 16th century hermitage in the depths of the forest, awesome in its contrasting aura of deprivation and austerity.

With camping gear you can camp in the lovely forest, all of which is preserved parkland. The campsite lies about 5 km outside Sintra, near the Convento. Facilities are basic, the surroundings lovely and natural. A vehicle would be necessary for getting into town. Sintra itself has plenty of places to stay. One good, affordable option for families is to stay in a private home. Inquire at the local tourist bureau. We found a wonderful place this way, an entire suite with two bedrooms, livingroom, kitchen and bath, located in a farmhouse on the edge of town. The children were delighted with the country setting, still only a short walk from the central square. Food shops were easy to find and the whole experience the height of luxury after weeks of camping.

The best time to visit, as with most places, is off-season, in spring or early fall after the inevitable tourist influx. Allow about three days to really enjoy the place. This will give you a chance to see the sights, preferably on foot, and to not feel rushed or make the children miserable. If your children are like ours, they'll want to play games every step of the way, a definite deterrent to seeing a place quickly. Weather can be a bit damp at times, another good reason to allow extra time. This is why the area is so unbelievably green and lush, the perfect setting for its palatial elegance.

RESOURCE SECTION

TOURIST BUREAUS
Portuguese Council for Tourism Promotion, 51, Rua Alexandre Herculano, Lisbon, Portugal 1200   Tel: 681174.
Portuguese National Tourist Office, 590 5th Ave., New York, NY 10036   Tel: (212) 354-4403.
Portuguese National Tourist Office, 60 Bloor St. W., Ste. 1005, Toronto, ON M4W 3B8, Canada   Tel: (416) 921-7376.

CONSULATES
Consulate General of Portugal, 630 5th Ave., New York, NY 10020   Tel: (212) 246-4580.
Consulate General of Portugal, 2020 University, Ste. 1725, Montreal, QUE H3A 2A5, Canada   Tel: (514) 499-0359.
Portuguese Consulate, 121 Richmond St. W., 7th Fl., Toronto ON M5H 2K1   Tel: (416) 360-8260.

NATIONAL AIRLINES
TAP Air Portugal, 399 Market St., Newark, NJ 07105   Tel: (800) 221-7370 .

SUGGESTED READING
Real Guide: Portugal by Ellingham, Fisher, Martin, & Kenyon. Prentice Hall Travel, New York.
Cadogan Guide to Portugal by D. Evans. Globe Pequot Press, Chester, CT.
Insight Portugal by A.F. Hill. Prentice-Hall, Englewood Cliffs, NJ.

SUGGESTED MAPS
Spain & Portugal, Hallwag, Scale: 1:1,000,000.
Spain & Portugal, Freytag & Berndt, Scale: 1:1,000,000.
Spain & Portugal, Michelin, Scale: 1:1,000,000.

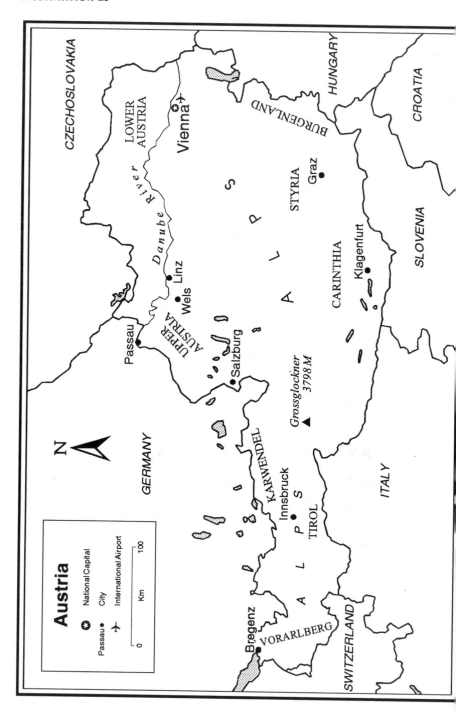

Austria

One of Europe's most charming countries, Austria is dominated by mountains and valleys, pierced by the undulating blue ribbon of the Danube. Less touristed and expensive than neighboring Switzerland, yet equally lovely, Austria has an authenticity, a sense of depth below its picturesque surface. Music and culture pay homage to a once-great empire and to a time when Austria was one of the creative meccas of the Western World.

Despite abundant opportunities for outdoor activities, the country seems best made for walking, along the numerous trails that ramble through the countryside, around lakes, and up mountains. Few places match the potential of Austria for easy, enjoyable family hiking.

GENERAL DESCRIPTION

Location. Austria is located in central Europe. A landlocked country, it borders Hungary to the east, Czechoslovakia and Germany to the north, Italy and Slovania to the south, and Switzerland and Liechtenstein to the west.

Terrain. Largely dominated by mountains, much of Austria lies in the heart of the Alps, a lovely area of steep mountains, high peaks, and deep valleys. To the east the land becomes more gentle, culminating in part of the vast Central European Plain. From high alpine meadows and rocky scree to dense lowland forest and clear lakes, the land is varied and exquisite, each region with its own distinctive flavor.

Climate. Austria enjoys a pleasant climate year round, with comfortable summers and sunny, cold, snowy winters. Summer weather features hot days and cool nights, particularly in the mountains. Both spring and fall are pleasant times to visit and escape the crowds of summer, but July and August are best for hiking in the Alps.

Culture & Lifestyle. Once part of the vast Holy Roman Empire, then ruled by one of Europe's most powerful monarchs, Austria emerged early as a cultural leader. Creative expression reached its zenith during the 17th and 18th centuries when Vienna became a cultural center of Europe, cultivating a music and architectural heritage that is still revered today. Music festivals and Baroque architecture, palaces and art-filled museums, the famous Vienna Choir Boys and equally renowned Lippizaner Horses all pay tribute to a rich cultural heritage. Today, city life is cosmopolitan, imbued with an Old World gentility, while country life remains equally steeped in tradition, with small family farms and miniature villages. There is a timeless quality to life in Austria, both rural and urban, as though the country had found its niche and paused there for eternity.

PRACTICAL CONCERNS

Political Background & Safety. Once part of two great empires and ruled by the powerful Hapsburg family, Austria obtained its present modest size and democratic form of government following World War I. Other than a seven year period when the country was annexed to the German Reich, Austria has remained independent and peaceful. The country is a completely safe place to visit, with a relaxed lifestyle and friendly people.

Travel Documents. Citizens of the United States, Canada, and Australia need only a passport to visit Austria for up to 90 days. EC nationals require only some form of identification.

Money. Local currency is the Austrian schilling, equal to 100 groschen. Travelers checks are widely accepted and the best way to carry money. Most major credit cards are acceptable in tourist areas. Banks are in all large towns and open Monday-Friday, with an hour closing at midday. Changing money is also possible at train stations, including on weekends, but be forewarned that the service charge is high.

Travel Costs. As with most European countries, Austria falls in the slightly expensive travel bracket. On the other hand, Austria is noticeably less expensive than neighboring Switzerland and Germany. Low-budget families will have to be a bit careful to keep costs down. As always, the best way is to camp, travel by public transportation (or bicycle), and do your own cooking. Trains offer various fare reduction plans designed for families. Hiking from hut to hut in the Alps, one of the most exciting outdoor activities, is not inexpensive, although membership in an Austrian alpine club cuts costs in half. The experience, however, is well worth the additional cost. Food prices are reasonable, particularly when shopping and doing your own cooking.

Language. German is the national language, spoken with a variety of dialects that can leave your high school German in a state of confusion. English is generally spoken by people in the tourist trade, but don't expect it in the countryside. Children are your best bet if trying to make yourself understood. Most learn English in school, beginning at an early age.

Health. There are no health concerns when visiting Austria. Water, food, and hygiene are all excellent, and medical supplies and facilities easy to find. Carry a sufficient (but lightweight) first aid kit when hiking in the Alps. Staffed huts are well-equipped for emergencies. Bring sunscreen for alpine hiking, as sun exposure can be intense.

Food. Food in Austria is delicious, filling, and reasonably priced. Food shops are plentiful, with a tempting array of goodies destined to undermine all your best intentions. Most alluring are bakery items, gorgeously displayed in shop windows. You should have plenty of trouble getting your children past those. Best buys include homemade baked goods, yogurt, cheese, sausage, staples, fruit (in season), and meat. Just about everything is available, making this an easy country to find things in. If eating out, try the delicious soups that are inevitably part of the menu. Combined with bread, they make an excellent, inexpensive meal for the whole family.

Clothes. Bring a cross-section of clothing, with something for hot and cool weather. Summers are generally T-shirt and shorts weather, although early morning and evening can be cooler in the mountains. Include at least one warm set of clothes (long pants, sweater). Hiking can be very hot in summer, due to the sun. Both bathingsuits and raingear are a must. For hiking, be sure to bring good boots for the whole family, ones with appropriate treads and ankle support. Sneakers or running shoes are not sufficient for this type of hiking. Austria has lovely clothes for sale, although most are quite expensive. Among the most tempting are those in traditional design, like the famous dirndls and handknit sweaters (terrific ones for children).

Laundry & Bathing. Laundromats are easy to find in sizable towns, and laundry facilities available at many campgrounds. Pensions can usually make arrangements for doing your laundry as well. Bring a piece of line and a handful of pins for drying clothes. This way you can even do small handwashes in the sink, something you'll see people doing at mountain huts. Hot water is always available for bathing, in pensions, hotels, and campgrounds. Freshwater lake swimming will also help keep your children clean.

Baby Needs. Babies are never a problem when traveling in Austria. All baby-related products are plentiful and local people welcoming to infants and toddlers. A number of towns have playgrounds and parks, always a hit with little children. Be sure to include an excellent child carrier for hikes into the mountains or countryside. Hut to hut hiking is possible provided your baby is a good sleeper. Diapers are easy to wash at frequent laundry facilities. Children under the age of six ride free on public transportation (provided they don't occupy a seat).

TRANSPORTATION

Getting There. Austria has international airports at Vienna, Innsbruck, Graz, Salzburg and Klagenfurt. Direct flights from North America usually go to Vienna (Icelandair lands at Salzburg). To reach one of the other destinations requires a change, usually in Germany. European airlines frequently use the other international airports. Austria is easily reached by train from all over Europe, with direct routing from as far away as London. Good highways also enter the country from Germany, Switzerland, Italy and Slovania.

Public Transportation. Public transportation is excellent, principally on trains. Austrian trains are fast, efficient, comfortable, and widespread, a real thrill for children to ride as they plunge through mountain tunnels and along cliff edges. Towns not serviced by train have bus connections from the nearest railway station. Various fare reduction plans are offered, including a discount mileage pass (Kilometerbank), ideal for families. Inquire at the ticket office. An updated train schedule is available from the Austrian Tourist Office. Children under six travel free (if not occupying a seat), then half fare to age 15.

Roads. Roads vary from dual-lane highways to narrow lanes. All are well-paved and easy to drive. Traffic is heaviest on highways and around cities. When bicycling, stick to local roads. Cars can be rented throughout Austria, but fuel is expensive. With such excellent public transportation, there's really no need for a car (many Austrians don't even own one).

ACCOMMODATIONS

Campgrounds. Abundant campgrounds are located throughout the country, frequently in lovely surroundings like the shores of a lake. Expect plenty of company during July and August. Many people use campers or RVs, but some campgrounds have allocated space for tents, always a nice bonus for we tent afficionados. Facilities are good, including hot showers and frequently washing machines for laundry (but no picnic tables). There are usually no designated sites, so space is allocated on a first come first serve basis. Prices are good, less than in many European countries, making this a very economical way to travel. Campgrounds are always within easy reach of public transportation.

Zimmer Frei. As with B&Bs, these offer reasonably priced accommodations in private homes. Rooms are always comfortable and breakfast generally included. Not only is the price better than hotels and pensions, but you have a chance to meet local people and see how they live. Children are always welcome. Just look for the sign *Zimmer Frei* posted outside homes, or inquire at the local tourist office. Breakfast is usually continental, with a heavy emphasis on bread and jam. Cheese, meat, fruit and muesli are also sometimes served. Payment for the night is usually required upon arrival, a standard procedure.

Farm Vacations. Farm vacations always provide one of the best opportunities for immersing yourself in the local culture. For families with young children, this offers a wonderful chance to enjoy the country without the rigors of moving from place to place, while also providing plenty of room for running around. Children of all ages love the farm atmosphere. Accommodations range from a few rooms to a whole private suite, depending on the place and what you want. Reservations are necessary and a minimum stay of a week required. Contact the Landesverband fur Tourismus (tourist office) in the capital of the province that interests you.

POINTS OF INTEREST

Natural. With its variety of high mountainous areas, abundant lakes, scenic rivers, and cultivated valleys, Austria is filled with natural points of interest. The best way to enjoy the landscape is on foot, something the

Austrians do at every opportunity. Although there are few parks and preserves, much of the land remains unspoiled and lovely. Villages are small and quiet, lakes clear and uncluttered, the hills and mountains a region of scenic splendor. Each region possesses its own natural wonders, from the high peaks and glaciers of Tirol to the vast eastern plain of Burgenland. The following are just a handful of the many regions worth visiting for their natural beauty.

• *Danube Valley.* A fertile valley region along the shores of one of Europe's most vital rivers, the area is best explored by bicycle, along the towpath that once served river barges. The scenery is beautiful, with vineyards and orchards, small villages and expanses of gentle countryside.

• *Tirol.* Located in the heart of the Austrian Alps, Tirol is a hiker's dream come true, offering the opportunity to explore the depths of this mountainous region on foot. The scenery is spectacular, a mix of dramatic peaks, alpine meadows, streams and lakes. Allow plenty of time to explore this breathtaking province.

• *Styria.* A mixture of mountains, river valleys and pine forests, gentler in many parts than the mountain regions to the west, Styria is easy to explore on foot, discovering its varied landscapes.

• *Carinthia.* Austria's southernmost province, the scenery here is diverse, with high mountains surrounding a central lake district. Included is the country's highest peak, the Grossglockner.

Cultural. Austria's rich cultural past and present are celebrated throughout the country, principally in the cities. Take in at least one of the following events if you get the chance. In the meantime, explore the cities and towns, villages and farms to discover the pleasant, Old World flavor that makes Austria so enjoyable.

• *Festivals.* Festivals flourish throughout the year, peaking in the summer months with traditional and classical music events, opera, theater, and dance. Given the country's extraordinary contributions to the music world, it's not surprising that many festivals feature the works of Austrian composers such as Mozart, Hayden, Shubert, and Strauss. Most prestigious is the Mozart Festival, held each summer in Salzburg.

• *Vienna Choir Boys.* Famous throughout the world for their incomparable voices, the Vienna Choir Boys perform weekly at the Imperial Chapel of the Hofburg Palace in Vienna. Children (and adults) will love this celebration of Austria's choral tradition.

- *Lippizaner Horses.* Any family will thrill to watch these elegant white horses, descendents from an ancient Ibernian line once bred by the royal family. Renowned for their strength and precise footwork, originally valued for military purposes, the Lippizaners today perform a spellbinding show in the ornate baroque hall of the Spanish Riding School in Vienna.

Historic. Austria's cities are the principal sites of historic points of interest. Even if you feel as we do and habitually avoid cities like the plague, don't miss the ones here, which are a far cry from the concrete urban sprawls we've come to associate with cities. Old World, charming and cultured, filled with ornate architecture, they paint a vivid picture of Austria's fascinating past.

- *Salzburg.* Small and intimate, this is one city that shouldn't be missed. Overshadowed by the dramatic Fortress Hohensalzburg, one of the largest medieval fortresses in Europe, the city speaks eloquently of its varied past. For hundreds of years the domain of the Catholic Church, the city is filled with historic points of interest, including the Fortress, numerous churches, the lovely Mirabell Palace and Gardens, Mozart's birthplace, and nearby Schloss Hellbrunn. Explore on foot, venturing down the narrow, picturesque streets that typify the old city.

- *Innsbruck.* Lying in the heart of the Inn Valley, sandwiched between two high mountain ranges, Innsbruck's setting is spectacular. Once an important trading post for Europe in the 12th century, the city evolved into a walled town. Today its Old Quarter appears much as it did in the Middle Ages, with narrow, winding streets edged with tall houses and arcades. Exterior architecture runs the gamut from austere medieval design to decadent rococo. Interesting sights include the Ottoburg, once a fortified gate tower on the city wall, the Imperial Palace, and the Golden Roof, designed for kings to watch city festivities from.

- *Vienna.* Austria's capitol and the ruling city of the Hapsburg monarchy, Vienna is an elegant place, steeped in its cultural past and present. The largest city in Austria, you might want to limit your time here with children, just taking in the key sights on a pleasant day outing. Don't miss a visit to Schonbrunn, the summer residence of Austria's last emperor and one of Europe's most elaborate royal residences. There are museums and churches, palaces and gardens, famous buildings and works of art, much built in the Gothic and baroque designs that once flourished here.

• *Graz.* More manageable in size than Vienna, Graz is a true historic town, with little that has changed through time. Most intriguing is the Old Town, with the narrow streets, arches, passageways, courtyards and arcades that typify medieval architecture. Wandering the area is fascinating and magical, like a fairy tale city for children, with many buildings sporting colorful, decorated facades. As with all ancient European cities, there are palaces and cathedrals, elaborate courtyards and gardens.

• *Lower Austria.* Due to the once vital importance of the Danube River, this region has more than its share of castles, palaces, churches and monasteries. Take a bicycle trip along the riverside bike path, exploring historic buildings along the way.

OUTDOOR ACTIVITIES

Hiking. Austria has some of the best hiking in the world, with a network of groomed trails that takes you through the heart of the mountainous countryside. Nearly every village has at least one footpath you can explore, offering an easy day's ramble through the hills and valleys. Inquire at the nearest tourist office to discover what's available, or just follow a footpath when you see one.

The most developed hiking is found throughout the alpine region, with well-marked trails and staffed "huts" offering food and accommodations. This is an excellent opportunity for families to discover the pleasures of long distance hiking without the need to carry anything more than a light backpack. Despite their popularity, trails are pleasantly deserted, with only the occasional hiker met along the way. Many trails are appropriate for even young children, with those eight and over capable of doing most routes, other than up peaks. Alpine hiking is something you'll find Austrian families doing with children of all ages, even on difficult routes when little children are roped between parents for safety. All mountain regions offer an extensive network of trails and are equally enticing. For more information on alpine hiking, see the sidebar *Hiking in the Karwendel.* Easier hikes are available over the gentler terrain of eastern Austria, including explorations along the trails through the Vienna Woods, a woodland park outside Vienna. Other gentle hiking possibilities are the lovely footpaths around many of the lakes throughout the country.

Bicycling. Despite a deserved reputation for being mountainous, Austria has some wonderful places to bicycle. The Danube area, with its flat terrain and scenic, pastoral beauty, has been developed for bicycling. There's a paved bike path all the way from Salzburg to Vienna via Passau and Linz. The bicycling is easy, with numerous villages to stop at and explore, castles to visit, and parks to relax in. Accommodations (including camping) and provisions are plentiful the length of the route. This is a good area for either pulling a trailer or having young children ride their own bikes. Only three-speed bicycles are needed throughout, the type that can be rented locally.

For more freelance touring, try exploring the eastern provinces, where the terrain is relatively gentle. Good areas include the Muhlviertel region in Upper Austria, with rolling hills and wooded highlands. Stick to backroads to avoid traffic.

Swimming. Be sure to bring bathing suits, as weather can be hot in summer and places to swim plentiful. Austria's many large lakes provide the best swimming, with clear water and attractive lakeside areas, including those at campgrounds. Many towns and cities also have wonderful swimming complexes open to the public.

Hiking in the Karwendel

Rising dramatically to the north like a fortress wall, the Karwendel mountain range towers above the wide Inn Valley in Tirol. At its base lies Innsbruck, the hiking center for Austria's alpine region and a charming town of medieval origin. In a country renowned for its imposing mountain landscape and extensive network of trails, the Karwendelgebirge stands out as one of the best places for family hiking. Easily accessed by public transportation, centrally located in the alpine region of Tirol, and convenient to Innsbruck, the trails here are manageable for children of all ages. There's no better place to introduce the whole family to the pleasures of hut-to-hut hiking, reveling in the challenge of exploring high places on foot without the added burden of carrying copious amounts of gear.

The landscape is diverse along any route: pine forests and mountain streams, flower-filled meadows and hidden patches of glistening snow; rocky, wind-blown passes and sheltered pastures. No matter what route you take, the hiking is safe and manageable, with minimal altitude difference once you reach the high mountain area. Each hut is strategically placed for comfortable day hikes, with plenty of time for picnic and play stops. Although trails are quiet and uncrowded, imbued with that sense of isolation that always attends high places, nightly gatherings at the huts are convivial, offering a pleasant opportunity to mix with like-minded outdoor enthusiasts.

As with all alpine regions, huts are staffed. With a wide deck and interior sitting room, there are plenty of places to relax after a day of hiking. If arriving late at a hut, expect to have quite an audience as earlier arrivals watch your progress from the confines of their deckchairs. The Karwendelhaus is a classic example, approached by a long series of switchbacks that leave you wondering if you'll ever arrive, while fellow hikers sit contentedly watching your laborious efforts. Sleeping arrangements in huts are usually in co-ed bunkrooms, with private rooms sometimes available for families.

Facilities are basic: an outhouse (equipped with newspaper), cold water, pillows, and blankets (bring a sleeping bag or bag liner with you). Meals, however, are wonderful. The best arrangement is to pack your own lunch and snack food, then rely on the huts for breakfast and dinner. As all food must be brought in, prices are fairly high. Hut etiquette dictates that you sign in upon arrival (this helps guarantee you a bed) and remove boots in the entry way. Late-comers are never turned away, but may end up in the annex or some such place. Even if you don't know a word of German, master the colloquial "Gruss Gott", the Austrian way of saying "Hello". Hikers passing on a trail always greet each other this way.

As for the trails themselves, they're wonderful in the Karwendel area, with none of the vertiginous or grueling stretches that can be encountered elsewhere. One excellent four-day tour begins at Scharnitz near the German border (an easy train ride from Innsbruck), winds the length of the mountain range, and ends at Aachensee, a high mountain lake to the east. Only the first day is a bit strenuous, principally along the last section, the infamous series of switch-backs to the Karwendelhaus. The rest of the day, however, is particularly lovely, delving deeply into the forested valley at the base of the mountains. From Karwendelhaus, the route is straightforward and simple, something even a six-year-old could do, with nightly stops at two lovely huts. The last day descends to Aachensee, surely one of Austria's most spectacular mountain lakes. Plan to spend a few days relaxing here afterwards, a lovely place with a pleasant campground, good swimming, and attractive villages. Children will love the tiny train that takes you back down from Aachensee to the main railroad line, and thus back to Innsbruck. Alternate trails in the Karwendel include some interesting day hikes from Aachensee (there's also a trail along the lake, with excellent berry picking), a dramatic three-day hike from the top of Haflekar overlooking Innsbruck (accessed by cable car), plus some shorter overnights.

Membership in the Austrian Alpine Club is well worth the cost, giving you a 50% discount at all huts, plus access to hiking information. To join, contact the Osterreichischer Alpenverein, Wilhelm-Greil-Strasse 15, 6010 Innsbruck, or attend to it when you get there. This is also your best source of maps and guidebooks. Don't worry

that the writing is in German. It won't take long to master the words for such vital features as vertiginous, wire rail, and metal steps. The entire route from Scharnitz to Aachensee is free of any such things, a real bonus when new to alpine hiking. With experience, you'll find the whole family develops an immunity to heights, similar to what Austrians seem to be born with. Children, of course, will be the first to adapt, just another example of their wonderful aptitude for adventuring.

RESOURCE SECTION

TOURIST BUREAUS
Austria Tourist Office, 500 5th Ave., New York, NY 10110 Tel: (212) 944-6880.
Austria Tourist Office, 2 Bloor St. E., Ste. 3330, Toronto, ON M4W 1A8 Tel: (416) 967-3381.
Other Austrian tourist offices are located in Chicago, Houston, Los Angeles, Montreal, & Vancouver.

CONSULATES
Austrian Consulate General, 31 E. 69th St., New York, NY 10021 Tel: (212) 737-6400.
Austrian Consulate, 390 Bay St., Ste. 2018, Toronto, ON M5H 2Y2.
Other Austrian consulates are located in major North American cities.

NATIONAL AIRLINE
Austrian Airlines (OS), 17-20 Whitestone Expressway, Whitestone, NY 11357 Tel: (800) 843-00002.

SUGGESTED READING
The Visitor's Guide To Austria by K. Allan. Hunter, Edison, NJ.
Mountain Walking In Austria by C. Davies. Cicerone Press, Cumbria, England.
Green Guide: Austria, Michelin. Michelin Tyer Public Limited Company, Middlesex, England.

SUGGESTED MAPS
Austria, Hallwag, Scale: N/A.
Austria 1 (Wien, Niederosterreich), 2 (Steiermark, Kamten), 3 (Tirol, Vorarlberg), a series of good regional maps, Freytag & Berndt, Scale: 1:250,000.
Austria, Michelin, Scale: 1:400,000.

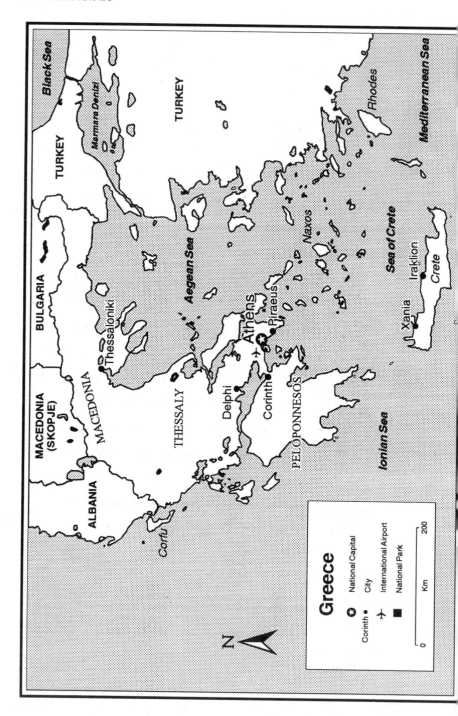

Continental Europe

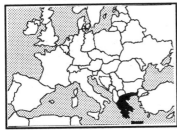

Greece

Greece is a land of contrasts, of sun-filled beaches and impenetrable mountains, sleepy villages and a once-great empire, of Old World simplicity and brilliant artistry. Above all, it is a place that every traveler dreams of traveling to, whether to soak up the warmth in some quiet corner of the Aegean, or to tread the paths of antiquity that permeate the land. For families new or old to adventuring, with children of any age, Greece offers a wonderful opportunity to pick a spot and stay a while, savouring the relaxed pace of life as you delve into its culture and rich heritage, its physical beauty and outdoor potential.

GENERAL DESCRIPTION

Location. Located in the southeastern corner of Europe, Greece reaches out into the Mediterranean. To the east lies the Aegean, to the west the Ionian Sea, while the north shares borders with Albania, the southern part of former Yugoslavia, Bulgaria, and Turkey.

Terrain. Mountains and the blue sea, pine forests and deep gorges, beaches nestled along rugged shores, and over a thousand islands form the dramatic landscape of Greece. On the mainland, high mountains stretch across much of the land, their grandeur accentuated by fertile valleys like the central plain of Thessaly. Mountains also dominate the Peloponnese Peninsula, its shores carved into bays, coves, and beaches. Islands lie scattered across the sea, each with its own distinctive characteristics, from the snow-capped peaks of Crete to the volcanic origins of Santorini. Populated and grazed for centuries, many islands have a barren, treeless look, thrown into relief by the colorful flowers, white-washed villages, and ever-present blue sky and water.

Climate. Greece enjoys a warm climate much of the year. Temperatures are most comfortable in the islands, with cooling breezes in the summer and moderate weather in winter. Deep winter months (December-February) can be wet and raw, with snow in the mountains. The best time to visit is spring or fall, with few tourists, better prices, more relaxed people, and good weather.

Culture & Lifestyle. Recognized as the cradle of Western civilization, Greece has a culture that goes back thousands of years. Today the country is very different from the years when Greek civilization was associated with political and creative leadership. Outside the cosmopolitan influences of Athens, a simple lifestyle prevails, where people revere the Old World values of family ties, village loyalty, and religious conviction. Much of the population still lives off the land, tending sheep, orchards, and fields.

The Greeks themselves are exuberant and excitable, open with their affections and emotions. Tavernas and cafes provide a social nucleus to village society, a place where women still remain in the background, where widows dress in black and are forbidden to remarry. Despite the overabundant presence of the tourist industry, foreign exposure has done little to undermine the strong cultural ties of the Greek people.

PRACTICAL CONCERNS

Political Background & Safety. Once a region of warring city-states, ancient empires, and continuous struggles for power and independence, Greece was finally united in its present state following World War I. With the abolishment of its monarchy, the country went through a period of military rule, finally emerging as a democracy in 1974. Despite successive periods of political instability, Greece has become a very safe place to visit, with a well-developed tourist infrastructure.

Travel Documents. No visas are required for visitors from North America or Australia. EC nationals need only some form of identification. Passports are stamped for a three month visit.

Money. Currency is the drachma, issued both in coins and notes. Travelers checks are always accepted, as are standard credit cards in touristed areas. Banks are open weekdays until about two p.m.. Watch out for Easter Week when banks are closed Tuesday afternoon through the following Monday.

Travel Costs. Greece rates as one of Europe's least expensive destinations, particularly off-season when prices can be very low. Campgrounds, pensions, food, and public transportation are all inexpensive and very good value. Archaeological sites cost little and dining out is well within the means of even budget travelers. The most expensive aspect of a trip to Greece is getting there.

Language. Greek is the national language, written with its own alphabet. Away from the tourist industry, few people speak English, particularly in the countryside. To get the knack of the Greek alphabet, practice with signs, often written phonetically in the English alphabet beneath the Greek words. Children will enjoy the challenge of unscrambling the confusion of Greek letters.

Health. Travel in Greece presents no health concerns. All water and food is fine, including dairy products, meat, and fish. Eating from street vendors is perfectly safe. First aid supplies are easy to find in ubiquitous pharmacies. Bring a good supply of sunscreen, as local products never seem to have a high SPF rating. Medical facilities range from the modern and well-equipped to the positively archaic. If you don't like what you see, find a private doctor (ask at the tourist office).

Food. Food is definitely one of Greece's greatest assets. Even on a strict budget you can eat well, revelling in the delicious foods that are available in shops, markets, and restaurants. Among the many excellent national dishes are moussaka, spanakopita and slovakia, all worth trying. For an inexpensive meal out for the whole family, order soup or fried fish, then fill up on the endless baskets of bread and huge servings of Greek salad that come with it. Shopping is done at markets, small grocery stores, produce shops, and bakeries. Best buys include dairy products (wonderful cheese and yogurt), meat (mostly lamb), seafood, olives, vegetables and fresh fruit. All the usual staples are easy to find: rice, noodles, eggs, oatmeal, canned goods, cereal. Fresh, powdered, and longlife milk are all available, the fresh sometimes in limited supply (find out when it's delivered.) Plan your cooking around produce, the cheapest, healthiest way to eat. Bread is excellent, baked fresh and sold from bakeries. If you're really lucky, you'll find one that still uses wood-fired ovens, fun for children to see and producing the best bread in the country.

Clothes. Bring ultra-lightweight clothing for summer, warmer clothes if visiting off-season. Winter and early spring can experience plenty of rain and cool, raw weather, even in the southern islands. By April you probably won't need anything warmer than a light sweater. Bathing suits, of course, are imperative. Bring along some money for buying cotton embroidered shirts, leather sandals, and straw hats.

Laundry & Bathing. Washing machines are in short supply, so count on learning the basics of handwashing. Bring a good bristle scrub brush and a piece of clothesline with pins. Bidets make great places for soaking laundry. Campgrounds usually supply laundry basins and communal clotheslines, if not a washing machine. Nothing ever seems to get stolen, even if left on the line overnight. If none of this appeals, ask around for someone who does laundry. Bathing facilities usually supply hot water, sometimes at extra cost. How hot it is can depend on what time of day you take your shower, as much of the hot water in Greece is supplied by solar-heated tanks on the roof. Electric water heaters mounted on the wall are another option, found in some rentals. Water is then preheated just before bathing.

Baby Needs. Greeks love babies, making this a wonderful country to travel to with young children. Expect your baby to be held, cuddled, plied with food, and generally regarded as the center of attention wherever you go. Babies are welcomed everywhere at all hours, so don't feel shy about taking yours out to a restaurant or someone's home for dinner. Everything you need is available: milk, baby food, cereal, diapers, clothes. Bring a baby sunscreen with you, plus a sunhat. A child carrier is a must if you plan any hiking or are traveling by public transportation. A stroller is fine if staying in one place. Babies ride free on all public transportation.

TRANSPORTATION

Getting There. Direct flights are frequent from all over the world to Athens. If coming from North America, use APEX to reduce costs. Taking the train or driving a car from northern Europe is currently not an option due to the political situation in former Yugoslavia. If coming from Europe, one of the easiest, most enjoyable ways is by boat, crossing to Pireas from Brindisi, Italy (with a stop at Corfu). Ferries also link Greece to Turkey, Egypt, Cyprus and Israel.

Regional Transport. Greece has an excellent network of buses and inter-island ferries. Olympic Airways also links the larger islands to Athens, but it's cheaper and more fun (except in winter) to travel by boat. Ferries are large, comfortable, and frequent. Travel deck class for the best price and most entertainment. You'll find yourselves sharing it with tourists, local families, and assorted livestock. Trains have limited, but good service on the mainland and the Peloponnese, with buses covering all remaining territory.

Remote areas can have something of an obscure bus schedule, so don't be surprised if a bus shows up that people insist doesn't exist. Children travel free or half fare, depending, it seems, on the driver. Buses are fast and efficient, when they're moving. Expect the intermittent stop for last minute shopping, mail delivery, or child pottying, all part of the experience. No smoking is strictly enforced on buses, despite a heavy cigarette dependency throughout the country.

Roads. Greece has good roads on main routes, deteriorating in quality as they become more remote. Driving is easy, the roads scenic, and traffic light away from cities. Car rentals and fuel are the usual prohibitive price and not really necessary. Consider renting a couple of mopeds for a few days to enjoy the independence and fun of riding the twisting mountain roads. Road surfaces are good for bicycling, but the riding is strenuous.

ACCOMMODATIONS

Campgrounds. Greece has plenty of choices for camping, from those licensed by the National Tourist Organization to numerous others. Licensed campgrounds are listed in the Tourist Board publication *Europa Camping and Caravanning*. Facilities range from basic to bordering on the vacation resort. Attractive surroundings are the norm, best enjoyed outside of peak-season when things can get crowded in popular areas. Showers (usually hot), laundry facilities, and some type of store are generally provided. Prices are very low as a means of accommodation for a whole family. Free camping is officially not permitted in Greece. Where there is no campground, there's invariably an inexpensive pension.

Pensions. Pensions tend to be inexpensive and easy to find in any town. The price always reflects what you get, so if dingy blankets, a communal bathroom across the courtyard, and wake-up-call at 2 a.m. by the local trashmen outside your window isn't to your liking, pay more next time. Some have communal cooking facilities, a nice bonus for families trying to save on eating out. The best rooms are those with a spacious balcony or roof deck just off your room (unless it's the kind of pension that rents out roof-top sleeping space). Renting by the week is usually the least expensive option. Prices tend to be significantly lower off-season.

Renting. Greece is a wonderful place to rent for a while. Off-season is best, with tourist villas and bungalows empty and available for a fraction of the cost. More spacious than pensions, they provide a welcome measure of independence for families with young children. Inquire locally and something should turn up. Always check the amenities first before booking.

POINTS OF INTEREST

Natural. Dominated by mountains and sea, Greece has a wild ruggedness that belies its thousands of years of civilization. It is a landscape of dramatic contrasts: mountain peaks and fertile plains, pine forests and barren hillsides, river-carved gorges and sun-washed beaches. From the smallest island to the depths of the mainland, Greece projects the many facets of nature.

• *Mainland Greece.* Predominantly mountainous, much of mainland Greece remains wild and unspoiled. Pick an area and explore it in depth: the fertile plain of Thessaly with its dramatic rock formations of Meteora; the fir tree forests of Evritania, the wooded peninsula of Halkidiki, or the mountain ranges of Macedonia.

• *Santorini.* Volcanic in origin, the main harbor is dramatic, once the crater of a volcano and lined with 300 meter-high cliffs. Boats make the trip to the nearby Kamenes Islands, with volcanoes that are still active. Beaches have black volcanic sand.

• *The Peloponnese.* A mountainous peninsula, the Peloponnese could be a destination in itself, with abundant natural splendors. Explore the wild Arcadian mountains, the scenic west coast, the caves of the Diros region, and the lovely Mani Peninsula.

• *Islands.* With six distinct island groups, there's no end to natural points of interest. As always, mountains predominate, thrown into relief by sparkling water and sand beaches, wildflowers and dazzling sun. Many are stripped bare of trees, the result of centuries of overgrazing, yet they still possess their own unique beauty. Some rise from the sea like fists of rock held aloft, while others exhibit a gentler side of nature, with orchard-covered hillsides and numerous sheltered coves.

Cultural.

• *Festivals.* With its rich sense of culture, Greece celebrates many festivals and special events, a number of them based around religious holidays. With their flamboyant temperament, Greeks are famous for their ability to have a good time, a facet of their nature you can experience to the fullest at a festival.

• *Gardens & Flowers.* Like many of the Mediterranean countries, the Greeks love to grow things, turning even the smallest plot of land into productivity. Resourceful and ingenious, blessed with an ideal climate, even the poorest, most hardworking family seems to take the time to grow flowers and fruit trees, vegetables and herbs, revelling in a love of nature's beauty that says much about them as a people. Flowers spill over the tops of empty olive oil cans, line windowsills and sit atop walls. Tiny yards bloom with fruit trees and grape arbors, miniature vegetable plots and bursts of flowers. It is one of the most lasting impressions of the Greek culture, this flair for growing things, for instilling beauty into even the tiniest corner of the land.

Historic. It's almost impossible to know where to begin when visiting this cradle of modern civilization. Despite an abundance of unsurpassed ruins, famous throughout the world, it is often the small, unexpected ones that leave the most lasting impression. Visit some of the great ones, but also take the time to explore those discovered on your own, pieces of antiquity happened upon when you least expect it. Children often find it easier to absorb smaller ruins than the larger, more popular ones. The Greek Tourist Organization publishes an excellent pamphlet on archaeological sites around the country.

• *Athens.* Despite being a large, crowded, noisy city, Athens is worth a short visit just to see its famous Acropolis. Rising above the city in ancient splendor, it contains a wealth of famous ruins, including the Parthenon that dominates the city skyline.

• *Delphi.* One of the country's most important and extensive historic sites, Delphi once served as the religious center of the Western world. Allow plenty of time to explore these dramatic ruins, overlooking the distant mountains of central Greece.

• *Minoan Ruins.* Remnants of one of the world's first great civilizations, the four Minoan sites on Crete bear testimony to an empire dating from 4,000 years ago. Knossos is the most reconstructed, Phaistos perhaps the most impressive and authentic, remaining in its excavated state. Even little children seem to gain a sense of awe at the ancient splendor of these once great cities.

• *Castles & Forts.* Crusader's castles and Venetian forts are always a hit with children. Visit the exciting walled city and castle of Rhodes, once a principal headquarters of the Crusaders. Venetian forts are equally exciting, with well-preserved ones on islands scattered across the sea.

• *Monasteries.* Historically a country steeped in religion, the coming of Christianity produced abundant churches, monasteries, and convents across the land, many built in isolated, inaccessible locations that are a wonder to visit. See the extraordinary monasteries of Meteora, built atop the perpendicular rock pinnacles of the Thessaly Plain.

OUTDOOR ACTIVITIES

Hiking. Hiking is the best way for families to explore the outdoors in this country where donkey trails and footpaths permeate the countryside. No matter where you go, it's almost always possible to find somewhere to hike, wandering through a pastoral landscape as fascinating as it is beautiful. The exposure is totally different from the often-touristed coastline, even just a mile inland where sleepy villages can be linked by pleasant rambles through hills and beside streams, among orchards and across rocky pastures.

Children will love this kind of hiking, with plenty to see and do. Take sufficient water, food and sun protection. Begin early in the morning on all day hikes, then take a break in the middle of the day to avoid peak sun hours (children will always welcome another opportunity to play). With young children, consider taking a bus up to a high point, then hiking back down on assorted trails. Don't worry about trespassing; the concept doesn't really exist in the countryside. For a challenging hike, try Samaria Gorge (18 km) on Crete, the country's most spectacular trail. The Greek Mountaineering Assoc. maintains a number of huts and trails in high mountain regions, best for experienced families with older children. Carrying all your own gear is required. For Families, probably the best option is to just pick an area and begin hiking. Despite the rugged terrain, paths are easy to follow, even for young children of six and up.

Bicycling. Much of Greece has a very mountainous terrain for bicycling. Roads are good, however, and traffic usually light away from cities. If based in one place, bicycles offer a wonderful means of local transportation, from market shopping to day explorations. Consider taking bicycles for an island hopping tour. Most islands are small, easy to bicycle (a number rent bikes), and accessed by narrow, rural roads with few cars. With bicycles you can not only see far more of each island, but avoid the need for taxis, buses, or rental cars. The sense of independence and adventure is tremendous. Bicycle touring is best in spring or fall, when weather is cooler. Bikes can easily be taken on ferries, but buses have no roof racks. If covering long distances, stick to coastal roads where terrain is usually the most level. Provisions and accommodations are always easy to find, with no major distances between stopping points. Bring spare parts and tools with you, although bicycle shops can be found in larger towns.

Sailing. Greece is in many ways a sailor's paradise. Made up of hundreds of islands, blessed with balmy weather most of the year, and culturally fascinating, the country offers a wealth of lovely places to explore. With a reputation for erratic winds, the Mediterranean can offer something of a challenge when it comes to actually sailing, a situation that is relieved by the relatively short distances between points of interest. Even those with little sailing experience can feel comfortable cruising here. Chartering is widely available, reflecting the popularity of the Greek Isles as a cruising ground. Areas with available boats include Corfu, Athens, Rhodes, and Cos. Be sure to choose a reliable charter company, as sailboat hire in Greece has been known to produce some less than desirable craft. Provisions are plentiful in most towns, and always within easy walking distance of the waterfront.

Docking Mediterranean-style is the accepted method, with the boat's stern toward the waterfront and an anchor secured off the bow. Privacy is minimal, but who cares when you have Greek village life to keep you entertained. For peace and quiet, head to one of the many lovely anchorages that dot the shores of most islands. Sailing is best during spring and fall (April-May and September-October) when weather is warm, skies blue, and the winds at their best. Summer tends to be very hot and windless, while winter can be uncomfortably cold and blustery. Prevailing winds in the Mediterranean blow from west to east, although each island seems to generate its own local conditions.

Swimming. Greece is justifiably known for its sun, sea, and beaches, making it one of the key places in the world for swimming. Some beaches are crowded and developed, others deserted and relatively undiscovered. The best are those away from town centers and tourist infrastructure, but expect at least a cafe or two on any beach in Greece (not always a bad thing when parents want to seek refuge from the sun while children indulge their endless capacity for beach time). Swimming in the Mediterranean is ideal for children, with no surf and predominantly warm water. Going topless (women and girls) is completely acceptable. Avoid swimming near large towns or cities, where water can be polluted. There's always a better beach around the next corner. Swimming weather begins in southern Crete in March, moving north with the spring. May to September are guaranteed swimming months.

The Island of Crete

An island of dramatic landscapes and fiercely independent people, Crete forms the southern boundary of Greece, separating the Aegean from the Libyan Sea. As with most far-flung places, it owes its first allegiance to itself, secure in its strong sense of cultural ties, of self-reliance and individuality, of regional identity. Wild and awe-inspiring, its mountains rise like alpine peaks, as unexpected as they are magnificent. The combination of snow-capped summits and Mediterranean beaches is almost ludicrous, endearing in its portrayal of nature's munificence. The people themselves are a mixture of gentle kindness and wild passion, famous for their feuds and fighting capabilities as well as their generosity and compassion. Self-contained and varied, filled with past glories and natural splendors, Crete makes a perfect destination for families, a place where the size is manageable and the scope endless, where any kind of adventure is possible.

No matter how long your visit is, the best plan is to spend time on both coasts, thus experiencing two very different facets of the island's character. The interior is equally fascinating, but can be easily explored from a coastal base. The north coast is by far the most developed, due in part to its easy accessibility. One of the most beautiful, natural regions is the Akrotiri Peninsula in the west, near Xania, a picturesque town built around a small, circular harbor. The area offers a bit of everything, from hiking and bicycling to explorations of historic ruins and present-day monasteries. Hike into the hills to witness village life and enjoy the exquisite combination of orange orchards and snow-capped mountains, blue sea and mountain air. For a wonderful, easy hike (22 km), take the bus from Xania up the enchanting Therisso Gorge to the mountain village of Therisso, hiking the dirt road from there to Laki, through villages and orchards, high mountain grazing land and rocky cliffs, always with a view of the distant sea. Children will find plenty to keep them entertained as they encounter herds of sheep wandering down the road, donkeys tethered to patches of grass, workers in the hills and fields, and frisky goats scampering among the rocks.

Another fascinating outing, ideal on bicycles, takes you to the tip of Akrotiri. A lovely area renowned for its abundant and diverse wildflowers (best seen in spring), the peninsula ends at two impressive monasteries, one at the base of the hills, surrounded by an ancient olive grove planted by the Turks, the other high in the mountains in rocky, windblown isolation. If you're lucky, the monks will invite you in, proudly displaying their interior courtyard gardens, hidden behind austere monastery walls.

Crossing the mountains to the south coast is dramatic, perhaps nowhere more so than on the road to Chora Sfakion, a region of fair-haired mountain people revered for their courage. It was here that the Resistance Movement thrived during World War II, as German occupation failed to tame these intrepid people. It was also here on the village pebble beach that Allied forces escaped the Nazi invasion. An exciting, isolated village, Chora Sfakion can also be approached by boat from Paleohora, returning back over the mountain road on leaving. This route takes in Crete's most extraordinary physical feature and spectacular hike, the 18 km Samaria Gorge, the longest gorge in Europe. Predominantly downhill the entire way, the trail is appropriate for even young children, with magnificent scenery and a perfect finish on the shores of the Mediterranean.

Due to snow conditions, the trail is only open from April-October. Start hiking early to beat the inevitable busload of group hikers. Boat transportation is available at the end, from Agia Roumeli to Chora Sfakion (there's no coastal road along this rugged piece of shore). Crete offers endless other places to hike as well, usually along the numerous donkey paths that have existed for generations. Some of the most impressive are made from carefully-laid stone, worn smooth after decades of use . To find somewhere to hike, just head out into the countryside, following any path that looks enticing. Interior regions all usually offer excellent hiking.

Delving into the island's interior, the Lassithi Plain is one of Crete's most extraordinary areas. Approached along a road that snakes through the hills, Lassithi suddenly emerges, a broad, flat plain ringed with mountains. Fertile and cultivated, edged with villages, the plain is most  distinctive for its hundreds of windmills, catching the breeze with their white cloth sails. Like giant pinwheels planted in the ground by children, they present an imposing picture, a picturesque merging of natural and human achievement.

No visit to Crete would be complete without a visit to a Minoan ruin. One of the world's earliest advanced civilizations, the Minoans thrived on Crete until their sudden destruction by the volcanic eruption on nearby Santorini. Perhaps the best ruin to visit is Phaistos, second in size to Knossos, yet more authentic in its unreconstructed state. Even very young children will be awed by the sense of a 4,000 year old history, of the grandeur that once existed here.

With the help of an accompanying guidebook, they can let their imaginations go wild, conjuring up images of what once existed.

Despite its distance from Athens, Crete is easy to reach by frequent ferry or Olympic Airways flights. Bus service is excellent on the island, servicing all communities linked by road. Bicycling is possible, but strenuous when crossing the central mountains between coasts. Moped rentals are frequently available, a good way to beat the cost of cars on the occasional day outing. Inexpensive pensions, rentals and camping are all available. The best time to visit is off-season, March-June, and September-October, with terrific weather, fewer tourists and lower prices. Swimming beaches are in most coastal areas. Try Agia Galini for a wonderful place to base yourselves for a while, with swimming, camping and a charming village. Food is outrageously good, moderately priced, plentiful, and locally grown. Expect Cretans to love your children, plying them with food wherever you go. You'll find Crete exciting and safe, with no crime other than the occasional family-related outburst.

RESOURCE SECTION

TOURIST BUREAUS
Greek National Tourist Organization, 2 Amerikis Street, Athens, Greece: GR-10110 Tel: 01 3223 111.
Greek National Tourist Org., 645 5th Ave., New York, NY 10022 Tel: (212) 421-5777.
Greek National Touist Org., Upper Level, 1300 Bay Street, Toronto, ON M5R 3K8 Tel: (416) 968-2220.
Other Greek tourist offices are located in Chicago, Los Angeles, and Montreal.

CONSULATES
Greek Consulate, 69 E. 79th Street, New York, NY 10021 Tel: (212) 988-5500.
Greek Consulate, 100 University Avenue, Toronto, ON M5G 1V6.
Other Greek consulates are located in Atlanta, Boston, Chicago, New Orleans, San Francisco, and Montreal.

NATIONAL AIRLINE
Olympic Airways, 647 5th Avenue, New York, NY 10022 Tel: (212) 838-3600.

SUGGESTED READING
Real Guide: Greece by Ellingham, Jansz, Fisher, Dubin, and Salmon. Prentice Hall Travel, New York.
Let's Go Greece by L. Chao & D. King. St. Martin's Press, New York.
Companion Guide to Mainland Greece by B. Jongh. Harper Collins, New York.

SUGGESTED MAPS
Greece, Freytag & Berndt, Scale: 1:650,000. This map has a cultural guide to Greece in English on the back.
Greece, Hallwag, Scale: 1:1,000,000.
Greece Regional Maps, Freytag & Berndt, Scale: varies.
Crete Touring Map (topographic), Nelles Verlag, Scale: 1:200,000.

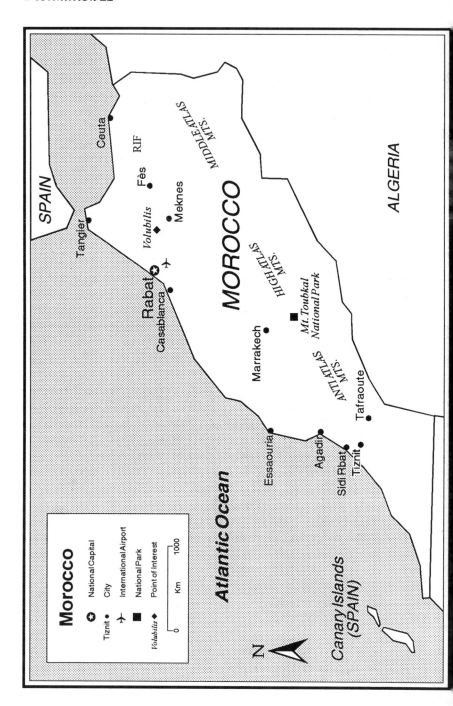

North Africa &
The Island of Madeira

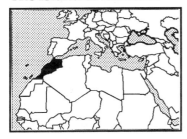

Morocco

Separated from Europe by a narrow ribbon of water, Morocco is world's apart, offering an easy window into the Moslem world of North Africa. Dominated by mountains in the north and desert in the south, the country is one of contrasts: modern cities and mud-built villages; Western clothing and robed, veiled women; shimmering heat and snowcapped peaks. It is an enjoyable, fascinating country for families to explore, one where children will elicit a positive response everywhere. Getting out of the cities into the countryside will show you a Morocco far removed from the reputed aggressiveness of Tangier.

GENERAL DESCRIPTION

Location. Morocco forms the northwest corner of Africa. Bordered by the Straits of Gibralter, the Atlantic Ocean, the Atlas Mountains, and the Sahara, the country is physically isolated, a fertile band of land between ocean and encroaching sand.

Terrain. The country covers a wide variety of terrains. Mountains dominate, forming a near-impenetrable barrier between Morocco and Algeria. The High Atlas mountains of central Morocco are the tallest in North Africa and second highest in the continent. To the west lies an expanse of arable land, fed by rainfall from clouds trapped along the high

mountain range. Beaches line much of the Atlantic coast, edged by cultivated fields. In the south, the Sahara stretches away, the gateway to Black
Africa.

Climate. Morocco is known as a cold country with a hot sun. Daytime
temperatures can be hot with nights cold, even in the desert. With the
exception of the extreme south, daytime temperatures along the coast are
pleasant throughout most of the year. Inland and in the mountains winters
are cold, with snow during midwinter months. Travel there is only possible
in summer. The best times to visit are early fall (after the summer heat) and
spring. Winter and early spring are best for the extreme south near the
desert.

Culture & Lifestyle. Culturally, the country has evolved from two
distinct groups: Arabs and Berbers. Berbers, the indigenous people of this
area, have always inhabited the mountain regions and fertile plains, living in
small villages and cultivating the land. With the spread of Islam, Arabs
arrived from the Middle East, converting Berbers to their religion. Today
the two groups are less easily discernible, as each intermingles with the
other, knowing no prejudice. The indigenous culture is most pure in the
Atlas mountain regions, where the clothes and speech, architecture and
agricultural pursuits, physical appearance and social codes are distinctly
Berber. Women here are afforded a far more visible role than the traditional
Islamic role of women. Assisted by years of French colonialism, parts of
urban Morocco also have a decided European flavor, particularly around
Casablanca and Rabat.

PRACTICAL CONCERNS

Political Background & Safety. Once colonized by both France and
Spain, Morocco has been independent and ruled by a monarchy since 1956.
Despite an on-going dispute over the Sahara with Algeria and very visible
police force, Morocco is extremely safe for travel. The theft and aggressive
hustling that one tends to hear about are most pronounced in Tangier,
unfortunately too many people's one exposure to the country as they
execute a lightening visit across from Spain. The rest of the country is
friendly and relaxing (especially the south), and even Tangier seems a bit of
a joke after being in the country a while. Disregard dire warnings that your
children will be stolen and sold into white slavery. They're more likely to
make a host of friends.

Travel Documents. A passport is all that's needed for Canadian, U.S.
and most EC and Commonwealth citizens. Visas, if required, are issued for
three months.

Money. Currency is the dirham, equal to 100 centimes. Use travelers checks or credit cards (check in advance which credit cards are widely accepted). Banks are widespread and open Monday-Friday, with a midday closing. During the month of Ramadan, an extended religious observance, bank and store hours can change radically.

Travel Costs. Morocco is an inexpensive country to travel in, excellent for families on a budget. Accommodations are reasonable for a comfortable room, and campgrounds extremely cheap. On the whole, the south is less expensive than the north. If traveling on public transportation, camping, and doing most of your own cooking, trip costs can be very low. Gasoline prices are high, as are car rentals.

Language. Arabic is the official language. Berber is spoken locally, while French serves as an unofficial second language, with most information and signs written in both French and Arabic. English is rarely spoken, including in tourist areas.

Health. No inoculations are required. Employ all standard precautions for food and water. Wash, then peel or cook any produce. Keep children's hands clean when eating. Avoid market street vendors (who often have no water for cleaning purposes). Water in major cities is safe to drink. Bottled water is available in most places and commonly used. Otherwise boil, filter, or use iodine. This should only be necessary in really isolated areas. Hepatitis is present, but can be avoided by taking the preceding precautions. Bilharzia is present in fresh water in the far south, so avoid swimming or wading.

Food. Basic foods are available in any sizeable town. These include canned goods, grains, yogurt, eggs, meat, tea, coffee, cereals (the ubiquitous corn flakes and oatmeal), and bread. Milk is sold fresh in small plastic bags (a real challenge to open). Bread ranges from white French-style to round, flat wheaty Berber bread. Cheese is usually those little triangles of silver-wrapped processed cheese that show up on airplanes. Fresh produce is abundant and sold at local markets, called souks. Cities and coastal tourist areas have the most variety of all foods.

Clothes. Take clothing for warm and cold weather. Traveling throughout the country, you can find yourselves wearing everything from bathingsuits to warm jackets. Despite being a Moslem country, the dress code is very loose when it comes to tourists. Shorts and T-shirts are fine for women, if accompanied by your husband or children. Bikinis are common on the beach.

Laundry & Bathing. Laundromats are a rare breed, so expect to do your own or hire someone. Campgrounds all provide laundry basins, excellent places to acquire the proper handwashing technique. Bring a hard bristle scrub brush with you. Tide detergent or cakes of laundry soap are available everywhere, but biodegradable, concentrated liquid soaps such as Camp Suds are better for short-term use. If traveling by car, include a plastic bucket for pre-soaking clothes. Hotels and pensions can either provide the service themselves or point you to someone who does. Showers are always available in hotels, pensions, and campgrounds, although they are usually the cold variety. Fortunately, the predominantly warm weather makes a cold shower seem more like a refreshing treat than a test of endurance.

Baby Needs. Powdered and fresh milk, baby cereal and disposable diapers are all available; as is jarred food in cities. Bring a good baby carrier and something for an infant to lie on outside. Even campgrounds rarely have grass. Bugs usually aren't a problem when sleeping, so no netting is necessary for napping babies. Include sun protection if going to beach areas. Have toddlers wear sandals or shoes, and wash before eating. If camping, bathe them under a spigot - they'll have more fun (and not notice the cold water). Diapers can be laundered by hand or sent out for cleaning.

Women. There's no question that traveling with children is the best way for women to enjoy this Moslem country. Despite a relatively relaxed attitude towards female attire (veils are rarely worn), women invite a great deal of interest when alone, particularly foreign women. With children, however, they are respected and almost always left alone. Traveling with my blond twin sons, I was positively revered.

Ramadan. The holy month of Ramadan warrants some understanding before choosing when to visit Morocco. During this period, which varies from year to year, but always lasts a complete month, fasting is meticulously observed from sunrise to sunset, or approximately 12 hours. Consequently, the whole country seems turned upside down, with shops and restaurants only open in the evening, people sleeping during the day and partying half the night, and a basic breakdown in things like food deliveries. Traveling through the countryside, it's almost impossible to get anything to eat or drink until nightfall. Then, just as you're trying to go to sleep, someone starts blowing a trumpet and celebrating outside your window. Children under the age of 14 are exempt from fasting, as are tourists, of course. Eating in the presence of an abstaining populace, however, takes some subtlety. Our advice is to avoid Ramadan. We didn't, and finally fled to Europe in quest of a fresh loaf of bread.

TRANSPORTATION

Getting There. Flying is the only way to get to Morocco other than by boat from Spain or Gibralter. The national airline, Air Moroc, offers reasonable fares. Use APEX to reduce costs, more effective the longer you stay. Boats cross the Straits of Gibralter many times daily from Spain to Tangier and Ceuta. Despite its popularity, we don't recommend the Tangier route as it lands you in Morocco's toughest, most aggressive town, an experience that can be intimidating. Leaving the country that way is fine. By then you will have acquired some savvy in dealing with the hustle scene that predominates. If coming from Europe, take the boat to Ceuta, a small Spanish enclave.

Regional Transport. Travel around Morocco is easy, whether by car or public transportation. Buses go just about everywhere. By Third World standards, they're comfortable, prompt, and relatively fast. Costs are miniscule and seats always available. Luggage is carried on the roof, including bicycles (don't be tempted to put it underneath in the lockers—those are for livestock). Be prepared to pay anyone who puts your luggage up on the roof or lifts it down; many will try to get on the payroll. It really isn't a bad system and you'll be helping out the local economy, but to avoid extra costs insist on doing some of the lifting yourself. Trains are excellent and the better option where they exist, primarily between cities in the north.

Roads. All main roads are paved and in good condition. Traffic is sparse, mostly buses and taxis driven at maniacal speed. Most challenging are roads through the High Atlas, a true engineering feat that can leave you breathless (whether driving or riding). If renting a car, rentals are cheapest in Casablanca.

ACCOMMODATIONS

Like all true budget travel destinations, Morocco offers everything from five-star hotels to first class dives. For a family, decent rooms can usually be found at reasonable prices. Even a fancy hotel room will cost about the same as a moderately-priced motel in the States. Camping is the cheapest way to go, with campgrounds available in most of the main tourist areas around the country.

Campgrounds. The best thing about Morocco's campgrounds are their price. Amenities are mostly limited to bathrooms (the Eastern kind where sitting isn't an option), water spigots, cold showers, laundry basins, and a small food shop or cafe. Surroundings range from the elegant green privacy of Meknes to the stark walls and sandy lot of Sidi Rbat. All have guardians, so leaving gear is no problem. Campgrounds are friendly meeting places, offering a haven to foreigners from inquisitive stares. Children will have plenty of room to play, and all are located in attractive, safe areas.

POINTS OF INTEREST

Natural. Morocco is a country of grandiose natural beauty, from its rugged, peaked Rif Mountains in the north to the desert fringes of the south. The countryside changes dramatically as you travel, always dominated by the high mountain range that borders the east. The following are a few of the country's most interesting areas:

• *High Atlas.* Located east of Marrakech, these offer wonderful hiking and a chance to visit remote mountain Berber villages on foot. Particular points of interest include Toubkal National Park, the lovely Ourika Valley, and Mount Toubkal, the second highest mountain in Africa.

• *Anti Atlas.* Travel to this part of Morocco is a must. Most pronounced are the strange rock formations and stark, arid mountains. Tafraoute makes the ideal base for explorations.

• *Kasbah Route.* Following the southern edge of the mountains where they meet the Sahara, this route traverses an area once dominated by Berber tribesmen. As with the other mountain areas, the landscape is overwhelming in beauty and a sense of nature's dominance.

• *Sidi Rbat.* The site of a coastal nature preserve, Sidi Rbat is beautifully located in isolation between ocean, sand beach, and a wide, marshy river mouth. Birdwatching is excellent.

Cultural. Morocco offers a great deal of cultural interest, particularly in the south where European influences are less pronounced: the Arab villages of the plains and mountain Berber villages; the traditional hooded robes worn by both men and women; the colorful clothes of Berber women and the exotic, provocative ones of Arabs. For a real taste of culture, explore a city medina, or old quarter, where narrow alleys twist and turn endlessly, lined with a tempting array of wares. Weekly village souks are equally fascinating, with people arriving from miles around on donkeys to buy and sell. The south (Marrakech and points south) is definitely friendlier, and therefore more culturally comfortable than the north, so concentrate your travels there if possible.

Historic. The country is filled with areas of historic interest, from kasbahs and forts to Roman ruins and sultans' palaces. All cities have numerous historic buildings worth visiting. Among the best are Meknes, Fes, and Marrakech, all historic capitals of previous rulers. The Kasbah Route in the south is just what it says, a road linking many of the great kasbahs that once featured so vitally in the country's defence. The following are among the best areas for historic sites.

• *Marrakech.* The traditional capital of southern Morocco, Marrakech reached its height of importance during the rule of the Saadians in the 16th and early 17th centuries. Historic points of interest include the Saadian Tombs (beautifully located beside a flower-filled garden), the ruins of El Badi's Palace, the Menara and Agda Gardens, and the Koutoubia minaret, Marrakech's most prominent architectural feature.

• *Meknes.* The capital of Morocco during the reign of the notorious Moulay Ismail, this small city reflects the wealth and extravagance of this imposing ruler. Historic points of interest lie within the original Imperial City area, including the awesome, cavernous Heri as-Souani, the Bab Mansour gate, and Dar el Kebira palace ruins.

• *Volubilis.* Impressive ruins of what was once the farthest settlement of the Roman Empire. Located in the gently hilly countryside outside Meknes, this is well worth a visit, with beautiful surroundings, many ruins to explore, and an overwhelming sense of isolation. Includes some lovely mosaics as well as assorted buildings.

• *Fes.* Morocco's most ancient capital, Fes remains the best preserved medieval Arab city in existence. The entire old city, or Fes el Bali, is worth exploring, with its abundant mosques and minarets, medressas and gateways, narrow walled streets and ancient buildings. Take a good day and don't be afraid to ask for help if you become hopelessly confused.

Wandering the old city on your own is not nearly as "life-threatening" as potential guides would have you believe.

OUTDOOR ACTIVITIES

Hiking. There are plenty of places to hike throughout much of the country, particularly in mountain areas. Both the Middle Atlas and High Atlas have a handful of designated trails, including one long circular tour around Mount Toubkal from village to village. Footpaths criss-cross the countryside, a local means of transport that provides scope for walking. Heat is definitely the biggest factor, especially in the south and coastal regions, so don't overestimate your, or your children's, capabilities. Hiking in the Middle and High Atlas is only possible during the summer months and early fall. Bring backpacks and good boots for hiking in these mountainous regions. This is best for children with experience, or families with babies that can be carried in backpacks.

Bicycling. Despite its mountainous terrain and hot climate, Morocco offers good opportunities for bicycling, including some possibilities for family touring. Bicycles can be carried on trains or buses for covering long or difficult distances. As bicycling is a major means of local transport, guardians are supplied at all public places like markets. Roads are good and traffic sparse, with drivers considerate towards bicyclers. Babies in bicycle seats or a trailer would be fine. Travel is best in the south where you receive a warmer welcome. Coastal roads are easy and flat, mountain areas very ambitious. Rudimentary bicycle shops are available in all large towns. Bring plenty of spare parts. Distances between towns are usually workable for touring. Some good routes include the south coast (Essoirra and points south), Marrakech Valley, north coast (Tangier to Ceuta; many ups and downs), and the Tafraoute area.

Swimming. Morocco has wonderful swimming practically year round, with excellent beaches along both coasts. Winter months feature swimming at the lovely sand beaches along the southwest Atlantic coast, principally at Agadir (a popular tourist area, excellent for families) and Tarazoute (very low-key, with camping). Both beaches are ideal for young children, with almost no surf. Best of all, for those who like natural surroundings, is the wonderful beach at isolated Sidi Rbat (camping and rooms beside a nature reserve). Summertime swimming is possible at the many beaches along the north and northwest coasts. All are appropriate for children. Bikini-clad mothers with children are left blissfully unbothered by peddlars, hustlers, and assorted men that frequent the popular tourist beaches.

Marrakech - City of Surprises

Lying in the heart of Morocco, Marrakech is the gateway to the southern half of the country, a region typified by magnificent mountains, the encroaching sands of the Sahara, and friendly people. Once the country's capital during the reign of the Saadians, the city has retained its Old-World charm and exoticism despite years of French colonial rule and present-day modernization. Even those not thrilled with most cities will be enchanted. More a town than a city, its size is small and personable, the atmosphere friendly, the setting spectacular. Situated in the midst of a vast central plain, Marrakech is shadowed by the High Atlas Mountains, rising to the east like a snow-tipped fortress wall. Approaching from a distance, your first glimpse is of the Koutoubia, a slender minaret piercing the shimmering horizon. It is a city full of surprises: flowers and horse-drawn carriages, low-lying buildings and narrow, twisting lanes, the exotic medina and open parks. Small and compact, the city can comfortably be explored on foot, even with little children in tow.

Marrakech is really two cities in one, the Medina, or old city, and the Gueliz, or new town, built during French occupation. The latter is attractive, with spacious, quiet streets, elegant homes, a profusion of trees and flowers, and the inevitable abundance of outdoor cafes. It is the medina, however, that continually lures you back, down its labyrinth of narrow walled streets, past tiny, crammed shops and wandering street vendors, robed figures and laughing, playing children. Here the traditional culture prevails, an endless source of fascination for visitors. Homes lie hidden behind stark walls, their interior elegance and spaciousness only guessed at from the outside. Women stroll past, feminine in their colorful, silken robes with peaked hoods. Historic sites abound, from the mysterious Saadian Tombs with their ornate decorations and lovely courtyard to the grandiose ruins of the once-great El Badi Palace. For children, the medina serves as a rich catalyst for imaginative play, conjuring images of sheiks and sultans destined for future games.

Take a ride in a horse-drawn carriage, always a thrill for children. More than just a tourist attraction, they provide a taxi service for the local populace, combining elegance with practicality. Depending on inclination, various options are offered, from scenic tours to direct deliveries. Tourists are automatically charged about four times the going rate, so feel free to do some bargaining. This is welcomed and considered all part of the fun in Morocco.

Indulge in the pleasant afternoon ritual of tea at an outdoor cafe. Moroccan tea is delightful, a strong infusion of mint leaves served heavily sweetened from oddly shaped pots. Children will love it, finding the whole occasion as exciting as an evening out, particularly if they get their own tea.

For inexpensive accommodations, consider camping at the attractively situated campground, just off the Avenue de France. Enclosed within a wall and continually manned by a guardian, the campground offers a nice oasis for Westerners in the midst of a foreign culture. There's plenty of room for children to play and women can safely relax in bikinis or skimpy outfits without causing a riot. After a day spent wandering the streets or countryside where you continually feel on display, the campground offers a welcome respite, somewhere you can still be outdoors, but private. Seen at first glance, the surroundings can be a bit of a shock (no grass, very basic facilities, etc.), but it grows on you. A small food shop at the entrance carries all the basics, including good fresh milk and yogurt. Produce can be bought a few blocks away. Security is excellent and no Moroccans permitted entry without invitation from a camper. Facilities include cold showers and laundry wash basins. Other affordable accommodations are located all over town, with even fancy hotels charging comparably reasonable rates.

Wonderful day and overnight outings can be done into the surrounding countryside. Take bicycles (or find some to rent - bicycling is very popular in Marrakech, with bikes rivaling cars in sheer quantity) and bike one of the narrow roads radiating out from the town. One energetic day can take
you through the
rolling countryside
south of the city to
a lovely reservoir,
another towards
the exquisite
Ourika Valley, a
spectacular
destination in itself.
Allow three or four
days for a complete bicycle   tour up the valley and back.

Excellent hiking is possible at nearby Toubkal National Park, an easy bus ride away. The park is a fascinating area of Berber villages, a marked cultural contrast to the urban world of Marrakech.

If you're really lucky and visit during March, you might be in Marrakech for the Feast of the King Day, an event your children will never forget. Black desert tents are erected in the field at the edge of town, important dignitaries (including the king) arrive, people pour in from the countryside, and the proceedings begin. These consist mainly of white-robed soldiers riding up and down the field on horseback, shooting their guns off in the air; a definite thrill for young and old alike.

RESOURCE SECTION

TOURIST BUREAUS
Office National Marocain du Tourisme, 22 Ave. d'Alger, Rabat, Morocco.
Moroccan National Tourist Office, 20 E. 46th. St., #1201, New York, NY 10017   Tel: (212) 557-2520.
Moroccan National Tourist Office, 200 Rue Universite, Ste. 1460, Montreal, QUE H3A 2A6, Canada   Tel: (514) 842-8111.
Other Moroccan tourist offices are located in Beverly Hills, CA & at Epcot Center, FL.

CONSULATES
Moroccan Consulate, 437 5th Ave., New York, NY 10016   Tel: (212) 758-2625.

NATIONAL AIRLINE
Royal Air Maroc, 55 E. 59th. St., New York, NY 10022-0012   Tel: (212) 750-6071.

SUGGESTED READING
Morocco, Algeria, & Tunisia: A Travel Survival Kit by G. Crowther & H. Finlay. Lonely Planet Publications, Berkeley, CA.
The Real Guide: Morocco by M. Ellingham & S. McViegh. Prentice Hall Travel, New York.
Cadogan Guide to Morocco by B. Rogers. The Globe Pequot Press, Chester, CT.

SUGGESTED MAPS
Morocco, Hildebrand, Scale: 1:900,000.
Morocco, Michelin, Scale: 1:1,000,000.
Morocco, Hallwag, Scale: 1:1,000,000.

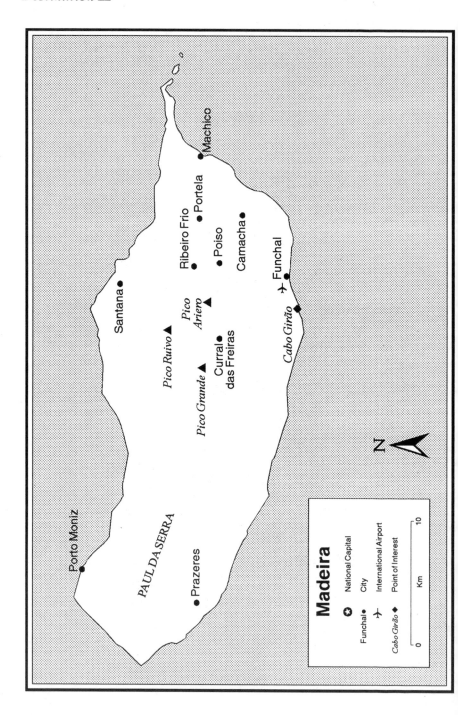

Madeira

National Capital
Funchal● City
✈ International Airport
Cabo Girão ◆ Point of Interest

0   Km   10

Machico
Portela
Ribeiro Frio
Poiso
Camacha
Funchal
Santana
Pico Ariero
Pico Ruivo
Curral das Freiras
Pico Grande
Cabo Girão
Porto Moniz
PAUL DA SERRA
Prazeres

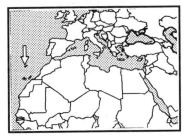

The Island of
Madeira

Rising from the sea in isolated splendor, Madeira is an island of renowned beauty. Mountainous and inspiring, it is a place of harmony between nature and man's will to survive, where wildflowers and rugged peaks rub shoulders with terraced fields and a 500-year-old irrigation system. For visitors, the island is a hiker's paradise, its terrain criss-crossed with footpaths that have long served the communities. Like all small islands, Madeira offers adventure on a manageable scale, a place where the culture,

landscape, and outdoor potential can all be easily sampled in these exquisite surroundings.

GENERAL DESCRIPTION

Location. Located 250 miles off the west coast of Morocco, Madeira is a tiny piece of Portugal flung out into the Atlantic. Together with its four smaller neighbors, only one other of which is inhabited, it forms an enclave of Portuguese culture north of the Spanish-owned Canary Islands and south of the Azores.

Terrain. A veritable mountain in the sea, Madeira climbs relentlessly from sea level to a series of high peaks. Only 50 km long, its small size is deceptive. By road the trip takes hours, negotiating each bend and twist, cove and cliff of this tortuous coastline. Little on Madeira is level, other than the multitude of terraces hacked from the hillsides. Left to its own devices, the land rises sharply, reaching up over mountain ridges, then plunging down again to the sea below. The south coast is gentler, a region of sun and soft breezes, fields of bananas and sugarcane, fruit orchards and vineyards. On the north, the onslaught of waves and constant onshore winds have carved a rocky, barren coast, a place where roads are few and villages more isolated. Inland, the mountains dominate, scored with a myriad of streams, rivers, and man-made levadas that irrigate the fields.

Climate. With such an extreme range of altitude, the island runs the gamut of four temperature zones, from subtropical to high alpine. When hiking in the countryside, it's possible to go from banana groves to blossoming apple orchards to windswept sheep meadows, all in an easy day's hike. The south coast is warmest, with summer temperatures most of the year. The north shore warms slowly, victim of winter winds and "northers". Wind-driven clouds, trapped by the mountain tops, frequently dump rain or snow on high areas. In the south in winter, it's possible to be warm in Funchal, a mere 10 km from snowline in the mountains. The best time to visit is March-November, when hiking is possible throughout the island.

Culture & Lifestyle. Madeira's culture is Portuguese, flavored with the strong sense of identity that only comes from island living. The prevalent sentiment is one of belonging to Madeira first and Portugal second. Due to the island's unique topography, a lifestyle has been dictated, one dominated by mountains and physical isolation. Agriculture still forms the basic structure of society, with narrow terraced fields mounting the steep hillsides like giant steps. Madeirans themselves are immune to heights, tilling the land right to cliff-edged drops of epic proportions. Streams have been harnessed into levadas, a system of man-made canals that extent over 500 miles, bringing water to terraced fields.

Hardworking and tireless, the people of Madeira walk everywhere, endlessly toiling up and down their mountains along narrow footpaths that access the fields and parallel each levada. In addition to a wide variety of fresh produce, Madeirans cultivate grapes for their famous Madeira wine and wicker, used to fashion everything from lunch baskets for school children to furniture destined for export. The lifestyle remains simple and labor intensive, with people living in small coastal or mountain villages.

PRACTICAL CONCERNS

Political Background and Safety. Discovered and settled over 500 years ago, Madeira became a frequent port of call for ships from all over the world. Today it is a safe, friendly place, with no notable crime. Children can safely roam even the streets of Funchal at night. Theft is not a problem.

Travel Documents. In most cases, only a passport is required, including citizens of the United States, Canada, and most of the EC and Commonwealth countries. A two month visa is issued upon arrival.

Money. Currency is the Portuguese escudo. Travelers checks and charge cards are widely accepted. Banks are in major towns and open weekdays. One word on begging children in Funchal: don't encourage them by giving handouts. Well-meaning, but misguided, tourists have perpetrated this problem by giving local children money. No one, their parents most of all, wants to see this behavior pattern spread. Happily, village children do not beg, not having been taught by tourists to do so.

Travel Costs. Madeira is a mixture when it comes to travel costs. Long popular as a tourist destination, particularly with the British, accommodations are expensive, even in small, unappealing pensions. There are no bargains here. With only one campground, there's not much you can do to avoid the (comparatively) high price of a place to stay. Renting is the best option, something that's easy to do on Madeira where the island is so small you can stay in the same place your entire visit. Rentals are equivalent to those in North America or Europe. Prices in the small villages are better, but places are harder to find. Everything else about Madeira is a bargain: public buses, food, restaurants, island made products, and activities.

Language. Portuguese is the official language. Spanish works almost as well. English is spoken anywhere tourists frequent. Learn some rudimentary words and phrases, always popular with village people, when shopping at the market, etc.

Health. Madeira has no health concerns. Medical supplies and services are available in Funchal.

Food. Food selection is excellent, better than in most parts of Portugal. Funchal is definitely the main provisioning place on the island, with various supermarkets, all of which have a wide variety. Some are cheaper than others, so look around. Food prices are surprisingly low for an island. Milk is available fresh or powdered. Unsweetened orange juice can be made from bottled concentrate. Bread, including whole wheat, is baked fresh daily. All the usual foods are easy to find and of good quality: eggs, meat, cheese, yogurt, cereals, grains, pasta, and canned foods. For fresh produce, shop at the market. Prices and quality are excellent and the market a beautiful sight, located in an open-roofed building. Saturday is main market day, with farmers arriving at dawn from all over the island. There's amazing variety due to Madeira's broad range of climates. Outside Funchal, food is more limited, so stock up if traveling around the island.

Clothes. Bring a variety of clothing, with the emphasis on warm weather. Funchal and the south coast are usually warm to hot, while the north coast and mountains can be quite cool except in mid-summer. Include one pair of long pants and a warm sweater or jacket, as well as raingear. Swimming gear is less important, as Madeira has no beaches (see the section on swimming).

Laundry & Bathing. It's always possible to make arrangements for someone to do your laundry. Rentals often include a washing machine, particularly in Funchal where many people have them. Clotheslines in apartment buildings are usually strung on balconies and the sight of a neighborhood festooned with drying clothes a common one. Out in the countryside women do laundry by hand in rivers and community washtubs, also a frequent sight. Anywhere you stay will have ample bathing facilities with hot water.

Baby Needs. Take a good child carrier, one that's comfortable on long walks or hikes. Skip a stroller. There's not enough level ground to want to push one around. Baby food, fresh and powdered whole milk, diapers and other paraphernalia are all available in Funchal. If your baby is at the toddler stage you might want a harness for limiting mobility while walking levada trails (ie. falling in the levada).

TRANSPORTATION

Getting There. Flying is the best way to reach Madeira unless you sail there on your own boat. Domestic flights all originate in Lisbon and are on TAP Air Portugal. Coming from North America, flights stop at the Azores and Lisbon (where you change planes). The flight from Lisbon is short, the landing terrifying. With only one short runway cut from the mountainside, a portion of which extends out over the water, there's no other way to describe your arrival.

Regional Transport. The island's bus system is a phenomenon. Buses are frequent, comfortable, fast, low-cost and rarely crowded (avoid early morning weekdays when they double as school buses). Children ride free.

Almost all buses originate in Funchal, making this an easy place to base yourselves for island explorations. The bus service is so excellent, there's really no need to pay the cost of a rental car, although rentals are widely available.

Roads. Three main roads service Madeira, all well-paved. One circumnavigates the island along the coast, the other two cross the mountains from north to south. Practically all vehicle traffic is limited to these three areas, principally the coastal road. Terrain ranges from very hilly to near vertical, making for some interesting bus or car trips. One section on the north shore was even cut from the cliff edge, not for the faint hearted.

ACCOMMODATIONS

Campgrounds. There's only one campground on Madeira, on the northwest coast. Unless you plan to base yourselves there for a while, bringing camping gear is hardly worth it.

Pensions. These range from reasonable to expensive, about the cost of an American motel. Efforts to find something cheaper are more likely to land you in unappetizing surroundings. Funchal has by far the most to offer, with many places having recently been built to accommodate tourists.

Rentals. This is probably the best solution for budget travelers, particularly if you plan to spend more than a few weeks. Prices are always lower this way. In Funchal it's possible to find an apartment rental with hot water, shower, washing machine, and kitchen for what it would cost you in North America. Inquire at real estate offices or the tourist bureau.

POINTS OF INTEREST

Natural. The combination of mountains and sea makes this an island filled with natural beauty. No matter how far you venture into the interior, it seems you can always see the water. Everywhere is lovely: the  high, craggy mountains, sometimes dusted with snow; the constant rush of streams tumbling down the hillsides; the deep green of the land filled with splashes of colorful flowers; the coast, with huge cliffs that plunge into the sea from incredible heights. Madeira's wildflowers, for which the island is renowned, grow everywhere in lush, untamed grandeur. Huge poinsettias, tangles of bright nasturtiums, wild hydrangea, and the yellow flower of the century plant that only blooms once every hundred years. Take to hiking the countryside along the many levada trails to capture the essence of Madeira's immense natural beauty.

• *Cabo Girao.* The second highest cliff in the world, this is well worth a bus ride to the top.

• *Botanical Gardens (Funchal).* Visit here to familiarize yourselves with the local plant life.

• *Queimades Park.* Located on the north side of Madeira near the scenic village of Santana, with lovely walks through a veritable island rainforest.

Cultural. The life that Madeirans have forged for themselves on this rugged island is intriguing. Settled over 500 years ago, the people have created an agricultural lifestyle by harnessing both water and land, channeling the water into levadas and forming the land into terraces. The sight of both, built by hand, speaks eloquently for the fortitude and determination of these people. The lifestyle is best seen while exploring the countryside on foot. Local island products include wicker work, beautiful hand embroidery, and the wine that made the island famous. Wicker can frequently be seen growing in fields, drying in graceful stacks alongside village homes, or being worked with in small local "factories". Another common sight is village women, seated together under a makeshift suncover, doing their intricate embroidery. For a literal taste of the wine culture, visit one of the many wine lodges. All welcome visitors for free, children included, culminating in a wine tasting exercise (also including the children).

Historic. Madeira has only a small handful of historic sites, including some lovely churches in Funchal and a museum or two. More interesting, however, are the hand-built levadas and terraces, carved from the mountainside, the laboriously made cobblestone streets and old-fashioned wicker sleds that once served as principal transport down the mountain from the town of Monte to Funchal. It is these things, still in use today, that define the history of this small, determined island.

OUTDOOR ACTIVITIES

Hiking. Hiking here can only be described as superb. It has everything: endless potential, good variety, visual stimulation, well-groomed trails, plenty for children to see and do, and excellent public transportation to and from trails. It's possible to take a bus to one spot, hike all day, and come home from another, thus negating the boredom of retracing your route. As most paths follow levadas, children have the constant presence of water to keep them occupied. Sailing stick "boats" is always a popular way to keep them moving as they rush off down the path in hot pursuit. Nearly all trails are appropriate for children. Bring a good child carrier for carrying young ones. Temperatures usually stay cool enough to keep from getting unpleasantly hot, especially in spring and fall. Hiking season is from March-November. Because hiking trails are integral to the communities, you'll find yourselves sharing them with the local inhabitants as they go about their work. Hiking here is not only a wonderful outdoor activity, but an intimate view into island life. For an excellent resource on Madeira hiking, buy a copy of *Landscapes of Madeira* (usually available in Funchal, but it's best to bring it with you if possible; listed under Suggested Reading in the Resource Section), with numerous outlined walks around the island. Hiking descriptions include useful information on bus schedules to and from hikes.

Bicycling. We can't really recommend bicycling on Madeira. The only somewhat level road around the island experiences too much traffic to make this a good touring choice. Nor would you be seeing the best of the island. Most roads are extremely steep and hardly something your children would enjoy. With such a good bus system and a natural emphasis on hiking, it's not worth bringing bicycles.

Sailing. Although the island offers no sailing potential due to its inhospitable shore, it is a popular stop for sailboats on either transatlantic passages or en route to and from the Canaries. Consequently, Funchal always has an international fleet of sailboats in its well-protected harbor. Coming from Europe, this makes an excellent stop, one from which you can explore the entire island while living aboard your boat. Dockage is provided along the breakwater, with boats rafted two and three deep. Fees are moderate. Centrally located in Funchal, the breakwater forms the city's attractive waterfront area, with outdoor cafes and plenty of room for children to play. All types of provisions are within an easy walk. Allow at least a two week layover to really explore the island.

Swimming. With no beaches and the deep Atlantic lapping at its shores, Madeira has little to offer in the way of swimming. Many of the fancier hotels in Funchal include pools, and there's a large, attractive municipal complex in one of the town parks. If you want to swim there, chose a time when the local children are in school. Their unsupervised poolside behavior leaves much to be desired.

Ribeiro Frio Hike

This is one of Madeira's most exciting hikes, a lovely four hour walk through mountains and meadow, overshadowed by high peaks, and overlooking the rugged north coast. Nothing typifies Madeira hiking more than this ability to be following a high mountain trail while still enjoying a panoramic view of the ocean, a breathtaking combination.

Catching the early morning bus from downtown Funchal gets you to Ribeiro Frio, high in the mountains, by about 8:00 a.m. With young children, bring along a small pillow or special "friend" to help them sleep on the bus. The ride is beautiful, up into the forests and mountains, with the coast dropping rapidly away behind you. Looking back, it's sometimes possible to see a cruise ship anchored just offshore, its rigging illuminated dramatically with strings of lights. Beyond Poiso, a small cluster of buildings at the mountain pass, the road plunges down the other side towards the north coast, twisting along a series of switchbacks that has you mentally braking the whole way. If you're the nervous type, you'll be only too glad to get off at Ribeiro Frio, the usual handful of buildings that qualifies as a roadside stop.

Bring warm clothing, as it's always cool at this altitude early in the morning. Branching off the main road just above Ribeiro, an easy, level, half hour walk brings you to the Balconies, a scenic overlook across the island's interior mountain range. In spring, snow still coats the peaks, feeding the myriad of streams that course down the hillsides. Mountain tops gleam in the early morning light, like alpine peaks rising from the sea. Below, the coastline lies spread out, its smattering of tiny villages clinging to the shore like forgotten toys. A rather rickety fence constitutes the barrier between you and a few-thousand-foot drop, evidence of the Madeirans' habitual disregard for heights.

Back along the path, a warm sunny spot provides just the right conditions for a picnic breakfast. We find this works wonders with children, packing breakfast along for the first stage of a hike. Ensured of an early start, we can anticipate and enjoy a relaxed, lengthy break, something children always welcome.

The official hike to Portela begins a bit further uphill beside the trout farm. Here, the clear waters of the Levada do Furado rush along eastward, accompanied by a wide, comfortable path through green trees filtered with sunlight. It's a lovely beginning to the hike, with glimpses of the blue ocean in the distance and the magical feel of

dense forest and moss-covered rock.
Rushing along on its trip to the sea, the levada carves a path through woods and rock, around waterfalls and across streams. The trail hurries along beside it, occasionally providing diversions as you find yourselves negotiating brooks on a series of stepping stones, or

debating a dip in an icy pool. Glancing back, the high peaks tower like sentinels, their imposing presence even more felt now than at the Balconies. The pace is easy, with plenty of time for frequent stops so children can climb around the rocks at various streams, or sail stick boats in the levada.

Lunch is a stop on some sunlit rocks. On hikes like this we find it amazing how much children can consume, even young ones. I finally learned to pack two complete lunches, one for lunchtime, the other for filling in the gaps.

Two-thirds of the way, the trail becomes a challenging cliff-hanger, winding along the rock face above an 850-foot drop. The steel railing, providing a measure of security in most spots, has an unfortunate tendency to deteriorate at inopportune moments. Most children, like Madeirans, will have little trouble with this, treating the vertiginous drops with characteristic aplomb, and scampering across areas that reduce their parents to neurotic wrecks. At a few places, even the levada engineers seemed overwhelmed, preferring to tunnel

through the rock rather than continue around the outside. The entire section is an impressive feat, built entirely by hand.

Beyond here, the path changes a third time, leaving the cliffs behind and coming out into open pasture filled with grazing cows and sheep. The land suddenly has the feel of a subtropical Scotland, with cropped grasslands rolling down to the sea. A gradual descent ends at Portela, the usual one restaurant and two shops that constitutes Madeira's idea of a town. Waiting for the bus back to Funchal (a one to two hour trip, depending on the bus), is pleasant outside the restaurant, with room for children to play and a panoramic view. Even the bus ride doesn't seem bad, a relaxing end to an active day as children nap and parents contemplate tea or coffee at one of Funchal's lovely waterfront cafes.

RESOURCE SECTION

TOURIST BUREAUS
Portuguese Council for Tourism Promotion, 51, Rua Alexandre Herculano, Lisbon, Portugal 1200.
Portuguese National Tourist Office, 590 5th Ave., New York, NY 10036 Tel: (212) 354-4403.
Portuguese National Touist Office, 60 Bloor St. W, Ste. 1005, Toronto, ON M4W 3B8, Canada Tel: (416) 921-7376.

CONSULATES
Consulate General of Portugal, 630 5th Ave., New York, NY 10020 Tel: (212) 246-4580.
Portuguese Consulate, 121 Richmond St. W., 7th Fl., Toronto, ON M5H 2K1, Canada Tel: (416) 360-8260.
Other Portuguese consulates located in most major North American cities.

NATIONAL AIRLINE
TAP Air Portugal, 399 Market St., Newark, NJ 07105 Tel: (800) 221-7370.

SUGGESTED READING
Landscapes of Madeira by J. & P. Underwood, Sunflower Books, London, England. We highly recommend this fantastic book to anyone wishing to hike the island trails.
Real Guide: Portugal by Ellingham, Fisher, Martin, & Kenyon. Prentice Hall Travel, New York.
Green Guide: Portugal, Madeira. Michelin Tyer Public Limited Company, Middlesex, England.

SUGGESTED MAPS
Great hiking maps for Madeira are included in the book *Lanscapes of Madeira* listed above. The tourist office in Funchal also has reasonable quality maps of the island.

Appendices:
Author's Recommendations

Best Places for Novice Traveling Families:
England, Scotland, Ireland, Newfoundland, Canadian
Maritimes, Florida, Madeira, Portugal

Exciting Places for Experienced Traveling Families:
Guatemala, Morocco, Newfoundland, Madeira, Norway,
Finland, Ireland

Best Places for Budget Travel:
Portugal, Morocco, Guatemala, Dominican Republic,
Newfoundland, Canadian Maritimes, Florida, Intracoastal
Waterway (if you have your own boat), Yucatan, Greece,
Ireland

Best Places for Winter Travel:
Greece, Morocco, Yucatan, Belize, Guatemala, Costa Rica,
Jamaica, Bahamas, Dominican Republic, Florida

Best Places for Spring and Fall Travel:
England, Scotland, Ireland, Canadian Maritimes,
Intracoastal Waterway, Portugal, France, Greece, Morocco,
Madeira

Best Places for Summer Travel:
Norway, Finland, Austria, Newfoundland

Best Places for Hiking:
Madeira, Austria, Norway, Finland, France, Greece, Cana-
dian Maritimes, Newfoundland, Ireland, Scotland,
England

Best Places for Bicycling:
Ireland, Canadian Maritimes, Austria, England, Scotland, France, Portugal

Best Places for Sailing:
Canadian Maritimes, Intracoastal Waterway, Bahamas, Florida, Greece, Scotland, Norway, Finland, Belize (if you have your own boat)

Best Places for Canoeing:
Canadian Maritimes, Newfoundland, Florida, Finland, Norway

Best Places for Camping:
Newfoundland, Canadian Maritimes, Florida, England, Scotland, Ireland, France, Portugal, Austria, Norway, Finland, Morocco

Best Places for Renting:
Guatemala, Dominican Republic, Jamaica, Portugal, Madeira, Greece, England, Scotland, Ireland

English-Speaking Destinations:
Newfoundland, Canadian Maritimes, Intracoastal Waterway, Florida, Bahamas, Jamaica, Belize, England, Scotland, Ireland

Spanish-Speaking Destinations:
Dominican Republic, Yucatan, Guatemala, Costa Rica, Portugal, (secondary language), Madeira (secondary language)

French-Speaking Destinations:
France, Morocco (secondary language)

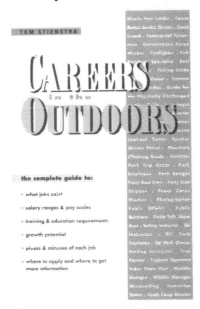